Getting Started in

CANDLESTICK CHARTING

The *Getting Started in* Series

Getting Started in Online Day Trading by Kassandra Bentley
Getting Started in Asset Allocation by Bill Bresnan and Eric P. Gelb
Getting Started in Online Investing by David L. Brown and Kassandra Bentley
Getting Started in Investment Clubs by Marsha Bertrand
Getting Started in Internet Auctions by Alan Elliott
Getting Started in Stocks by Alvin D. Hall
Getting Started in Mutual Funds by Alvin D. Hall
Getting Started in Estate Planning by Kerry Hannon
Getting Started in Online Personal Finance by Brad Hill
Getting Started in 401(k) Investing by Paul Katzeff
Getting Started in Internet Investing by Paul Katzeff
Getting Started in Security Analysis by Peter J. Klein
Getting Started in Global Investing by Robert P. Kreitler
Getting Started in Futures, Fifth Edition, by Todd Lofton
Getting Started in Financial Information by Daniel Moreau and Tracey Longo
Getting Started in Emerging Markets by Christopher Poillon
Getting Started in Technical Analysis by Jack D. Schwager
Getting Started in Real Estate Investing by Michael C. Thomsett and Jean Freestone Thomsett
Getting Started in Tax-Savvy Investing by Andrew Westham and Don Korn
Getting Started in Annuities by Gordon M. Williamson
Getting Started in Bonds, Second Edition, by Sharon Saltzgiver Wright
Getting Started in Retirement Planning by Ronald M. Yolles and Murray Yolles
Getting Started in Online Brokers by Kristine DeForge
Getting Started in Project Management by Paula Martin and Karen Tate
Getting Started in Six Sigma by Michael C. Thomsett
Getting Started in Currency Trading by Michael D. Archer and James L. Bickford
Getting Started in Rental Income by Michael C. Thomsett
Getting Started in REITs by Richard Imperiale
Getting Started in Property Flipping by Michael C. Thomsett
Getting Started in Fundamental Analysis by Michael C. Thomsett
Getting Started in Hedge Funds, Second Edition by Daniel A. Strachman
Getting Started in Chart Patterns by Thomas N. Bulkowski
Getting Started in ETFs by Todd K. Lofton
Getting Started in Swing Trading by Michael C. Thomsett
Getting Started in Options, Seventh Edition by Michael C. Thomsett
Getting Started in A Financially Secure Retirement by Henry Hebeler
Getting Started in Candlestick Charting by Tina Logan

Getting Started in
CANDLESTICK CHARTING

Tina Logan

JOHN WILEY & SONS, INC.

Published by John Wiley & Sons, Inc., Hoboken, New Jersey.
Published simultaneously in Canada.

For general information on our other products and services or for technical support, please contact our Customer Care Department within the United States at (800) 762-2974, outside the United States at (317) 572-3993 or fax (317) 572-4002.

Wiley also publishes its books in a variety of electronic formats. Some content that appears in print may not be available in electronic formats. For more information about Wiley products, visit our Web site at www.wiley.com.

Library of Congress Cataloging-in-Publication Data:
Logan, Tina.
Getting started in candlestick charting / Tina Logan.
p. cm. — (The getting started in series)
Includes bibliographical references and index.
ISBN 978-0-470-18200-0 (pbk.)
1. Stocks—Charts, diagrams, etc. 2. Stocks—Prices—Forecasting.
3. Investment analysis. I. Title.
HG4638.L64 2008
332.63'2042—dc22

2008002758

Printed in the United States of America

10 9 8 7 6 5 4 3 2

Contents

Preface

If the markets moved in a logical fashion, anyone could learn a few basics and make money trading. But that is not the case. It is the emotional crowd that moves markets. Traders' and investors' greed and fear, imprinted on charts, are like a road map to the markets. Those who learn to read and decipher the underlying messages of that price movement can gain a much-needed edge in a competitive environment.

That's where *Getting Started in Candlestick Charting* comes in. This book will provide you with a solid foundation from which to begin using candlestick charts. You'll learn to recognize candlestick reversal patterns and embed them in your mind through an understanding of how they reflect the messages of crowd sentiment. Candlesticks will help you gauge the strength of price moves and spot potential reversals early, before the crowd reacts.

If you have steered clear of candlestick charting until now because it seems like there is a mind-numbing number of patterns to learn, you can put that concern to rest. It is not necessary to learn dozens of candlestick patterns. This book narrows the focus to several commonly formed candlestick reversal patterns that you can learn to recognize in short order. You can start right away utilizing candlesticks to improve your chart analysis skills, and, of course, to increase your profitability.

You will find this book very helpful if you desire to:

- Learn candlestick charting but don't want to get overwhelmed.
- Learn to recognize high probability trade setups.
- Improve your swing trading techniques. Candlestick charting is a stellar tool for fine-tuning swing trading strategies.
- Learn how to improve the timing of your entries and exits.
- Develop a knowledge base in classic Western technical analysis and understand the role of candlesticks within that broader framework.

Every effort was made to produce this important learning resource in a user-friendly format. The chapters are organized in a manner in which they build one upon the other. The content is written in layman's terms with a level of detail that ensures understanding by beginning and intermediate-level traders.

I make no apologies for defining technical terms and describing concepts that advanced level chartists might consider to be familiar territory. However, even advanced chartists who choose this book with the intent of adding candlesticks to their technical skill set will find that it suits their purpose. Since a picture is worth a thousand words, there are numerous illustrations and real-world charting examples included throughout the chapters. Through careful dissection of the charts, and the commentary and analysis included with them, you'll already be recognizing the key Japanese candlestick patterns and Western technical events before you finish the last page of this book.

In Part I of the book you'll learn about candlestick charting. Chapter 2 demonstrates how the candlestick lines are constructed. In Chapter 3 you'll be introduced to several common candlestick reversal patterns. You'll learn their definitions and the psychology behind each formation. The patterns are well illustrated to help you train your eye to recognize them when analyzing charts. A summary of the candlestick patterns presented is included in Appendix A. Once you have thoroughly studied the details of each pattern in Chapter 3, use this guide for quick reference until you are so familiar with the patterns that you no longer need it. Chapter 4 will solidify your understanding of how the reversal patterns are formed and factors that may impact their signals. Chapter 5 wraps up Part I with a discussion of "tails" and how their presence sends a message about the current market sentiment.

Part II of the book shows you how to put candlestick charting to work. You'll learn how to blend Eastern candlestick charting with classic Western technical analysis. Candlesticks are not a complete trading system. In order to recognize their full potential you must understand how they fit into the broader picture. It is crucial to realize the important roles played by volume, volatility, trends, gaps, support, and resistance. These topics are covered in Chapters 6 through 9. If you are new to chart analysis in general, you'll find these chapters to be invaluable. Even if you are already well versed in Western technical analysis, you'll learn how to merge candlestick charting with Western techniques to gauge market movement and locate high probability setups. Chapter 10 shows you how to find the reversal signals and how to put them to work in your trading strategies.

After gaining new knowledge, it is imperative that you immediately practice applying what you have learned. To assess your newfound skills, several practice sets are included in Chapter 11. There is an old proverb that states: "I hear and I forget. I see and I remember. I do and I understand." You'll test your ability to recognize the candlestick patterns and Western technical occurrences introduced throughout the book. It will be time well spent. The answer keys and author's commentary are provided for you to check your work.

As its title suggests, *Getting Started in Candlestick Charting* will provide you enough detailed instruction to get right to work using candlestick charting techniques. Once you have mastered the common reversal signals, if you wish to learn more patterns there are several resources listed in the bibliography at the back of this book. *Getting Started in Candlestick Charting* will also help you start to build your foundation of knowledge of Western technical analysis. If you wish to add to that foundation with more advanced analysis, trade management techniques and implementing trading strategies, I offer additional training in these areas. Feel free to contact me by e-mail at tina@tinalogan.com or visit my website at www.Tinalogan.com.

I sincerely wish you the best of luck with your trading.

TINA LOGAN
San Diego, CA
2007

Acknowledgments

First I wish to thank Steve Nison for his perseverance in bringing candlestick charting to the Western hemisphere. His groundbreaking books *Japanese Candlestick Charting Techniques* and *Beyond Candlesticks* convinced me to add candlestick charting to my repertoire of technical analysis skills. I've never looked at a chart the same since. Stephen Bigalow was also instrumental in my candlestick journey. His candlestick books are written based on his experience using the candlesticks in the trading trenches. Mr. Bigalow generously invited me to contribute a chapter to his second book *High Profit Candlestick Patterns*. Thanks also to authors Gregory Morris and John Person for their fine contributions on the subject of candlestick charting.

Special recognition goes to two traders who, thankfully, arrived just at the right times in my trading career. First, Chris Manning who is responsible for getting me hooked on technical analysis. He had a knack for taking a tough, and sometimes dry, subject and making it come alive. His teachings were instrumental in encouraging me to develop a strong knowledge base in Western technical analysis. Later I was introduced to Herbert Otto, a nearly 40-year veteran of the markets. I continue to marvel at, and appreciate, how he generously shares his vast knowledge of both fundamental and technical analysis.

Without the support of my dear friends Michele Furlong and Jelaine Whipple, who believe in me and constantly encourage me, I may not have survived the writing of this book! Pat Johnson and Donna Love deserve praise for all they have done in assisting me in so many ways. They have a genuine interest in helping people and it does not go unnoticed. And thanks to my friends and colleagues at the Anthony Robbins Companies. I am certain that I would not be trading today had I not made that critical stop in my life's journey.

Thanks to my family for not complaining as I indulge my obsession with the markets. Although they may not share my enthusiasm for analyzing stock charts for countless hours each week, they seem to have accepted that I will continue to do so.

I would like to recognize three amazing women who were mentors at pivotal times in my life: Mrs. Muriel Gamble, Mrs. Roberta Cave, and Dr. Deborah Ballard-Reisch. They all contributed greatly to pushing me forward and upward.

Thank you to Jennifer MacDonald and the John Wiley & Sons team, who were willing to give me this opportunity to make a contribution to their *Getting Started in* series of books. I am amazed at all that goes into writing a book and how organized they are at getting the final product to the presses.

And last but not least, thanks to my many special clients. Their loyalty and encouragement has allowed me to continue to indulge my passion for training and trading.

Part 1

Candlestick Charting

Chapter 1

Introduction to Candlestick Charting

When I first began using technical analysis years ago, I used the standard bar chart. Eventually, though, I discovered the candlestick chart with its unique display of price action. Just switching from bar charts to candlestick lines alone helped my chart analysis tremendously. Candlesticks light up the chart's canvas, making it very quick and easy to see price trends and changes in the sentiment of market participants.

The next step was to learn the candlestick patterns with their unusual yet interesting names. After I understood the psychology behind the various patterns, I never went back to using bar charts. Once you learn to put this powerful charting tool to work, I am confident that you, too, will get hooked on candlesticks.

As valuable as candlesticks are as a chart analysis tool, they are simply that—one tool. They should not be viewed in isolation, but instead in the context of the surrounding chart landscape. Japanese candlestick charting should be blended with classic Western technical analysis methods rather than replacing them. It is the synergy of the two methods—Eastern merged with Western—that provides the means for superior technical analysis.

Getting Started in Candlestick Charting will not only provide you with an introduction to candlesticks, but will show you how to analyze them with the aid of Western techniques. It will guide you down the path toward advancing your charting skills and improving profitability.

Evolution of Candlesticks

Japanese candlestick charting is a centuries old methodology that was a secret of the Far East for generations. Candlestick charting took root in Japan, where the first rice exchange was set up in the 1600s. Eventually the exchange was institutionalized and the Dojima Rice Exchange in Osaka, Japan opened for business. Initially, the merchants dealt only in the exchange of the actual product: rice. In the early 1700s, the exchange shifted to the use of rice coupons. Rice coupons were sold against future rice deliveries resulting in the creation of futures contracts. The Dojima Rice Exchange was Japan's largest rice exchange, and the world's first futures market.

The legendary Japanese businessman Munehisa Homma made a considerable contribution to the early development of what we know today as candlestick charting. In 1750, Homma was granted control of his family's business, which included a large rice farming estate. He began trading at the local rice exchange in Sakata, Japan, a busy port for the collection and distribution of rice, and still an important port city today.

Homma accumulated a great fortune trading in the local and regional rice exchanges. It was said that he set up a network that stretched from Sakata to Osaka (a few hundred miles), which consisted of men using flags to communicate from rooftops. Homma kept records of his observations of the psychology of rice traders, as well as a historical record of weather conditions and rice prices. The trading rules and principles that Homma developed were instrumental to the evolution of candlestick analysis.

It wasn't until a few centuries later that candlestick charting was introduced in the United States. Candlestick charts have become extremely popular since first being introduced in the West in 1989 by author Steve Nison. The first edition of his groundbreaking book *Japanese Candlestick Charting Techniques* was released in 1991 (New York Institute of Finance). Before that time, candlesticks were virtually unknown in America. If not for Mr. Nison's perseverance and passion for the subject matter, the Western hemisphere may have continued to be unaware of this remarkable analysis tool.

Fortunately for us, Mr. Nison spent an immense amount of time and effort researching this charting methodology. This was no easy task. He began his research and study of candlesticks before the advent of mainstream charting programs, and as such, initially had to create the charts by hand. In addition, it also involved the tedious and difficult translation from Japanese to English. Add to that the challenge of interpretation, and some subjectivity that is an inherent part of technical analysis, and you can see the magnitude of this undertaking. As with most great endeavors, he accomplished those tasks with the help of key contacts he developed in the United States and abroad.

Traders who are new to candlestick charting will enjoy the benefits of Nison's persistent efforts, as well as the contributions by other authors who followed his lead. As candlesticks took hold in America, traders embraced them and helped integrate this technology into the realm of Western technical analysis.

The use of candlestick charts has now become so common that nearly all charting programs include them. With the widespread use of computerized chart analysis, the candlestick chart has become as well known as the bar chart. In fact, almost every trader that I know uses candlesticks; so I'd surmise that the candlestick chart has caught up with the bar chart in popularity, and perhaps even surpassed it.

If a technology is not effective it will not last. Experienced traders will eventually abandon a methodology if it does not prove worthy as an analysis tool, which, directly or indirectly, enhances their profits. The fact that candlestick charting has been around for centuries is a testament to its effectiveness.

Strengths of Candlesticks

Candlestick charts are superior to bar charts. That is only my opinion, of course, but it is one that is shared by many skilled chartists. Compare a bar chart (Figure 1.1) to a candlestick chart (Figure 1.2) and you'll see that they include the same price data: the open, high, low and closing prices. The candlestick line, however, provides insight into the current psychology of the investing crowd, which is not as easily identified in a bar chart. Once you become comfortable with the candlesticks, and understand their implications, you may find that a standard bar chart looks incomplete.

Since the candlesticks include the same price data as bar charts, you can utilize any of the popular technical analysis tools and techniques that can be used with bar charts, such as moving averages and trendlines.

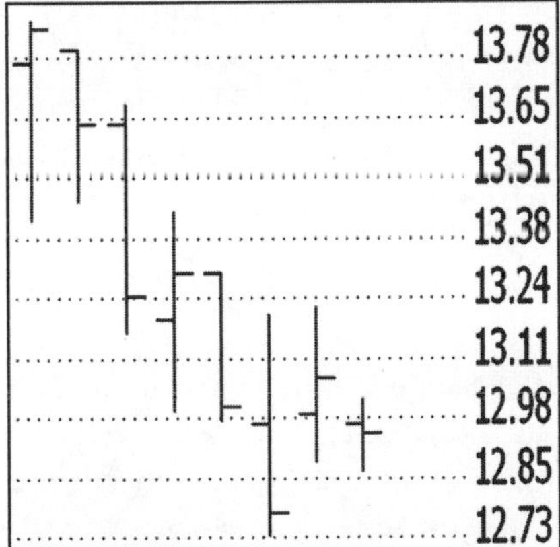

FIGURE 1.1 Bar chart
Source: TeleChart 2007®

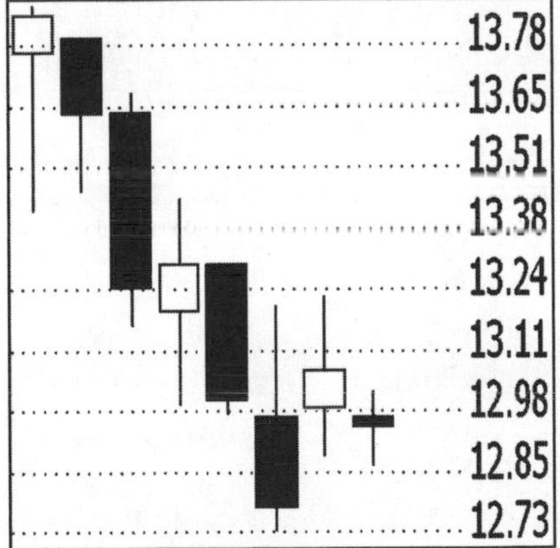

FIGURE 1.2 Candlestick chart
Source: TeleChart 2007®

Candlesticks make analysis quicker and more efficient. Since the area between the opening and closing prices is boxed and colored, it is obvious whether the bar is bearish (black) or bullish (white). In addition, the length of the boxed area tells us how dominant the bears or bulls were during a trading session. You don't have to stop and "think it through."

Candlesticks are tremendous for signaling turning points. They help identify the sentiment of investors as price becomes overextended or tests support and resistance levels. Their signals are often received earlier than those from traditional Western indicators or reversal patterns, which make them a strong tool for timing entries and exits.

Although the notion of candlesticks providing primarily short-term signals may be seen as a weakness by some traders, that trait can actually be put to good use by swing traders. Swing traders tend to take profits after short-term price moves. Precision entries and exits can make a substantial difference to their bottom line. Candlesticks provide short-term signals, so they are an excellent swing-trading tool. It is one of the primary ways in which I use them.

Limitations of Candlesticks

Candlesticks are not perfect. Like any technical analysis tool, they do have their limitations and weaknesses as indicated below:

Because of their boxed construction, candlestick lines take up more space on a chart. When a chart is tightly compressed, it may be difficult to see the detail of each candlestick line. This is not usually a major hindrance for most chartists though. Modern charting programs offer the ability to quickly zoom out or zoom in to see more or less data on the chart.

Most candlestick patterns provide only a short-term glance into investor psychology. Candlestick signals that form on daily charts may be more beneficial for shorter-term trading than for longer-term investing. However, since candlesticks can be employed on any time frame, investors may benefit from utilizing them on weekly charts.

Candlestick patterns do not provide price targets. However, Western technical analysis does provide techniques for projecting targets, which is a strong argument for blending the two methodologies.

Candlestick reversal patterns do not predict the duration, or magnitude, of a price move. They simply alert chartists to a potential change in the direction of price.

With certain setups, by the time a candlestick signal is confirmed price may be well off its low (bullish pattern) or well off its high (bearish pattern). Therefore, an entry should not be initiated for a new long or short position based solely on the pattern. The reward compared to the risk should always be considered when taking any trade.

Most candlestick advocates will agree that the benefits of candlesticks far outweigh their limitations and weaknesses.

Getting Started with Candlestick Charting

Choosing candlesticks as your chart type, *and really implementing candlestick analysis,* are two different things entirely. Although numerous traders now prefer to view price action displayed as candlestick lines, there are still many users who are not proficient in their interpretation. In addition, many traders fail to take advantage of the candlestick patterns.

Some traders just feel overwhelmed by the number of patterns, along with their unusual names, that they must commit to memory and learn to recognize. Others may not understand the message of the emotional crowd that is evident in the candlestick lines and patterns, and which makes them so valuable. And still other users may not be well versed in Western technical analysis and, as a result, fail to use candlesticks in the proper context.

Getting Started in Candlestick Charting tackles those challenges. It will provide you a strong foundation of the following:

- The construction of the candlestick lines and how the candles can provide insights into market behavior. By using candlesticks to display data, you should see an immediate improvement in your chart analysis skills.
- An understanding of the psychology of investors that underlies the formation of several common reversal patterns. You'll learn how to identify those patterns, which will help you to select higher probability trading setups and also improve the timing of your entries and exits.
- An introduction to several key Western technical analysis concepts. This knowledge will give you a broader view of price action in contrast to the narrower view provided by candlesticks.
- Blending candlestick charting with Western technical analysis in order to enhance their signals. By doing so, you'll enjoy a higher level of success than using either Japanese candlesticks or Western technical analysis in isolation.

A common complaint that I hear from traders is that they just get overwhelmed by all there is to be learned in this business. I encourage them to remain steadfastly focused on the outcome of trading, which is to make money. The outcome is not to fill your mind with an exhaustive amount of data. You must learn to sift through what appears to be a mountain of information and hone in on the key areas that will achieve the outcome of increasing profits and reducing risk. That is precisely the intention of this book. That "sifting" process has been done for you with the goal of shortening your learning curve.

In the beginning, it is better to learn a limited number of candlestick patterns, and to learn them very well, rather than trying to absorb several dozen patterns by rote memorization. If you really dig in deep and understand the meaning behind a pattern, and then practice identifying it using real-time charts, that knowledge will be lasting rather than fleeting. Once you have a strong foundation of understanding in place, you'll find it easy to add more candlestick patterns later if desired.

Although there is no way around putting in the time needed to learn a new subject, there are ways to learn that can expedite the process. *Getting Started in Candlestick Charting* will save you an invaluable amount of time by putting your focus in the key areas that will have an immediate and significant impact on your trading.

Learning a new subject, especially a technical one such as chart analysis, takes time and practice. You may need to review this book more than once in order to become proficient at utilizing candlestick charts. Remember that repetition is the mother of skill. The benefits you'll reap will far outweigh the initial outlay of time and effort.

Additional Introductory Comments

The term *candlestick charting* is often abbreviated to *candlesticks* or *candles.* The terms are interchangeable and are all used throughout this book.

Mention of Western technical analysis, bar charts, or chart patterns refers to techniques that have been used in America for many decades. Reference to Japanese or Eastern technical analysis refers to candlestick lines and candlestick patterns that have been used in the Far East for centuries. Whenever the term *reversal pattern* is used, it should be construed to mean a candlestick reversal pattern. If a Western reversal pattern is referenced, it will be clearly stated as such.

The daily chart is the most commonly viewed time frame. Most of the discussion and chart examples in this book refer to daily charts; therefore, the term *day, session,* or *trading session* is often used to reference a candlestick line. (A trading session is one day of trading from the opening bell to the closing bell.) Candlestick charting can be used on any time frame. If a time frame other than daily is referenced, it will be clearly noted. The term *bar, period,* or *trading period* may be used in reference to a candlestick line in such cases.

The discussion and illustrations in this book focus on U.S. stocks. Therefore, the word *price* is used often; for instance, to describe a price advance or a price decline. However, candlestick charting can be used as an analysis and timing tool in most markets. Candlesticks are commonly used in the futures markets. As long as the prices, or values, that are needed are available, a candlestick line can be constructed. For example, the opening, high, low, and closing prices are used to construct candle charts for stocks. Index charts, such as the Dow Jones Industrial Average, do not have prices. Those four price points are represented by numerical values for an index.

In most charting programs, the chart can be compressed horizontally and vertically. The level of compression may impact the look of the candlesticks. In addition, the chart adjusts to accommodate new higher, or lower, price points. Therefore, if you are looking back from the right edge at historical data, it may look different than it did when it was at the right edge of the chart. Make sure to move the chart back when analyzing candlestick lines or patterns using historical data. Most mainstream charting programs allow you to back up the chart; however, free online services may not offer this feature.

All chart examples in this book were produced with permission by TeleChart 2007®, a registered trademark of Worden Brothers, Inc., Five Oaks Office Park, 4905 Pine Cone Drive, Durham, NC 27707; phone (800) 776-4940 or (919) 408-0542, www.worden.com.

For ease of instruction, the terms *trader* and *investor* may be used interchangeably to refer to persons who execute trades, either short or long term. However, it should be noted that *trading* typically applies to holding short-term positions and *investing* generally refers to a longer-term strategy that may include the analysis of a company's fundamentals. The term *bulls* refers to bullish market participants either holding, or considering, long positions. The term *bears* refers to bearish market participants holding or considering short positions.

The term *security* or *securities* may be used generically to refer to either equities, securities or both. The term *trading instrument* may be used to refer to anything traded on the markets other than stocks, for instance: bonds, currencies, futures, and so on.

There are many chart examples included throughout the book. Their inclusion is for educational purposes only. Reference to any individual stock should not be construed as advice to buy or sell shares of that stock.

Chapter 2

Constructing Candlestick Lines

A Western price bar, shown in Figure 2.1, is constructed using the open, high, low, and closing prices of a trading session. The range from high to low is represented by a vertical line. The length of that vertical line shows visually how far the stock was run up, and down, during the trading session. The opening price of the session is shown as a short horizontal line drawn to the left of the vertical line. The closing price is drawn to the right.

range
A price bar's range is the difference between the highest and lowest prices reached during a given trading period, for example, a daily session.

A Japanese candlestick line is shown in Figure 2.2. The term *candlestick* is often shortened to candle. Although the candlestick line has a more striking appearance than

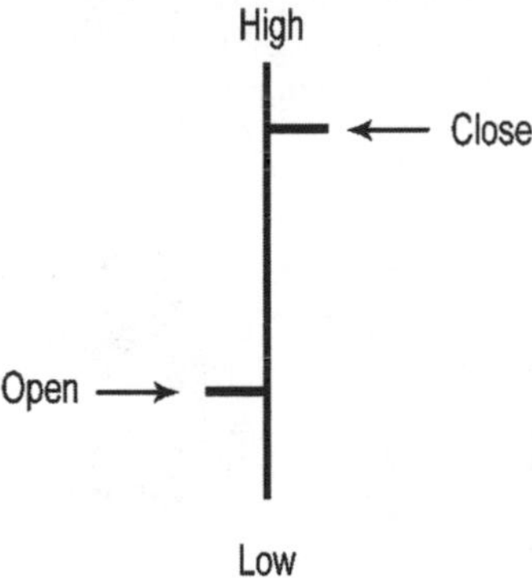

FIGURE 2.1 Western bar

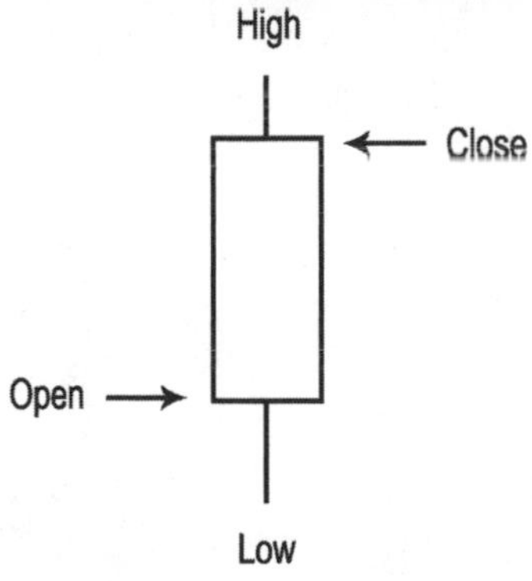

FIGURE 2.2 Japanese candlestick

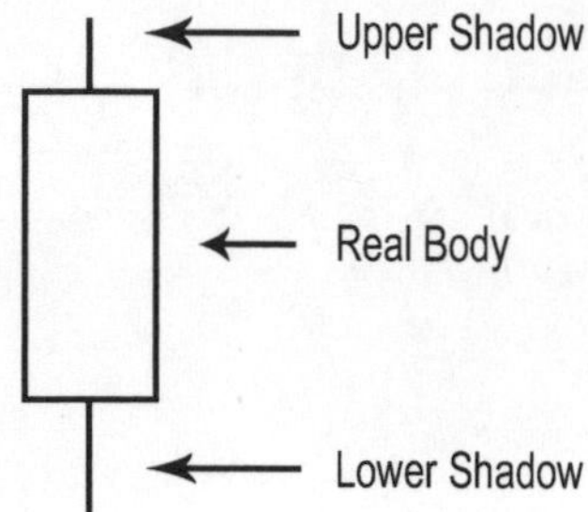

FIGURE 2.3 Candlestick line

the Western price bar, it is comprised of the same data. The opening, high, low, and closing prices are plotted along a vertical line. The difference is that, rather than showing the opening and closing prices as small horizontal lines, the area between those two price points is boxed.

The candlestick line is so called because it actually resembles a candle. The boxed area is referred to as the *real body*, or body (Figure 2.3). The thin vertical lines drawn above and below the real body are called *shadows*. A shadow is sometimes called a wick because it looks like a wick that extends out either end of a candle.

The shadows represent the price extremes of the trading session. The vertical line above the real body, referred to as the upper shadow, represents the difference between the top of the real body and the highest price of the session. The vertical line below the real body, referred to as the lower shadow, represents the difference between the bottom of the real body and the lowest price of the session.

If price closes *higher* than it opens, the session is bullish and the candle's real body is white (hollow), as shown in Figure 2.4. If price closes *lower* than it opens, the session is bearish and the candle's real body is black (filled), as shown in Figure 2.5. The terms *black* and *bearish* are used interchangeably throughout this book, as are the terms *white* and *bullish*. Figures 2.4 and 2.5 also illustrate how the price data of the Western bar translates to the candlestick line.

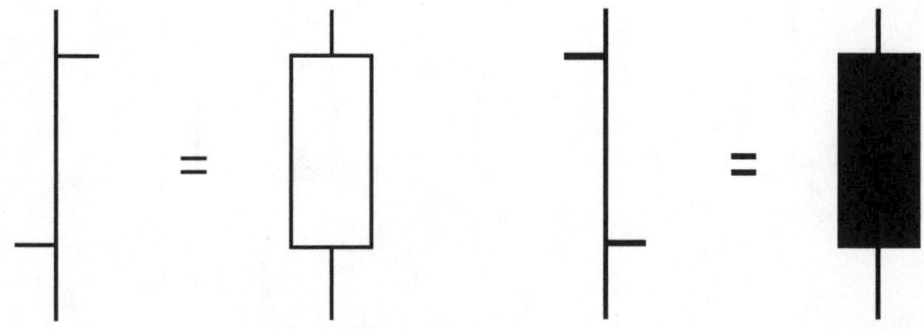

FIGURE 2.4 Bullish (white) candle **FIGURE 2.5** Bearish (black) candle

Smart Investor Tip

Many charting programs allow the option of changing the candlestick colors. Some traders may prefer to use colors other than black and white. For instance, they may choose green for bullish days and red for bearish days.

The height and color of the candlestick's real body tells a story about the direction, and the momentum (or lack of), of the price move. The shadows show how far the bulls and bears were able to drive price up and down during the session.

In this chapter you may see mention of a certain type of candlestick pattern, for example, a doji. Any pattern mentioned here is for reference only. The patterns will be explained thoroughly in Chapter 3.

Distinguishing between the Real Body and the Range

The Japanese tend to put a lot of emphasis on the real body—the area between the open and the close. In Western technical analysis, the bar's range is often emphasized, which is the distance from the high to the low. The difference between the range and the real body is illustrated in Figure 2.6.

In Western technical analysis, a bar with a long range from high to low may be referred to as a wide range bar, regardless of the difference between the opening and closing prices. However, when the Japanese refer to a long or tall candle, they are referring to the length (height) of the real body, not the range from high to low of the session. The Japanese have specific names for candlestick lines that include long shadows, for example, a hammer or a long-legged doji.

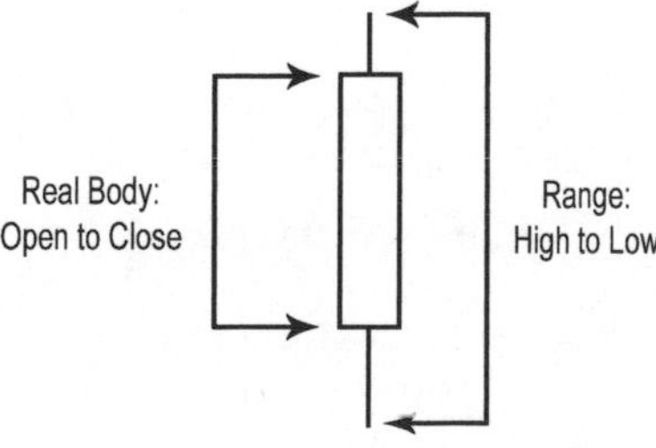

FIGURE 2.6 Real body versus the range

Even though the Japanese place a lot of emphasis on the candlestick line's real body, the shadows also provide pivotal insights when analyzing charts. In the discussion of the candlestick reversal patterns in Chapter 3, a certain shadow length is indicated for many of the formations.

Importance of the Open and the Close

amateur hour

The first hour of the trading day is referred to by many experienced traders as *amateur hour.* Amateur traders often make knee-jerk reactions during the opening frenzy.

In both Eastern and Western analysis, the opening and closing prices of each trading day receive a lot of attention and deservedly so. The daily chart is the most commonly referenced time frame and represents a full day of trading activity. Emotions tend to run high during the first hour of the trading day (after the market open) and the last hour (before the market close). You'll generally see higher volume during those times than throughout the remainder of the day.

There is usually a flurry of activity during the first 30 to 60 minutes of trading each day. That is the time of day when the following occurs:

- Traders respond to company or industry news, or global events that occurred between the prior trading day's close and the current day's open.
- Various U.S. government economic reports are released on certain days each month. Many of those reports are released prior to the market open.
- Reactions to news, events, or economic reports often provoke a strong surge, or a gap open to the up or down side, in individual stocks and/or market averages.
- Queued-up market orders are filled, most of which are placed by amateurs after the close of the previous session.
- Traders assess the opening activity to determine their intraday strategies.

Smart Investor Tip

Only limit orders are filled outside of normal trading hours. Therefore, market orders that are placed after the prior day's close or before the current day's open are held until the opening bell.

A lot of trading activity also occurs during the last 30 to 60 minutes of the trading day. That is the time of day when the following occurs:

- Many trading strategies, especially computerized trading systems, may call for executing "on close" orders for entering or exiting trades.
- Many breakout strategies require that price close above resistance for a long position, or below support for a short position. This is referred to as *waiting for confirmation.* Those trades are executed late in the trading day.
- Day traders close out their accounts to cash before the close of market. Much of that activity occurs during the last half hour of trading.
- In the futures market, margin calls are determined based on the closing price.
- A lot of "big money" moves in or out of the markets late in the day.

The close is a very important price. In fact, many traders believe it is the most important price of the day. The close tells us the current market value of the stock. The close is also the price most commonly used for chart analysis, to calculate moving averages of price, and so on.

The opening and closing prices of candles on intraday charts are not as significant as they are on the daily time frame. Intraday data, which is often called real-time data, flows in a steady stream over the Internet throughout the day. So with the exception of the opening price of the first intraday bar, the open of one intraday period is usually not much different than the close of the prior period.

Smart Investor Tip

Traders who employ strategies that call for executing trades on a closing basis usually don't wait until the actual close of market to do so. Waiting until the closing bell may result in the order's not being filled. Therefore, those who *manually* place their orders often do so between approximately 3:45 PM and 4:00 PM Eastern time. *Automatic* "on close" orders that are executed by computer are usually filled as near as possible to the closing price.

Distinctive Candlestick Lines

Candlesticks not only make it easy to see the trend, but also the force behind the move. Candlesticks with average to long real bodies highlight the strength of the dominant party. A stock may be making higher highs and higher closes, which would look bullish on a standard bar chart. However, if those higher highs are no longer being made with strong bullish candles, and instead by diminishing real bodies, or if long upper shadows are forming, the upswing may be losing strength. The reverse is true for a downside move.

If you look across a chart's canvas, you'll see a variety of candle lines with real bodies and shadows of differing lengths. Many of the candle lines will look to be about average length. Some of the candle lines will have noticeably longer or shorter real bodies than average, and some will have long or short shadows. These are relative terms. What constitutes average, long, and short may vary widely from one stock or index to another. As a general rule, you can look back from the right edge of a chart at the data for the past few weeks and get an idea of what these terms represent for that particular stock or index.

By themselves, the distinctive candle lines mentioned in the following pages tell a story about the current psychology of investors. As you study the reversal patterns outlined in Chapter 3, you'll recognize that certain of these distinctive candle lines are also components of reversal patterns.

Long Candles

If the real body of the candle line is extended, it is referred to as a *long*, or *tall, candle*. It represents a significant price move for the session and leaves no doubt of the bullish or bearish sentiment. Since *extended* is a subjective term, as a general rule, in order to be considered long, the length of the candle's real body should be about two times the length (or longer) of an average real body for that stock or index.

A long white candle opens near the low of the session and closes near the high, leaving little or no upper and lower shadows (Figure 2.7). It is a clear indication that the bulls were in control of the session.

One or more long bullish candles may form during an uptrend. Although the candle line itself shows a strong bullish sentiment during that particular session, its location in context with the surrounding price action may dictate whether the uptrend continues or reverses. Consider the following two scenarios:

1. A long white candle may form after a downtrend and signal a potential bullish reversal. One or more long bullish candles may form as a new uptrend emerges. It is a sign of bullish interest and strength and the uptrend may be just getting started (bullish reversal).
2. A long white candle may form near the end of an uptrend, or after a swift upward move, and signal a potential exhaustion move (bearish reversal). The long bullish candle may actually be the last surge of buyers into the stock and may be followed by a sell-off.

FIGURE 2.7 Long bullish candle

FIGURE 2.8 Long bearish candle

The reverse is true for a long black candle (Figure 2.8). Price opens near the high and closes near the low, indicating strong bearish sentiment during the session. The same two scenarios mentioned above may be applicable, but in reverse:

1. A long black candle may form after an uptrend and signal a potential bearish reversal. One or more long bearish candles may form as a new downtrend emerges. It may be the start of a sell-off that corrects the prior uptrend.
2. A long black candle may form near the end of a downtrend, or after a sharp downside move, and signal capitulation. A final last blast of selling pressure is often followed by a bullish reversal.

capitulation
A phenomenon in which investors "give up" and are willing to sell a declining stock at almost any price in order to exit their long positions. True capitulation involves very high volume and a sharp decline as panic selling occurs. Capitulation is often followed by a change in the direction of the trend.

In Western analysis, the shadows would be included in a reference to a bar's being long. A long bar would be referred to as a *wide-range bar,* regardless of the difference between the open and closing prices. In Japanese candlestick charting, reference to a long candle should be interpreted as a long real body. Therefore, a small-bodied candle with long shadows would qualify as a wide-range bar in Western technical analysis; while to the Japanese it would not qualify as a long candle because its real body is small. Such a candle would be given a different name, for example, a *high-wave candle.*

Most long candles have short upper and lower shadows. Periodically you'll see a candle that has a long body, and long upper and/or lower shadows (see the candle numbered 2 in Figure 2.14 for an example). As long as the real body is extended, such a candle may still be considered long. However, the smaller the shadow(s), the more obvious the domination of the prevailing side (bulls or bears).

Short Candles

If the length of the real body is undersized, it is referred to as a *short,* or *small, candle* (Figure 2.9). What qualifies as short is subjective; it may vary from one stock or index to another. The real body of a short candle would be noticeably shorter than that of an average real body when looking back over the past few weeks of price data. A short candle will have small upper and lower shadows or, in some cases, no shadows. If the real body is small, but there are longer upper and/or lower shadows, it will be distinguished by a specific name, such as a *spinning top* or a *high-wave candle.*

Unlike a long candle, which shows clear leadership for the session, a short candle shows a lack of leadership. The stock trades in a narrow range all day with neither the bulls nor the bears making much headway.

A short candle is a component of several bullish and bearish reversal patterns. For example, if, after the formation of a long bullish candle, price gaps up during the next session and forms a short candle, it is called a *bearish star.*

In Western technical analysis, a short candle may be referred to as a *narrow-range (NR) bar.*

Shaven Candles

If there is no shadow extending from either the top or bottom of the candle's real body, the candle is referred to as *shaven* or *shaved.* Some traders may call these candle lines flat tops and flat bottoms. The Japanese often refer to them as *marubozu,* meaning "close cropped."

If there is no upper shadow present, regardless of whether the real body is black or white, the candle line is said to have a shaven head (Figure 2.10). If there is no lower shadow present, regardless of color, it has a shaven bottom (Figure 2.11). Periodically, you will see a candle line with both a shaven head and a shaven bottom, as shown in Figure 2.12.

FIGURE 2.9 Short candles

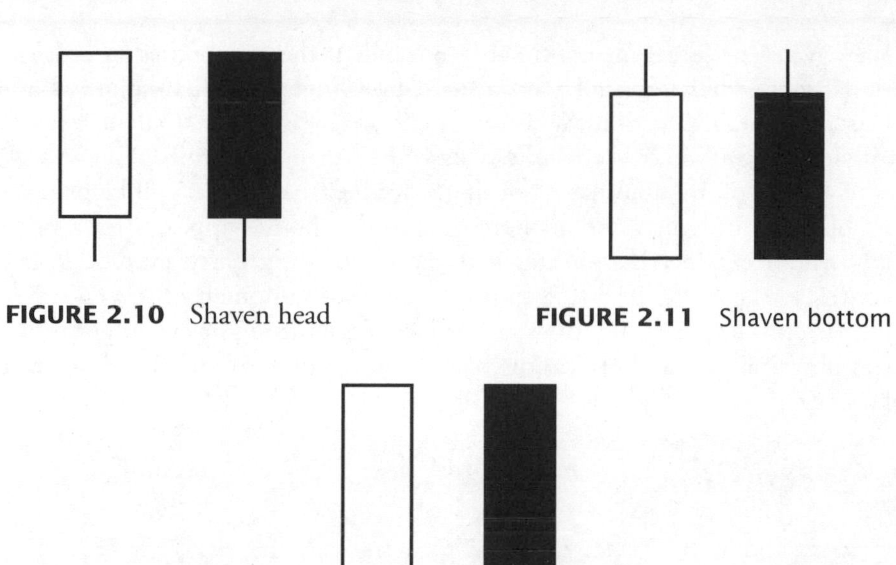

FIGURE 2.10 Shaven head

FIGURE 2.11 Shaven bottom

FIGURE 2.12 Shaven head and shaven bottom

Spinning Tops

A spinning top is a candlestick line that has a small real body. The real body can be either black or white. According to some resources, the real body of this candle line should be small *in comparison to* its shadows. In other words, the upper and lower shadows are longer than the candlestick's real body. However, according to Steve Nison in his book *Japanese Candlestick Charting Techniques* (New York Institute of Finance, 2001, p. 26): ". . . the sizes of the shadows are not important. It is the small size of the real body that makes these spinning tops."

By Nison's definition, a short candle (mentioned previously) would be a spinning top, as would a candlestick line with a small real body and shadows that are longer than the real body (Figure 2.13). Regardless of which definition you choose to follow, the appearance of a small real body after a directional move, or after a long candle, represents a loss of momentum. (A *directional move* refers to price moving either up or down, but not sideways.)

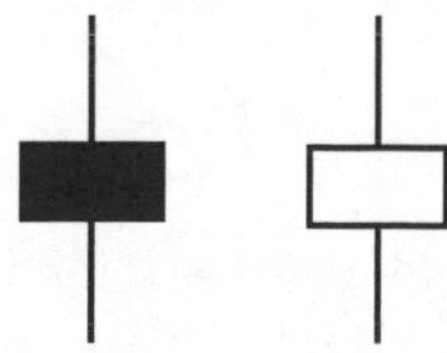

FIGURE 2.13 Spinning tops

When price action is primarily one-sided, the real bodies in a directional move will generally be average-sized or longer and their color will reflect the trend's direction. When the bulls are dominating while a stock is rallying, for instance, the candlesticks will be primarily white. Conversely, when the bears are dominating during a decline, the candles will be primarily black. Thus, when one or more diminishing bodies appear after a price advance or decline, it indicates that the dominating party may be losing control of the move. In fact, a spinning top is a component of several reversal patterns. For example, the star portion of a morning or evening star is a spinning top (or a short candle), as is the second candlestick line in a harami.

Example

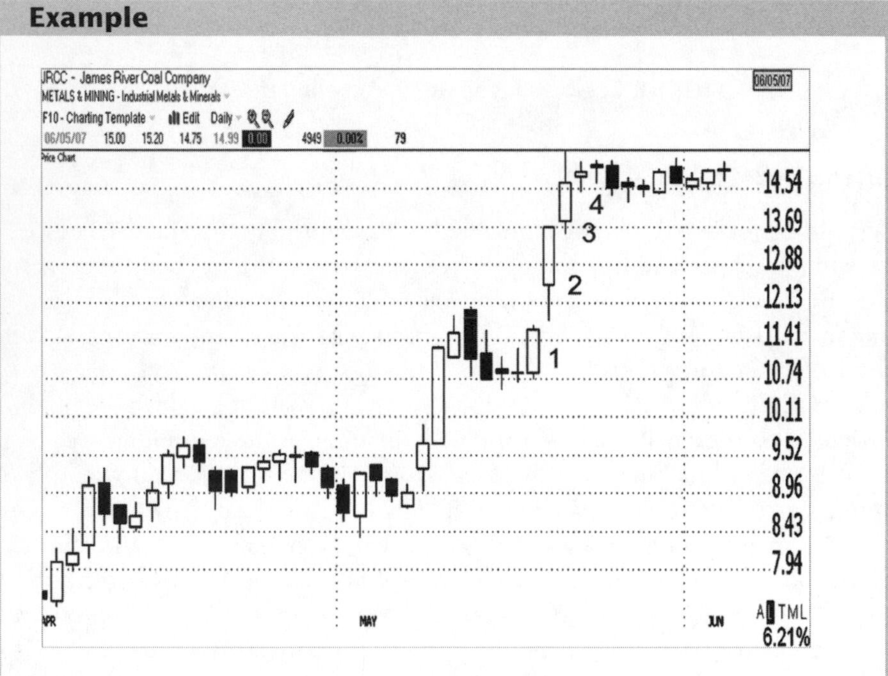

FIGURE 2.14 Spinning top formed after an upswing warning of a loss of momentum
Source: TeleChart 2007®

Figure 2.14 shows a swift upward price move (numbered 1–4) on the chart of James River Coal Company (JRCC) from May 17 to 21, 2007.

(continues)

Example *(continued)*

Note that the candlestick line numbered 1 opened near its low and closed near its high, clearly indicating the bulls' dominance during the session. Candlestick 2 was another strong bullish candle. It had a long real body and closed on its high, forming a shaven head. Candlestick 3 formed another bullish real body; however, the long upper shadow indicates that price backed off from its high before the close of the session. That was the first sign of caution. Candlestick 4 formed a spinning top indicating that the rally's momentum was fading.
Price consolidated for two weeks following the spinning top. The combinations of candles 3 and 4 create a bearish star pattern, which you will learn about in Chapter 3.

When the real body is small and the shadows are unusually long, the candle line is called a *high-wave* candle (Figure 2.15). This uncommon candlestick line is similar to the long-legged doji, which will be covered in Chapter 3. The difference is that the doji has no real body and the high-wave candle has a small real body. Think of the high-wave candle as a long-legged spinning top. Its long "legs" (shadows) indicate that there was quite a power struggle between the bears and bulls during the session, with neither side emerging as the clear victor.

A long-legged candlestick line visually shows us that there was a lot of volatility during the session.

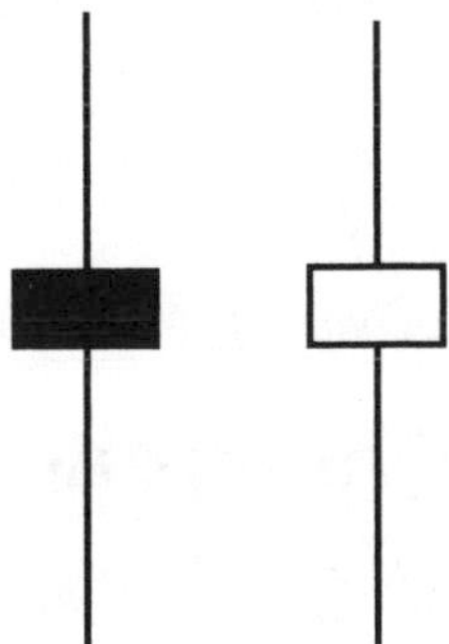

FIGURE 2.15 High-wave candles

Example

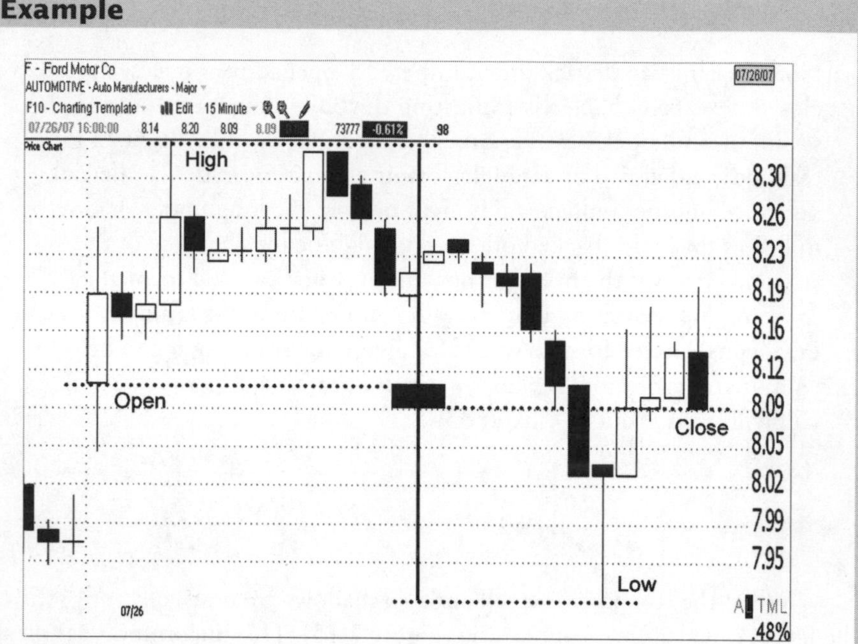

FIGURE 2.16 Daily high-wave candle overlaid on the 15-minute chart demonstrates the session's volatility
Source: TeleChart 2007®

Figure 2.16 shows a 15-minute chart of Ford Motor Company (F) on July 26, 2007, which was a day where a high-wave candle formed on the daily chart. The daily high-wave candle is overlaid on the intraday chart for demonstration purposes. The dotted lines show where the open, high, low, and closing prices from the daily chart correspond to intraday price action. The intraday swings to the high and low points along the vertical line resemble a roller coaster ride as the bulls and bears battled throughout the day to maintain control. By the close of the daily session, the result is basically a stalemate.

Candle Lines Evolve throughout the Session

Viewing a closed candlestick line on a daily chart tells you how the day's battle ended. For instance, if the candlestick has a white real body, you know that the bulls had control by the close of the session. However, that does not tell you if the bulls had control during the entire session. If you want to see the details of the day's battle, you'll need to view the price action on an intraday chart.

Example

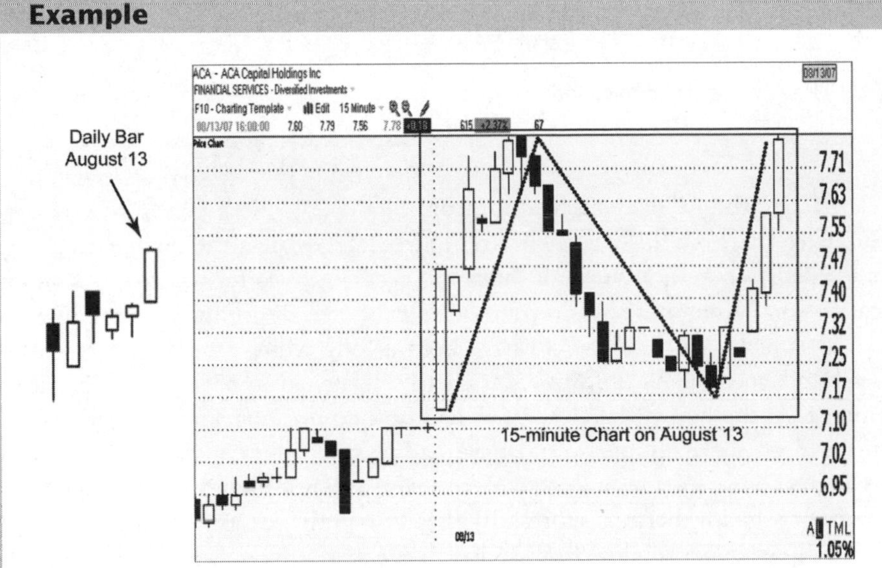

FIGURE 2.17 Shifting from a daily chart down to an intraday time frame defines how the battle between the bears and bulls unfolded throughout the session

Source: TeleChart 2007®

Figure 2.17 shows a chart of ACA Capital Holdings Inc (ACA) on August 13, 2007. On the left side you can see how the daily bar looked. It was a long white candle with a very small upper shadow. One might think that after opening at the low (a shaven bottom) the bulls just ran the stock up all day long. That was not the case. By viewing the 15-minute chart on the right, you can see the intraday activity. The up and down lines show the price trajectory throughout the day. The bulls were in charge for the first 90 minutes of trading. The bears took over for the next few hours, reversing the morning's rally almost entirely. The bulls then took over again and ran price back up to close near the high.

After a stock opens for trading, the opening price of the daily candlestick line is set for the day. The open cannot change; however, the high, low, and closing prices are subject to change throughout the session. A candlestick line evolves throughout the trading session as buy and sell orders are filled. By the close of the session, the daily candlestick line that you see may have looked significantly different at intervals during the session.

Smart Investor Tip

The closing price is called the *last* until the actual close of market.

Using the ACA example again from Figure 2.17, let's take a look at how the daily chart would have evolved. Figure 2.18 depicts the change in shape of the daily candlestick line as the bulls and bears jockeyed for control throughout the session. When price was run up during the first 90 minutes, at the high of the session the daily bar would have been a long white candle with a shaven head and bottom. As the stock started to sell off, an upper shadow began to emerge. At the point where the bears had pushed price back to near the low of the session, the daily bar would have had a long upper shadow and a small white real body. As the bulls took over again, the real body became larger and the upper shadow became shorter. By the close of the session, all that remained of that long upper shadow from earlier in the session was its small tip between the close and the high.

If, at the close of market, a daily candlestick line shows a small real body near the high of the session with a long lower shadow, at some point during the session it had a long bearish real body. Buyers stepped in, putting upward pressure on price, causing the once bearish real body to morph into a long lower shadow (see Figure 2.19).

If, at the close of market, the daily candlestick line has both an upper and a lower shadow and a small real body, at some time during the session the bar

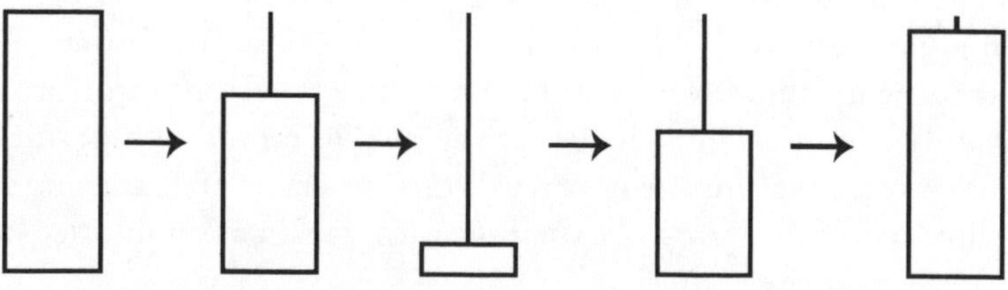

FIGURE 2.18 Daily bar changes shape throughout the session

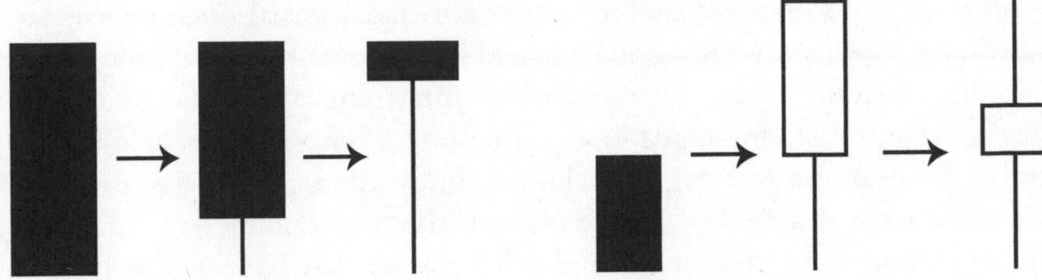

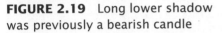

FIGURE 2.19 Long lower shadow was previously a bearish candle

FIGURE 2.20 Spinning top had both a longer bearish and bullish real body during the session

was more bullish and more bearish but closed near the middle of the range (see Figure 2.20). By the end of the session, the candlestick line formed a spinning top.

The same concept of drilling down from the daily bar to intraday time frames to see the detail can be applied to higher time frames. For example, a trader analyzing a weekly chart could shift down to the daily time frame to see the intraweek price action. To see even more detail, he could shift down to the hourly time frame.

Time Frames

The daily chart is the most widely viewed time frame. However, Japanese candlestick charting is applicable to all time frames. Investors who hold their positions long term may use candlestick charting on weekly and daily time frames. Swing traders, who hold for shorter periods, may use candlesticks on daily and hourly time frames. Day traders may employ them on the lower intraday time frames.

Intraday Charts

Candlestick lines can be constructed for intraday charts ranging from 1-minute to hourly. If you were to look at an hourly chart, for example, the opening price would be the first price of that hour. The highest and lowest prices reached during that hour would define the high and low of the candlestick line. The close would represent the final price of the hourly trading period.

Candlestick patterns may become less obvious on low intraday time frames, such as 1- or 5-minute charts. With the exception of the open of the first intraday bar, there is usually not much difference between the closing price of one bar and the opening price of the next. As such, certain candlestick patterns may not be as prevalent and some may not be as well defined on intraday charts, such as those that have a gap between the bodies of two consecutive bars. When distinctive candle lines and patterns form on intraday charts, their interpretation is the same as when they form on daily and higher time frames.

Recall from previous discussion the important events that occur during the opening and closing hours of a trading day. Those same events will not be applicable near the opening and closing times for each intraday period. Between the close of one day and the open of the next trading day, enough time lapses for traders to digest news and other events that happened overnight or over a weekend. Conversely, after the first intraday bar on lower time frames has formed, there is no time lapse between the close of one bar and the open of the next bar. The candlestick lines are formed from a steady stream of data. There is not sufficient time between each bar for traders to assimilate news or change their outlook. Therefore, there will not be as much emphasis on the opening and closing prices from one bar to the next on intraday charts.

Weekly Charts

If you are analyzing candlestick lines on a weekly chart, the open will be the opening price of the first trading day of the week. The high and low will be the highest and lowest prices achieved during the trading week. The close will be the closing price on the last trading day of the week.

It must be noted that some charting programs provide weekly data in the form of a "rolling" week. In other words, if you view a weekly chart on any given day, you are viewing the price action for the last five trading days. That means if you are viewing the weekly chart on a Wednesday, you are seeing the price action from Wednesday of the prior week to Wednesday of the current week. Some charting services may provide a standard week of Monday through Friday. In that case, if you view a weekly chart on a Wednesday, you are seeing price action from Monday through Wednesday of the current week. In either case, you won't know until the close on the last trading day of the week how the weekly candlestick line will appear.

The rolling week can be problematic in some cases because the current week's price bar, as well as the historical weekly bars, will adjust daily as the week unfolds. If your charting service utilizes a rolling week, be cautious about analyzing historical weekly charts mid-week because the candlesticks may look different than they would if you were to analyze them after Friday's close.

Chapter 3

Candlestick Reversal Patterns

In the previous chapter, you were shown how the candlestick line is constructed. The term *candlestick line* is a nonspecific term used to refer to any single candlestick on a chart. There are certain candlestick lines, or combinations of lines, that have specific names and criteria that identify them. They are referred to as *candlestick patterns*. A candlestick pattern may consist of a unique single line, such as a doji; or it may include two, three, or more candlestick lines. For example, an evening star pattern includes three candlestick lines in its formation. Candlestick patterns that provide reversal signals are the focus of this chapter.

Some traders may elect to simply make a shift to displaying data as candlestick lines instead of bar charts. That action alone should improve their chart analysis since candlesticks make it quicker and easier to interpret price action. However, most traders who are interested in adding candlestick charting to their technical arsenal will choose to delve deeper into the study of candlesticks by learning some, or all, of the candlestick patterns.

There are texts available by other fine authors on candlestick charting (some are listed in the bibliography at the back of the book). Depending on the resource you consult, anywhere from 55 to 68 candlestick patterns may be described. That includes reversal patterns, continuation patterns, and some distinctive variations of those patterns. Some of the patterns occur frequently, while others are rare.

I have found, through my own experience when I first began learning the candlestick patterns, and confirmed through discussions with dozens of my students, that trying to learn too many patterns at once can be counterproductive. After learning about half of those 55 to 68 patterns, it all starts to become sort of a blur. The result may be some knowledge of a lot of patterns, but a lack of thorough understanding and comprehension that allows you to put them all right to work.

In *Getting Started in Candlestick Charting,* the number of patterns, along with distinctive variations of certain patterns, will be limited to approximately 20 of the most common and best-known reversal patterns. The rare patterns are excluded, with the exception of a few that are distinct variations of commonly formed patterns. For example, a pattern called a *gravestone doji* is mentioned; however, it is just a variation of a doji. In addition, continuation patterns are not included. There is a reason the focus will be confined to reversal patterns. According to Gregory L. Morris, in his book *Candlestick Charting Explained* (McGraw-Hill, 2006, p. 312): "Reversal patterns occur about 40 times more often than continuation patterns." He goes on to say: "In this analysis, there were 65 reversal patterns and 23 continuation patterns, which make reversal patterns account for about 74% of all patterns."

Equally important, if not more so, to learning candlestick patterns is an understanding of how to actually put them to work in the context of the broader picture. That will be the primary focus of the chapters in Part II.

I believe that those of you who are new to this field of technical analysis will appreciate the "learn less, but better" approach presented in this book. And once you have that strong foundation in place, it will be easy for you to learn additional patterns, should you choose to expand your study of candlestick charting.

Common Reversal Patterns

The candlestick patterns discussed in this chapter are listed in Table 3.1 As the table illustrates, each bearish reversal pattern has a bullish counterpart. The patterns of the same name, for example, the engulfing pattern, can have either bearish or bullish implications, depending on whether the pattern forms after price has been rising or falling, respectively. There are also variations of some of the patterns presented along with the primary pattern descriptions.

TABLE 3.1 Common Candlestick Reversal Pattern

Bearish Pattern	*Bullish Pattern*
Hanging Man	Hammer
Shooting Star	Inverted hammer
Doji (northen)	Doji (southern)
Dark Cloud Cover	Piercing Pattern
Bearish Engulfing	Bullish Engulfing
Bearish Harami	Bullish Harami
Evening Star	Morning Star

The reversal patterns all share one common trait: they must follow a directional move. Bearish reversal patterns form after an upward move. They are considered to be bearish because they may be followed by a shift in price direction from up to down, or from up to lateral (sideways). Bullish patterns form after a price decline and may be followed by a change from down to up or from down to lateral.

directional move
A price move that is either up or down, but not sideways.

Don't let the idea of having to learn several patterns with their unusual names dissuade you. It is necessary to move past that and instead focus on what is important—to really understand what the candle formations tell you about the current psychology of market participants. Once you understand the value of the patterns, I'm sure you'll agree it is worth the time and effort.

Stocks and markets may vary in their price movement, as well as their volatility. Therefore, you may discover that some patterns occur more or less frequently in one market than another or from one stock to another.

Pattern Format

A standard format is followed for each pattern whenever possible in order to maintain consistency and ensure that each pattern is thoroughly explained. That format includes the following:

- The price action that precedes the pattern: either a price advance or a price decline.
- A description of the pattern and its criteria.
- An illustration of the pattern. Rising or falling lines will be displayed in the illustrations prior to the pattern example to indicate whether it forms after an advance (bearish pattern) or a decline (bullish pattern).
- The psychology behind the pattern's formation.
- A chart that contains a real-world example of the pattern shown in the context of the surrounding chart landscape.
- Variations of the pattern where applicable.
- A helpful hint for remembering the pattern's name where applicable.

The order in which the patterns are presented does not dictate their significance as reversal patterns.

For your convenience, a brief summary and illustration of each pattern is included in Appendix A for quick reference.

Nonideal Patterns and Variations

The illustrations that accompany the reversal pattern descriptions were drawn in order to show ideal examples. The purpose of providing textbook examples is so that you have a good benchmark from which to work. Although you will see some ideal patterns when you begin analyzing charts, you should also expect to see plenty of less-than-perfect formations. That does not mean they are not powerful. Even nonideal versions can provide important clues about shifts in investor psychology.

In the chart examples presented throughout the book, you'll view the candlestick patterns in the context of the broader chart rather than in isolation. That will give you a feel for their real-world applications.

For some patterns, an acceptable variation that differs slightly from the standard criteria will be shown. For instance, the ideal dark cloud cover, which is a bearish reversal pattern, will gap up open above the prior candle's *high*. However, if it only gaps open above the prior candle's *close*, it is an acceptable variation, although not quite as strong in some cases.

Just like most anything in technical analysis, there is also some subjectivity involved. One trader may look at a shooting star pattern and dismiss it because the upper shadow is only about one and a half times the length of the real body rather than two or more times the length as dictated by the criteria. Another trader may say that is trivial and it is long enough to generate a signal.

Some of the nonideal patterns and variations are just as strong as ideal patterns when viewed in the context of the bigger picture. For instance, if a mediocre pattern forms at a strong support or resistance area, it is still likely to follow through. That's where blending candlesticks with Western technical analysis can be especially helpful.

In summary, try not to be too rigid in your expectations or exclude valid signals that are not perfect setups, or you may miss many good trading opportunities and important warning signs.

Umbrella Lines: Hanging Man and Hammer

The Japanese refer to this formation as an *umbrella line* because it resembles an umbrella (see Figures 3.1 and 3.2). However, you'll rarely hear the term *umbrella line* passed around in conversations among traders in the United States. These patterns are simply referred to as the *hanging man* and the *hammer*.

These two reversal patterns have the same shape. The factor that differentiates one pattern from the other is whether it forms after a price advance (a bearish hanging man) or a price decline (a bullish hammer).

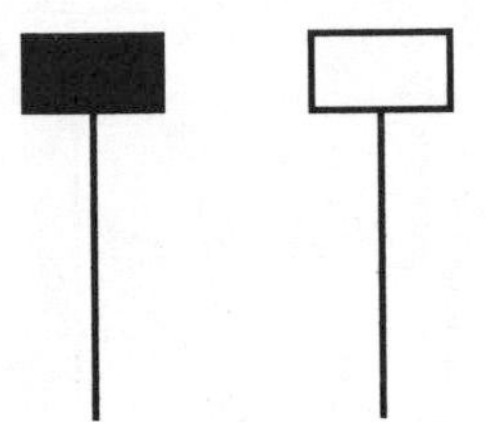

FIGURE 3.1 Umbrella lines: No upper shadow

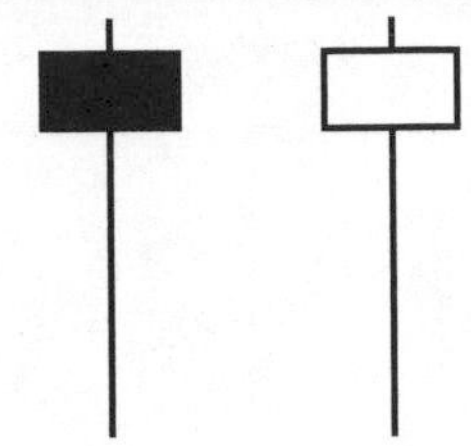

FIGURE 3.2 Umbrella lines: Small upper shadow

Pattern Description and Criteria

The hanging man and hammer are single-line candlestick patterns. They both include the following criteria:

- A small real body forms at, or very near, the upper end (the high) of the candlestick's range.
- The color of the small real body is not significant; it can be either black or white.
- The long lower shadow is typically two or more times the length of the real body.
- There should be no upper shadow (Figure 3.1) or a very small one (Figure 3.2). Price must close near the high of the range.

The long lower shadow indicates that the stock declined sharply during the trading session. In fact, at the time price was at the low, the candle had a long bearish real body with a shaven bottom. (Recall the discussion at the end of Chapter 2 about how the candlestick line changes shape throughout the session.) The bulls were able to grab control from the bears and push price back up to close near the high by the end of the session.

rally
A fairly sharp rise after a decline or a period of consolidation. Demand overwhelms supply resulting in a rise in value.

The smaller the real body, the shorter the upper shadow, and the longer the lower shadow, the more consequential the pattern.

Hanging Man

If an umbrella line forms after a price advance, it is called a *hanging man* and it is a bearish signal. A hanging man may appear after a short-term upward move, but it is more significant if it appears after a long or sharp rally or at an all-time high for the stock or index.

FIGURE 3.3 Hanging man (black body)

FIGURE 3.4 Hanging man (white body)

sell-off
Rapid selling of a stock or other trading instrument. Supply overwhelms demand resulting in a decline in value.

long (long position)
The purchase of a stock or other trading instrument with the expectation that the price will rise.

Although it does not matter if the small body is black (Figure 3.3) or white (Figure 3.4), a black body indicates that, even though the bulls did take control back from the bears intraday, they were not able to close the session positive. However, that does not necessarily mean that a bearish close will result in a higher likelihood of a top reversal than a bullish close.

Pattern Psychology The bulls have been benefiting from a price advance. Then a sharp sell-off occurs during the hanging man session, which gives them cause for concern. Some traders who already held long positions prior to the hanging man may use the intraday recovery to take profits near the high. Others will tighten their stop loss orders in order to protect the gains achieved during the prior run-up. Traders who entered new long positions during the hanging man session may be nervous. Some will have negative positions already, depending on where they entered the trade. If price declines after the hanging man pattern, many traders will be forced out of their long positions. Those holding short positions will be on the right side of the market, at least temporarily.

A long lower shadow after an upward move may be seen as a positive development because it shows that the bulls regained control during the session. Therefore, it is usually best to wait for more bearish confirmation before entering a short position based solely on a hanging man signal. To confirm the signal, the stock should trade below the hanging man's real body the following session, and ideally it should close below it.

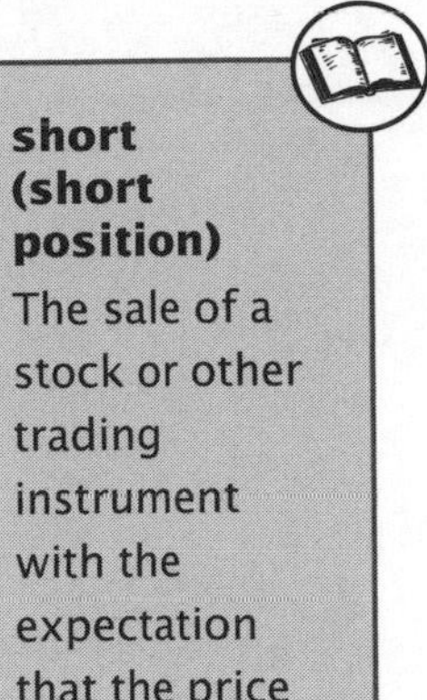

short (short position) The sale of a stock or other trading instrument with the expectation that the price will decline.

Chart Example Figure 3.5 shows a daily chart of Autozone Inc. (AZO). Three bearish hanging man patterns with short upper shadows formed within a five-week period. The first pattern (1) formed on June 5, 2007, after a several-day price advance off the May low. It was confirmed the following day with a lower close. The uptrend stalled for two more days before moving higher. The second hanging man (2) formed on June 19 after a few weeks of uptrend. The ascent of the uptrend was fairly steep and vulnerable to profit-taking. The hanging man's signal was confirmed the following session with a lower close. Price declined for several days. The third pattern (3) formed on July 6 and was confirmed the following session with a lower close. It became part of a larger bearish Western double top pattern that was created by the parallel highs in June and July. Price subsequently retraced a significant percentage of the prior trend.

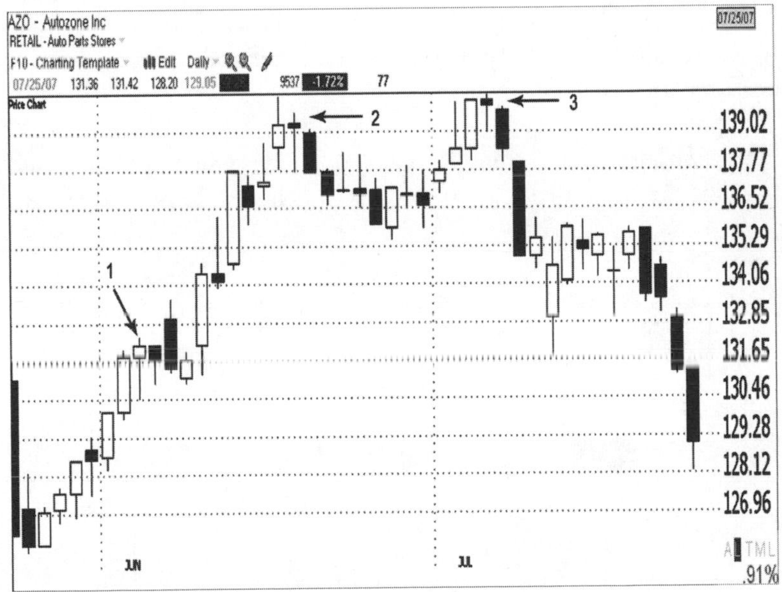

FIGURE 3.5 Bearish hanging man patterns formed after upward moves
Source: TeleChart 2007®

double top
A common bearish reversal pattern that occurs when two prominent, parallel (or nearly parallel) peaks form in an uptrend. The pattern resembles the letter "M." It is a valid reversal pattern when it is confirmed by a close below the middle of the "M."

The real bodies of the hanging man patterns labeled 2 and 3 were so small that they could also be interpreted as doji. Regardless, the signal is a bearish one. Doji are discussed later in this chapter. (*Note:* The plural of *doji* is also *doji.*)

Helpful Hint This pattern resembles a hanging man with his head at the top and his body hanging below. You may remember playing the drawing game called "hangman" as a child.

Hammer

If an umbrella line forms after a price decline, it is called a *hammer.* The hammer is the bullish counterpart of the hanging man. The hammer is a strong reversal signal. It is meaningful whether it forms after a short-term downside move or after a more significant decline.

Although it does not matter if the small real body is black (Figure 3.6) or white (Figure 3.7), a white body indicates that not only did the bulls wrestle control away from the bears, but they were able to close the session slightly positive. However, that does not necessarily mean that a bullish close will result in a higher likelihood of a bottom reversal than a bearish close.

Pattern Psychology The trend has been down when a sharp sell-off occurs, which, at first, further emboldens the bears. However, when the

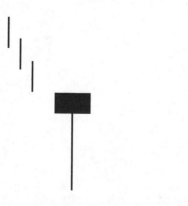

FIGURE 3.6 Hammer (black body) **FIGURE 3.7** Hammer (white body)

stop-loss order
An order placed with a broker to exit an open position if a stock reaches a certain price. The order is intended to limit the loss an investor takes if the stock moves against him. Stop-loss orders become market orders when triggered.

strong intraday reversal transpires, and price closes near its high, the remaining bears may be worrying over their positions. The long lower shadow indicates that bulls are stepping into long positions. Some traders who have short positions will either cover them or tighten their stop-loss orders in order to protect the gains achieved during the prior downswing. If price continues to rise following the hammer pattern, more traders will be forced to cover their short positions. Since short covering equals buying, and bulls will also be buying, it provides fuel for a rally.

It is not necessary to wait for further confirmation before entering a long position based on the hammer's signal. For traders who feel more comfortable doing so, though, confirmation occurs when price trades above the hammer's real body, and ideally it should close above it.

double bottom
A common bullish reversal pattern that occurs when two prominent, parallel (or nearly parallel) bottoms form in a downtrend. The pattern resembles the letter "W." It is a valid reversal pattern when it is confirmed by a close above the middle of the "W."

Chart Example Figure 3.8 shows a daily chart of Pediatrix Medical Group Inc. (PDX). A hammer with no upper shadow formed on June 8, 2007, following a sharp decline during the prior three sessions. The long lower shadow of the hammer was about three times the length of its small real body, indicating a strong bounce intraday. Price turned up over the next several days, but then rolled over and tested the hammer's low as support on June 25. The successful test of support at the hammer's low (dotted line) set up a larger Western double bottom reversal pattern.

cover (buy-to-cover)
An order placed with a broker to exit a short position.

Helpful Hint This pattern resembles a hammer with its long handle and its head set crosswise at the top. Think of it as the stock "hammering out a bottom."

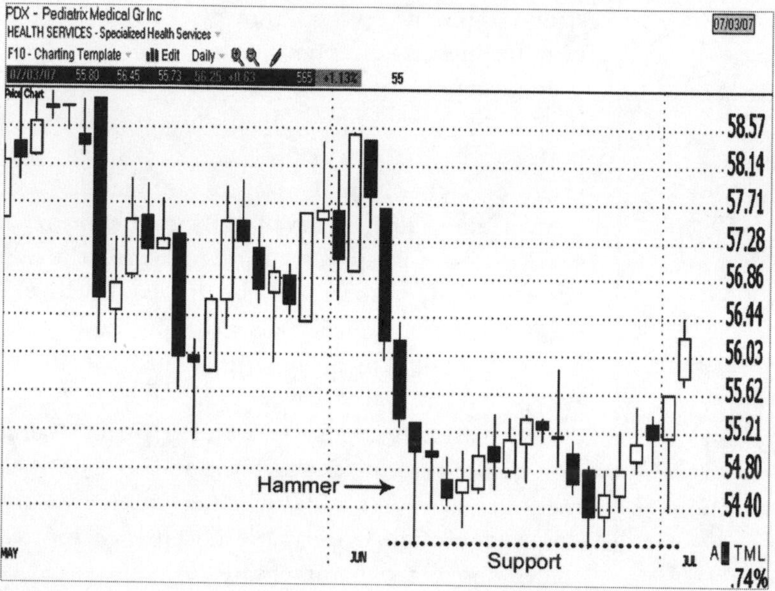

FIGURE 3.8 Bullish hammer formed after a price decline
Source: TeleChart 2007®

Shooting Star and Inverted Hammer

The long shadow of the shooting star and inverted hammer patterns points in the opposite direction to that of the hanging man and hammer. Thus, they are inverted umbrella lines. The factor that differentiates one pattern from the other is whether it forms after a price advance (a bearish shooting star) or a price decline (a bullish inverted hammer).

Pattern Description and Criteria

The shooting star and the inverted hammer are single-line candlestick patterns. They both include the following criteria:

- A small real body forms at, or very near, the bottom (the low) of the candlestick's range.
- The color of the small body is not significant; it can be either black or white.
- The long upper shadow is typically two or more times the length of the real body.
- There should be no lower shadow (Figure 3.9) or a very small one (Figure 3.10). Price must close near the low of the range.

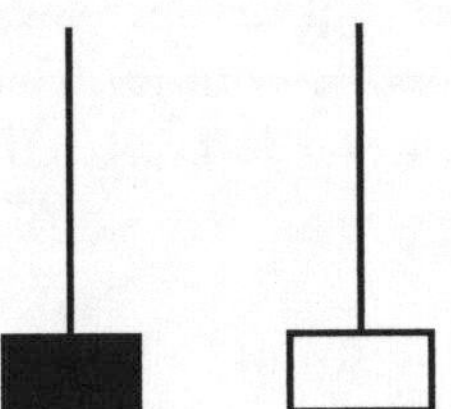

FIGURE 3.9 Inverted umbrella lines: no lower shadow

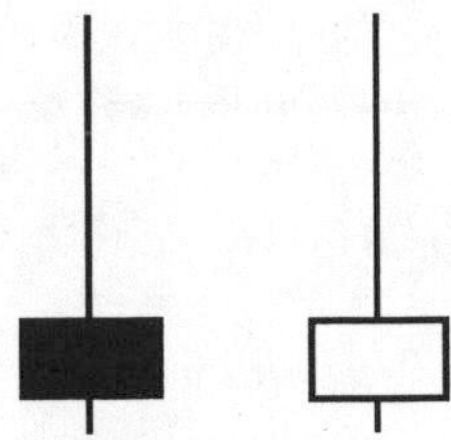

FIGURE 3.10 Inverted umbrella lines: small lower shadow

The long upper shadow indicates that the stock rallied strongly during the trading session. In fact, at the time price was at the high of the session, the candle had a long bullish real body with a shaven top. The bears were then able to force price back down to close near the low by the end of the session.

The smaller the real body, the shorter the lower shadow, and the longer the upper shadow, the more consequential the pattern.

Shooting Star

If the inverted umbrella type of pattern forms after a price advance, it is called a *shooting star,* and it has bearish implications.

Although it does not matter if the small body is black (Figure 3.11) or white (Figure 3.12), a black body indicates that not only did the rally fail but the bears were able to close the session slightly negative. However, that does not necessarily mean that a bearish close will result in a higher likelihood of a top reversal than a bullish close.

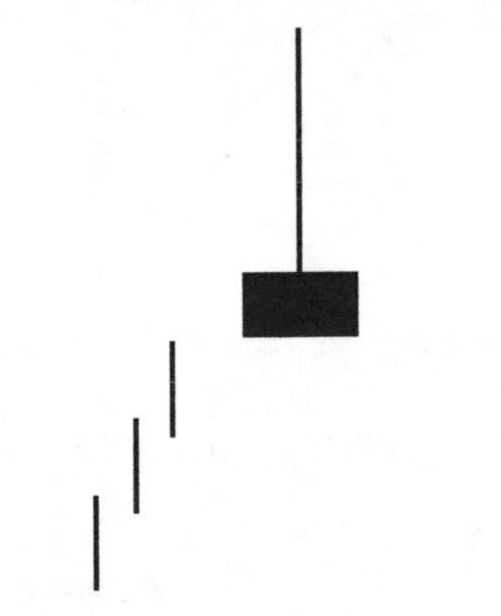

FIGURE 3.11 Shooting star (black body)

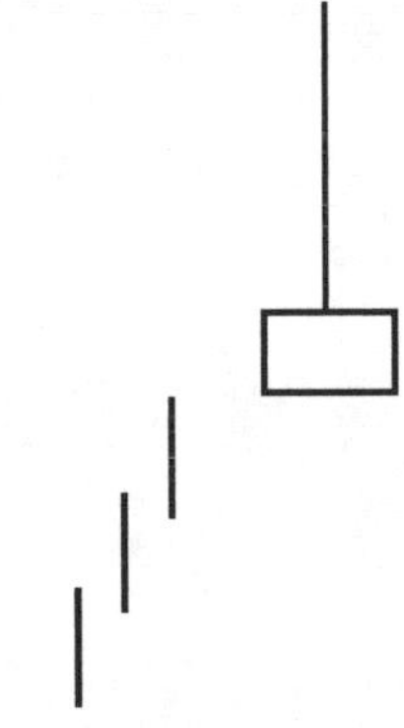

FIGURE 3.12 Shooting star (white body)

An ideal shooting star will have a real body that gaps up open away from the prior real body like the other star patterns discussed later in this chapter. It is acceptable, though, for the real body of the shooting star to overlap the prior candle's real body.

Pattern Psychology Price has been rising and another strong rally occurs after the open, encouraging the bulls. That bullish sentiment is challenged later during the session as price reverses direction intraday. Traders who had just entered new long positions during the shooting star session will feel even more anxious as many of them watch their trades turn negative. By the close of market, the day's rally has been erased as price closes at, or near, the low of the session. If price continues to decline following the shooting star's signal, many bulls will exit their long positions and more bears will establish short positions.

It is best to wait for confirmation before entering a short position based solely on a shooting star signal. To confirm the signal, price should trade below the shooting star's real body, and ideally it should close below it.

Chart Example Figure 3.13 shows a daily chart of MGP Ingredients Inc. (MGPI). On March 30, 2007, price gapped up open from the prior day's close, leaving a gap between the two real bodies and forming a shooting star

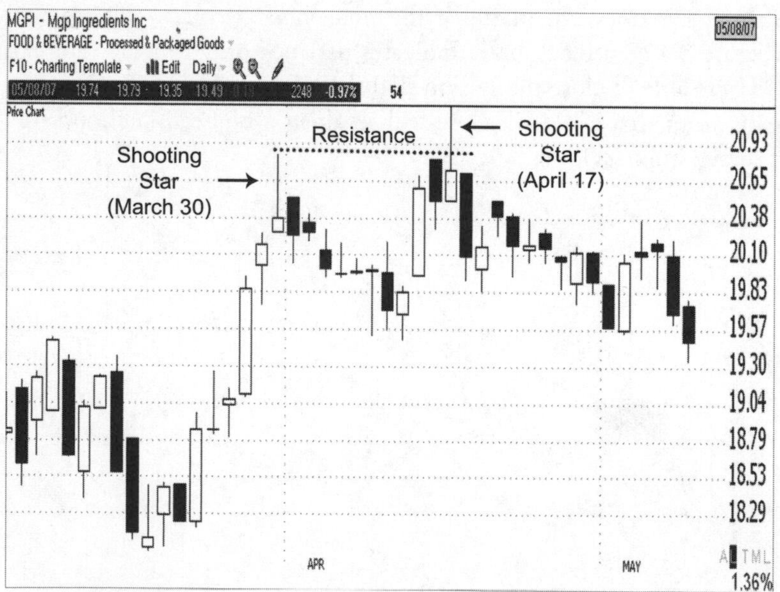

FIGURE 3.13 Shooting star patterns formed after upward moves
Source: TeleChart 2007®

with no lower shadow. (The prior session was a hanging man, although its lower shadow was not quite twice the length of its real body.) Price declined for several days following the shooting star's bearish reversal signal. Price moved up again, ending with another shooting star with a shaven bottom on April 17. Its real body formed within the prior bar's real body, so there was no gap up at the open like the first shooting star. However, it did meet the primary criteria for the pattern so its reversal signal should not be ignored, especially because it formed at resistance. The high of the first shooting star's upper shadow provided resistance for the second shooting star. Although price broke through that resistance intraday on April 17, it did not close above it. Price reversed direction again after the emergence of the second shooting star.

Helpful Hint The shooting star pattern looks like a star falling down from the sky with its long tail trailing behind it.

Inverted Hammer

If an inverted umbrella type of pattern forms after a price decline, it is called an *inverted hammer.* The inverted hammer is the bullish counterpart of the shooting star.

Although it does not matter if the small body is black (Figure 3.14) or white (Figure 3.15), a white body indicates that the bulls were able to rally the stock intraday and close the session slightly positive. However, that does not necessarily mean that a bullish close will result in a higher likelihood of a bottom reversal than a bearish close.

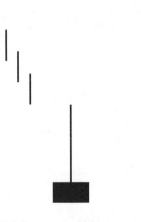

FIGURE 3.14 Inverted hammer (black body)

FIGURE 3.15 Inverted hammer (white body)

Pattern Psychology Price has been declining so the strong rally that occurs intraday will make some bears nervous. Even though the stock fell back and closed near the low, it is now evident that the bulls are showing interest. Astute traders may use the information the inverted hammer provides as motivation to cover their short positions. If price moves higher following the inverted hammer, a short-covering rally may develop.

A long upper shadow after a decline may be viewed as a negative development because the bulls were not able to sustain the strong rally that occurred intraday. Therefore, it may be best to wait for more bullish confirmation before entering a long position based solely on a signal from an inverted hammer. To confirm the signal, price should trade above the inverted hammer's real body the following session, and ideally it should close above it.

Chart Example Figure 3.16 shows a daily chart of Limited Brands Inc. (LTD). The long lower shadow that formed on May 15, 2007, was the first sign that the decline may be losing its force. The next morning price gapped down open and then rallied, but closed the session back near the low, leaving a bullish inverted hammer. The hammer that formed during the following session held support at the inverted hammer's low and closed above the inverted hammer's real body (confirmation). It was followed the next session by a strong white candle, which showed that the bulls had arrived in force.

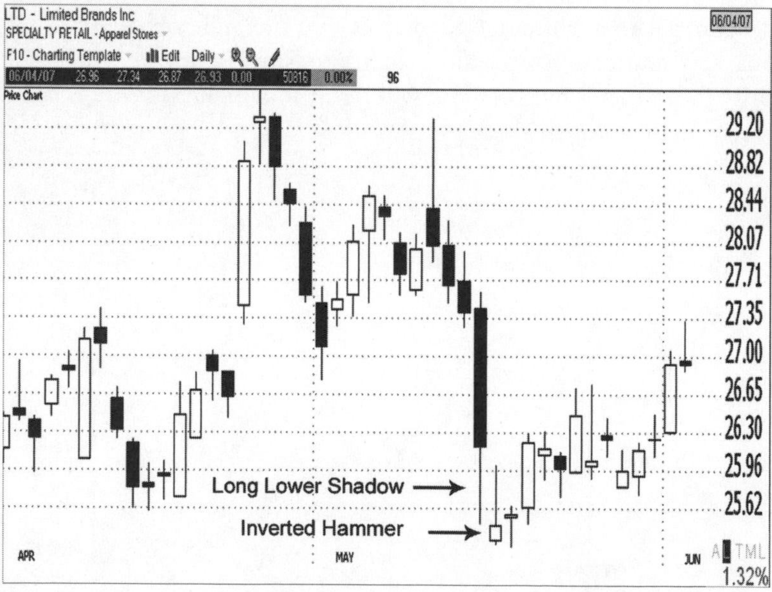

FIGURE 3.16 Bullish inverted hammer formed after a price decline
Source: TeleChart 2007®

Doji

Even though it is comprised of only a single candlestick line, the *doji* can be a very significant signal, especially if it forms at a top. The doji is probably the most commonly referenced candlestick pattern. It gets so much attention that some traders give it too much credit. Although its signal should not be ignored, its importance should not be overstated either. A doji should be considered a strong warning, but not a guarantee, that price may change direction.

Pattern Description and Criteria

The doji includes the following criteria:

- The pattern has no real body. The opening and closing prices are exactly the same, or nearly the same, and are plotted as a horizontal line that intersects the vertical range, as shown in Figure 3.17.
- The length of the upper and lower shadows can vary.

Although an ideal doji is formed during a trading session in which the opening and closing prices are exactly the same, that scenario is not very common. If the open and close are nearly the same, it is still considered a doji. If the real body is very small, it is sometimes referred to as a *near-doji* (Figure 3.18). It is important to note that "nearly the same" in reference to the open and closing prices is a relative concept.

Example

If the opening and closing prices are 5 cents apart, that would not be much difference for a stock trading at \$50. However, it would result in a larger real body on a stock trading at \$5. A higher-priced stock, say one trading at \$150, may have a difference of 20 cents or more between the open and close and still look like a doji, or a near-doji.

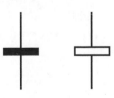

FIGURE 3.17 Doji (no body) **FIGURE 3.18** Near-doji (very small body)

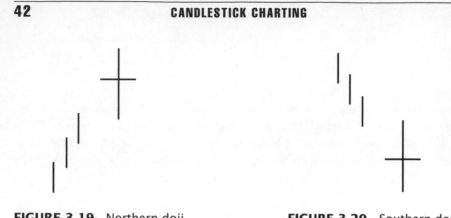

FIGURE 3.19 Northern doji (bearish)

FIGURE 3.20 Southern doji (bullish)

A doji that appears after an upward move should be viewed as a bearish signal. Its signal is stronger if it follows one or more long bullish candles. A doji that forms after a price advance is more potent and reliable than one that forms in a declining market. Steve Nison refers to a doji that forms after a price advance as a *northern doji* (Figure 3.19).

A doji that appears after a downward move may also result in a change in price direction; however, doji tend to lose some of their potency in a declining market. It is usually best to wait for more confirmation when a doji forms in a downtrend before entering a long position based solely on its signal. Nison refers to a doji that forms at the end of a price decline as a *southern doji* (Figure 3.20).

Pattern Psychology

After a directional price move, a candlestick with no real body forms, representing equilibrium between the bulls and bears. The doji represents indecision, which is not likely to sustain a move. Its appearance should be considered a warning that a change in the trend's direction may occur.

Chart Example

Figure 3.21 shows a daily chart of Marchex Inc. (MCHX). On June 7, 2007, a bullish southern doji formed after a downward move. Price consolidated for several days using the doji's low as support (dotted line) before rising back up to test the May high. On June 26, a bearish northern doji formed after the upward move. Price consolidated for three more days, using the doji's high as resistance (dotted line), before turning back down and filling the gap.

Helpful Hint

A doji resembles a cross.

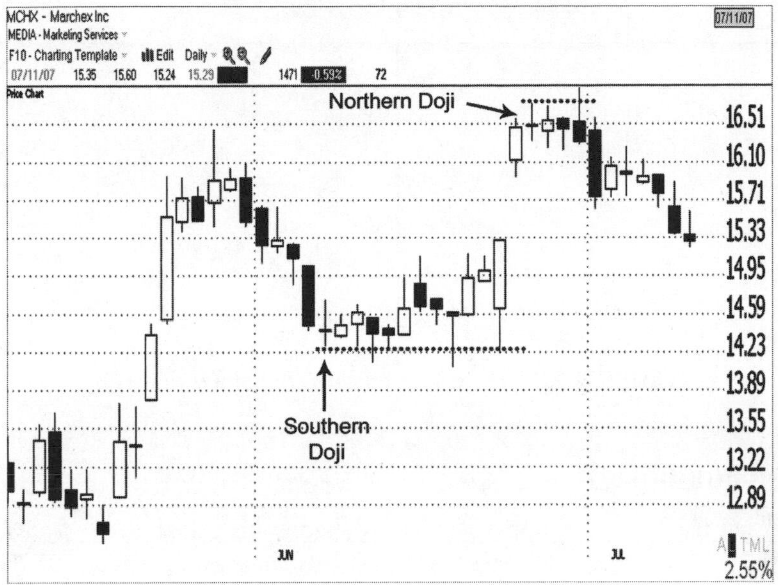

FIGURE 3.21 Northern and southern doji
Source: TeleChart 2007®

Doji Is a Component of Other Patterns

A doji can stand on its own merit, but it also is a component of other candlestick patterns. If a doji appears as part of another formation, it strengthens the signal. Some examples include the following:

- If the middle bar of a three-candlestick evening star is a doji, the pattern is more ominous. In that case, it would be referred to as an *evening doji star.*
- If a doji appears as the second candle in a harami, it will increase that pattern's implications and would be referred to as a *harami cross.*

Distinctive Doji

A doji may be referred to by a nickname, depending on the length of the shadows and where the opening and closing prices appear along the vertical line that forms the candlestick's range.

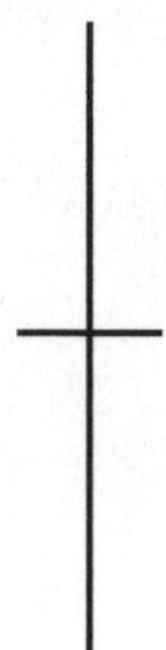

FIGURE 3.22 Long-legged doji (rickshaw man)

Long-Legged Doji

A doji that has very long upper and lower shadows is called a *long-legged doji* (Figure 3.22). It may also be referred to as a *rickshaw man.*

Pattern Psychology The long upper shadow indicates that the stock rallied at some point during the session when the high was established. The long lower shadow indicates that the stock also sold off sharply at some point during the same session when the low was established. By the close of market, neither the bulls nor the bears could claim victory. According to Steve Nison, in his book *Japanese Candlestick Charting Techniques* (New York Institute of Finance, 2001, p. 162): "These long shadows hint, as the Japanese say, 'the market has lost its sense of direction.'"

The long-legged pattern illustrates a volatile struggle between the bulls and bears during the session. If you view an intraday chart of the day's price action, it may look somewhat like a roller coaster ride. Refer back to Figure 2.16 in Chapter 2 to see an example of how a long-legged candle might look intraday.

Chart Example Figure 3.23 shows a daily chart of Infosys Technologies (INFY). A high-wave candle formed on March 30, 2007. The low of the high-wave candle provided support for the next day's session and a reversal followed. The high-wave formation is a long-legged spinning top. Another long-legged pattern formed on April 13. It had no real body; therefore, it was a long-legged doji. The high of the long-legged doji provided resistance during the next two trading sessions and a decline followed.

Gravestone Doji

When the horizontal line representing the opening and closing prices forms at, or very near, the bottom of the vertical line (the low of the session),

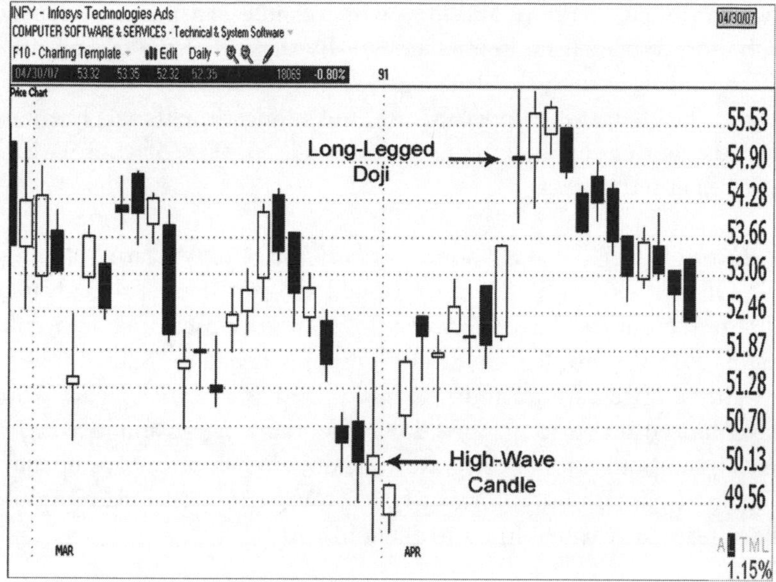

FIGURE 3.23 Long-legged doji compared to a high-wave candle
Source: TeleChart 2007®

with a long upper shadow, it is a distinctive variation called a *gravestone doji* (Figure 3.24).

When it forms after a price advance, the gravestone doji resembles a shooting star. If it forms after a price decline, it resembles an inverted hammer. The difference is that the shooting star and inverted hammer patterns both have small real bodies at, or near, the lows of their sessions. The gravestone doji has no real body because the opening and closing prices are the same, or very close to the same. The presence of a doji produces a stronger signal. As is usually the case with a doji, the gravestone pattern is typically stronger at market tops than at market bottoms.

Pattern Psychology The long upper shadow indicates that during the session the market rallied strongly. At the time price was at the high of the session,

FIGURE 3.24 Gravestone doji

there was no upper shadow. The long white candle had a shaven top (and a shaven bottom if there is no lower shadow). By the end of the session the bears were successful in beating the bulls back to the same point where the session had started. The longer the upper shadow, the stronger the signal. The Japanese say that the gravestone doji represents the gravestones of those who died defending their territory.

Chart Example Figure 3.25 shows a daily chart of Vulcan Materials Co. (VMC). On April 30, 2007, the stock gapped up open after a price advance and rallied strongly during the session. By the session's close, price had fallen all the way back to the low, leaving a very long upper shadow. Such a long upper shadow after a price advance must be interpreted as a bearish signal. You may also have noticed that price gapped down the following session, leaving a void on the chart on both sides of the gravestone doji. When price gaps up and then down again in this fashion, it forms a bearish Western reversal pattern called an *island top*. Gaps are covered in more detail in Part II.

Helpful Hint An easy way to remember this doji's nickname is by noting that the long upper shadow looks like the upright part of a gravestone and the horizontal line looks like the gravestone's base.

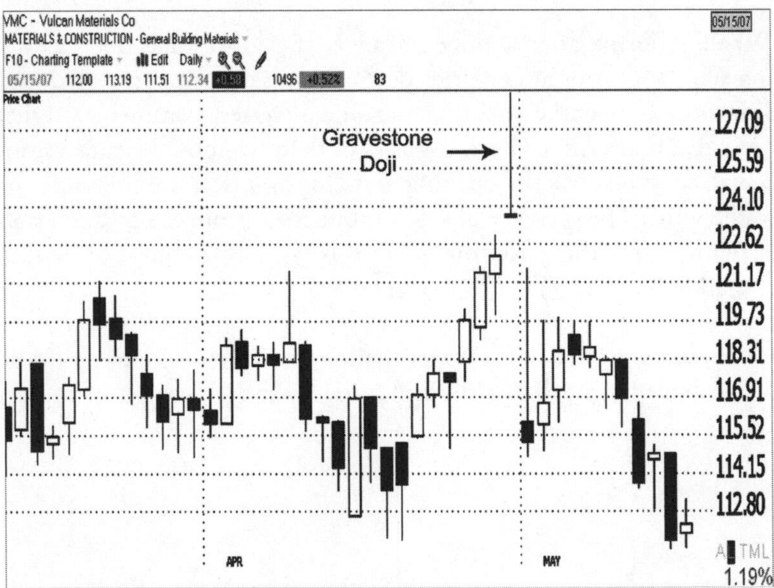

FIGURE 3.25 Gravestone doji formed after a price advance
Source: TeleChart 2007®

FIGURE 3.26 Dragonfly doji

Dragonfly Doji

When the horizontal line representing the opening and closing prices forms at, or very near, the top of the vertical line (the high of the session), with a long lower shadow, it is a distinctive variation referred to as a *dragonfly doji* (Figure 3.26).

The long lower shadow of the dragonfly doji points the opposite direction of the gravestone doji's shadow. When it forms at the end of a price advance, the dragonfly doji resembles a hanging man. If it forms after a price decline, it resembles a hammer. The difference is that the hanging man and hammer patterns both have small real bodies at, or near, the highs of their sessions. The dragonfly doji has no real body because the opening and closing prices are the same, or very close to the same.

Pattern Psychology The long lower shadow indicates that during the session the market sold off sharply. At the time price was at the low of the session, the long black candle had a shaven bottom (and shaven top if there was no upper shadow). By the end of the session, the bulls were successful in pushing price back up to the same point where the session had started.

Chart Example Figure 3.27 shows a daily chart of Wheeling-Pittsburgh Corp. (WPSC). On July 27, 2007, a dragonfly doji formed after a sharp decline back to support at the June low (dotted line). Although doji are typically better at calling tops than bottoms, in a situation like this where the doji formed at prior support, it increased the likelihood that price would change direction after the doji. The very long lower shadow shows the covering of short positions by bears and the willingness of the bulls to step into long positions at that support level. Note also in this example that a hammer formed two days prior to the dragonfly doji; however, it failed to confirm with a higher close the next session.

Helpful Hint An easy way to remember this doji's nickname is by noting that the long lower shadow resembles a dragonfly's long body. The horizontal line looks like its outstretched wings, which are closer to the top of its body.

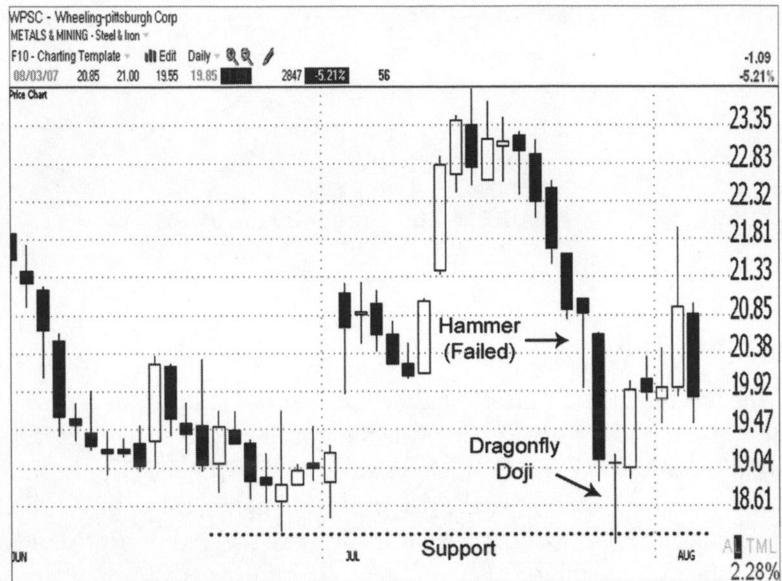

FIGURE 3.27 Dragonfly doji formed at support
Source: TeleChart 2007®

Dark Cloud Cover and Piercing Pattern

Both the dark cloud cover and the piercing pattern are reversal patterns that are formed from two candlesticks of the opposite color. They may be referred to generically as *piercing lines* because they both pierce the prior candle's real body.

Dark Cloud Cover

The *dark cloud cover* (Figure 3.28) is a strong reversal pattern that forms after a price advance.

Pattern Description and Criteria The dark cloud cover pattern includes the following criteria:

- The first candle has a strong bullish real body (at least average length, and often it is a long white candle).
- The second candle has a bearish real body. Price gaps up open above the prior session's high and closes deeply (ideally half-way or more) into the prior session's white real body. Because of this price action, the second candle's black real body will be at least average length, or longer.

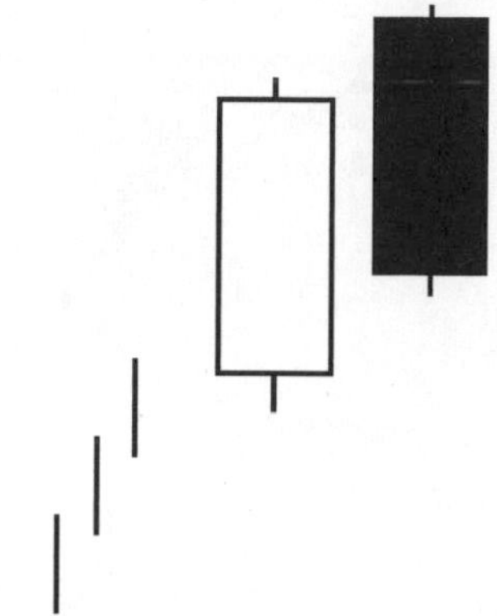

FIGURE 3.28 Dark cloud cover

The deeper the second candle's black real body penetrates the prior candle's white real body, the stronger the signal. If it engulfs the prior candle's entire real body, it is not a dark cloud cover pattern; it would be a bearish engulfing pattern.

If the second candle's bearish real body does not close at least halfway into the prior candle's bullish real body, it may be best to wait for additional downside confirmation before entering a short position based strictly on the dark cloud cover's signal. Confirmation comes when price trades below the dark cloud cover day during the following session, and even better if it closes below it.

It is not unusual to see heavy volume accompany this reversal pattern. If so, and if this pattern forms at a major market top, it is a climax move called a *blow-off top.*

blow-off top
A sharp upward thrust in an uptrend is followed by aggressive selling. The move is accompanied by heavy volume and often results in a change in the direction of the trend.

Pattern Psychology The trend is up and the formation of a strong white candle shows the dominance of the bulls. The market gaps up open during the following session with the bulls still in control. Then price turns down and a sharp sell-off occurs. In spite of the higher open, by the end of the session the bears have completely taken control away from the bulls and closed the session well below the prior session's close.

The pattern clearly demonstrates an abrupt reversal in market sentiment. It is a striking reversal pattern and will be noticed by many traders.

Chart Example Figure 3.29 shows a daily chart of Knightsbridge Tankers (VLCCF). After trending up for several weeks, price gapped up open to a new

FIGURE 3.29 Bearish dark cloud cover pattern was accompanied by heavy volume
Source: TeleChart 2007®

high on May 22, 2007 (circled). A sell-off began, and by the close of the session nearly all of the gains from the prior session's strong bullish candle had been wiped out. Volume was heavy leading up to the reversal signal, as well as on both days of the dark cloud formation suggesting a climax top. Price continued its decline in the following days.

Acceptable Variation Although it sends a stronger signal if the second candle gaps up open above the prior candle's high, it is acceptable if price only gaps up open above the prior candle's close (Figure 3.30). Because both candlestick lines of this pattern should have fairly long real bodies, the acceptable variation would include the following criteria:

- The first candle has a strong bullish real body and also has an upper shadow.
- The second candle gaps up open, not above the high of the prior session's upper shadow, but above the prior session's close. In other words, it opens within the prior candle's upper shadow.
- The second candle's black real body closes well into the prior candle's white real body.

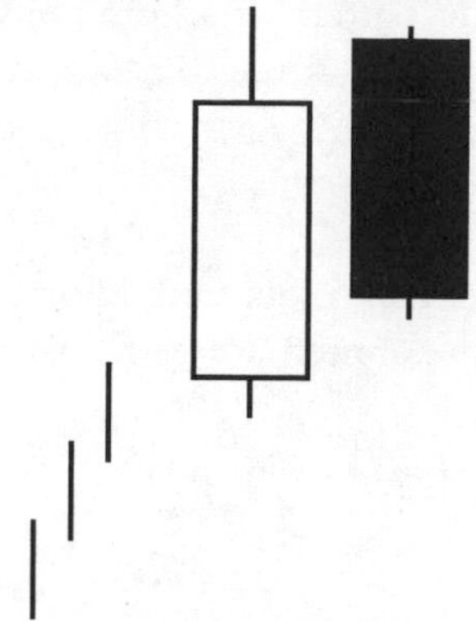

FIGURE 3.30 Dark cloud cover (variation)

Chart Example (Variation) Figure 3.31 shows a daily chart of Imperial Oil Ltd. (IMO). On May 22, 2007, a strong bullish candle formed with a long upper shadow (circled). The next session gapped up open above the prior candle's close but within its upper shadow. Price reversed direction and closed far into the prior candle's bullish real body. Heavy volume accompanied the bearish reversal formation. Price consolidated after the climax move.

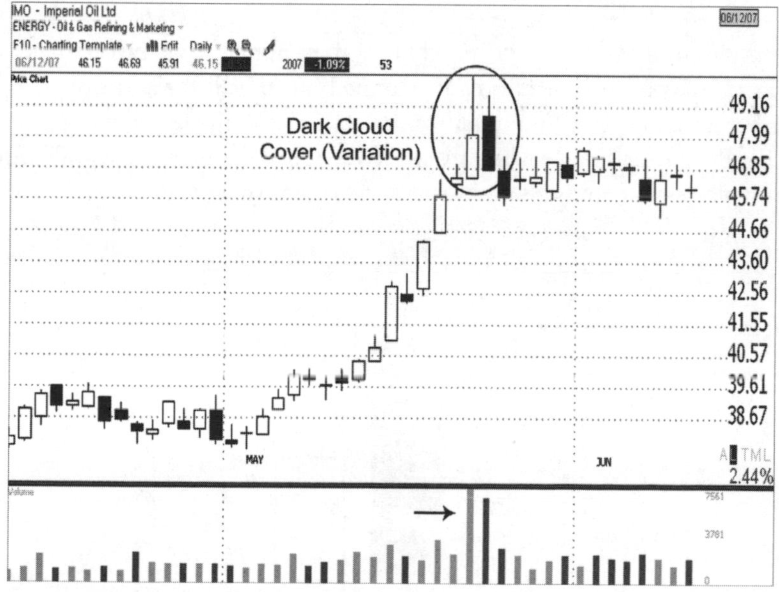

FIGURE 3.31 A variation of the bearish dark cloud cover pattern. Price opened above the prior bar's close rather than above its high

Source: TeleChart 2007®

Helpful Hint Think of this pattern as an ominous black storm cloud rolling in over a white cloud.

Piercing Pattern

The *piercing pattern* (Figure 3.32) is a strong reversal pattern that forms after a price decline. It is the bullish counterpart of the dark cloud cover pattern.

Pattern Description and Criteria The piercing pattern includes the following criteria:

- The first candle has a strong bearish real body (at least average length, and often it is a long black candle).
- The second candle has a bullish real body. Price gaps down open below the prior session's low and closes deeply (more than half-way) into the prior candle's black real body. Because of this price action, the second candle's white real body will be at least average length, or longer.

The deeper the second candle's white real body penetrates the prior candle's black real body, the more likely a reversal will occur. If it engulfs the prior candle's entire real body it is not a piercing pattern; it would be a bullish engulfing pattern.

If the second candle's bullish real body does not close at least halfway into the prior candle's bearish real body, it may be best to wait for additional confirmation before entering a long position based strictly on the piercing pattern's signal. Confirmation comes when price trades above the piercing candle during the following session, and even better if it closes above it.

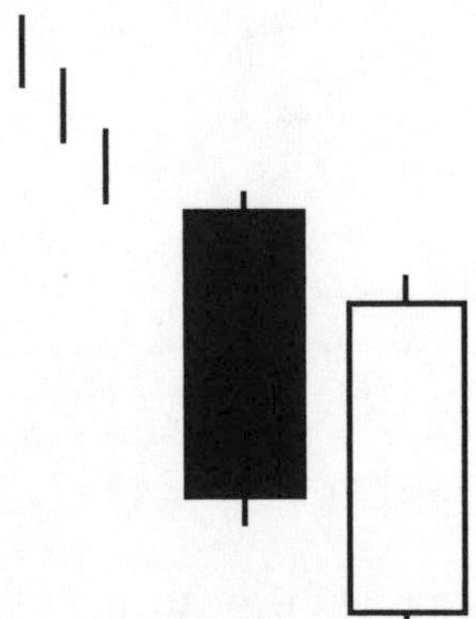

FIGURE 3.32 Piercing pattern

It is not unusual to see heavy volume accompany this reversal pattern. If so, it may point to a selling climax.

selling climax
A sharp sell-off in a downtrend is followed by aggressive buying. The move is accompanied by heavy volume and often results in a change in the direction of the trend.

Pattern Psychology The trend is down and the formation of a strong bearish candle further supports the dominance of the bears. The market gaps down open during the following session with the bears still in control. Then price turns up, and a strong rally ensues. By the end of the session, the bulls have been successful at closing price deeply into the prior black candle's real body.

One look at this pattern and it is obvious that there was an abrupt reversal in market sentiment. A weak (bearish) open is reversed, and price closes well above the prior day's close. The striking contrast is very noticeable on the chart and will be seen by many traders.

Chart Example Figure 3.33 shows a daily chart of Talisman Energy Inc. (TLM). After a fast decline, price gapped down open on June 27, 2007, below the prior session's low (circled). Price reversed direction intraday and by the end

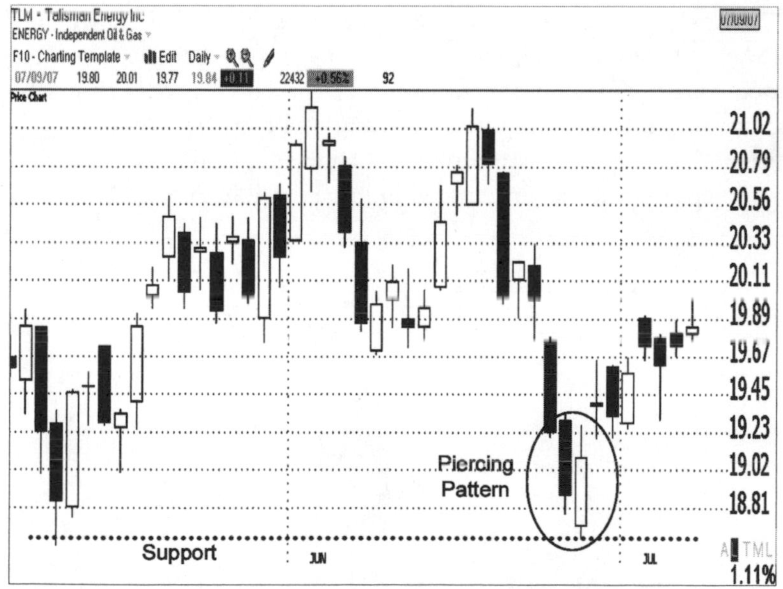

FIGURE 3.33 Bullish piercing pattern formed at support
Source: TeleChart 2007®

of the session closed well into the prior candle's long black real body. This pattern had a higher chance of changing the trend direction because it formed at support at the May low (dotted line).

Acceptable Variation Although it provides a stronger signal if price gaps down open below the prior session's low, it is acceptable if price only gaps down open below the prior session's close (Figure 3.34). Because both candlestick lines of this pattern should have fairly long real bodies, the acceptable variation would include the following criteria:

- The first candle has a strong bearish real body and also has a lower shadow.
- The second candle gaps down open, not below the low of the prior session's lower shadow, but below the prior session's close. In other words, it opens within the prior candle's lower shadow.
- The second candle's white real body closes at least halfway into the prior candle's black real body.

Chart Example (Variation) Figure 3.35 shows a daily chart of Intercontinental Exchange Inc. (ICE). After a fast decline from July 17–25, 2007, price gapped down open on July 26 (circled), to support (dotted line). Price did not gap open below the prior candle's low, but below its close and within its lower shadow. Price reversed direction intraday and closed well into the prior candle's bearish real body. This example had even more support below than that shown in Figure 3.33. Many traders will observe such strong support, which increases the likelihood that this pattern will follow through. This example shows how an Eastern signal (reversal pattern) can converge with a Western technical event (support) to increase the probability that a change in price direction will occur. Support and resistance will be discussed in more detail in Part II.

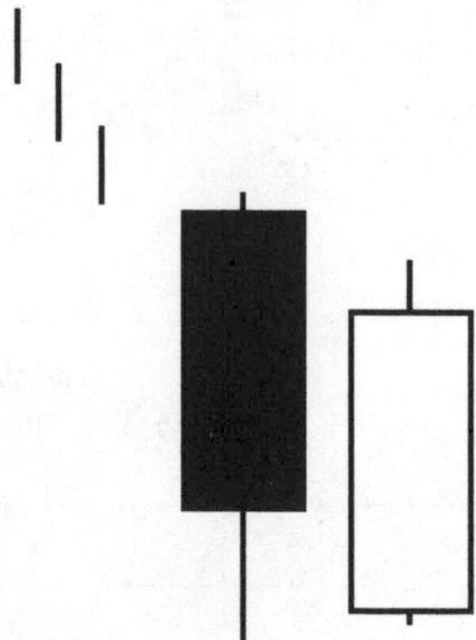

FIGURE 3.34 Piercing pattern (variation)

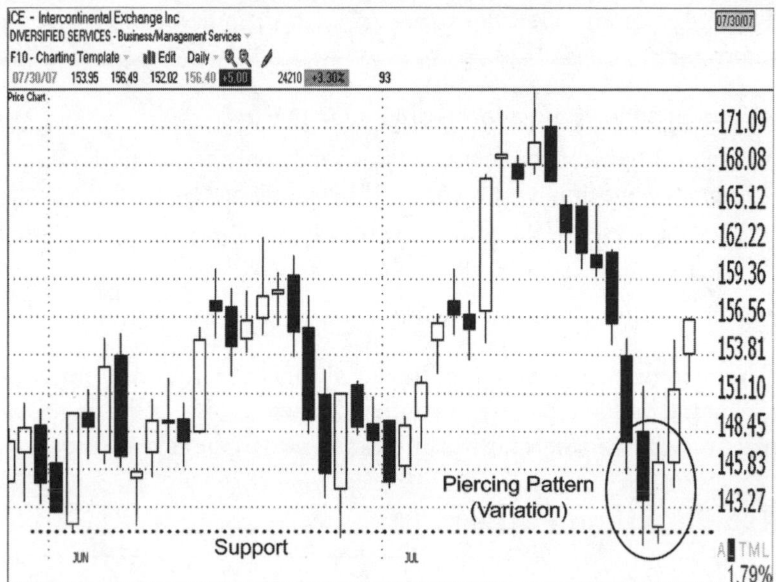

FIGURE 3.35 Variation of the piercing pattern formed at prior support. Price opened below the prior bar's close rather than below its low
Source: TeleChart 2007®

Engulfing Patterns

An engulfing pattern is a strong reversal signal that includes two candlestick lines of opposite color. The pattern forms after a directional price move, either up (bearish pattern) or down (bullish pattern). The trend that precedes the pattern may be short or longer term.

Pattern Description and Criteria

Engulfing patterns include the following criteria:

- The color of the first candle's real body should correspond to the direction of the current trend: white in an uptrend or black in a downtrend.
- The second candle has a longer real body and is the opposite color of the prior candle.
- The real body of the second candle must completely engulf (surround) the real body of the first candle. It is not necessary that the second candle envelop the prior candle's upper and lower shadows, just the real body.

Engulfing patterns are even stronger if one or more of the following factors are present:

- The engulfing candle forms after a long or steep trend.
- The real body of the first candle is very small, for example, a spinning top or even a doji, and is engulfed by a long real body.
- The engulfing candle has a long real body with little or no upper and lower shadows (shaven, or nearly so).
- The engulfing session is accompanied by heavy volume.

The engulfing pattern exemplifies an abrupt turnaround in investor psychology. By the time the pattern is confirmed by the close of the engulfing session, price may have made a fairly significant move in the new direction.

Bearish Engulfing Pattern

A *bearish engulfing pattern* forms after a price advance. The first candle has a bullish real body. The second candle has a longer bearish real body that completely surrounds the prior candle's white real body (Figure 3.36).

You will observe some bearish engulfing patterns where the close of the first session is the same, or nearly the same, as the open of the second session (Figure 3.37 left); or the open of the first session is the same, or near, the close of the second session (Figure 3.37 right). It is acceptable if the prices match at either end, but not at both ends. The second candle's real body should be noticeably longer than the first candle's. If the prices were to match at both ends, the real bodies would be the same size, which would not meet the engulfing pattern criteria (though it would still show an abrupt shift in market sentiment). The same scenarios shown in Figure 3.37 apply to the bullish engulfing pattern discussed later in this chapter except that the bullish pattern occurs after a downtrend and the colors are reversed (black followed by white).

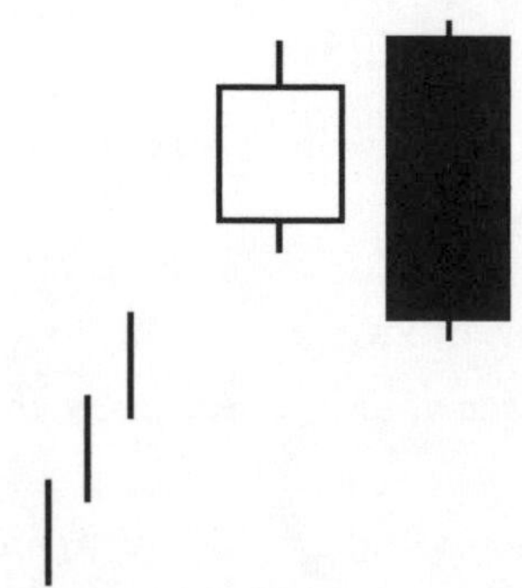

FIGURE 3.36 Bearish engulfing pattern

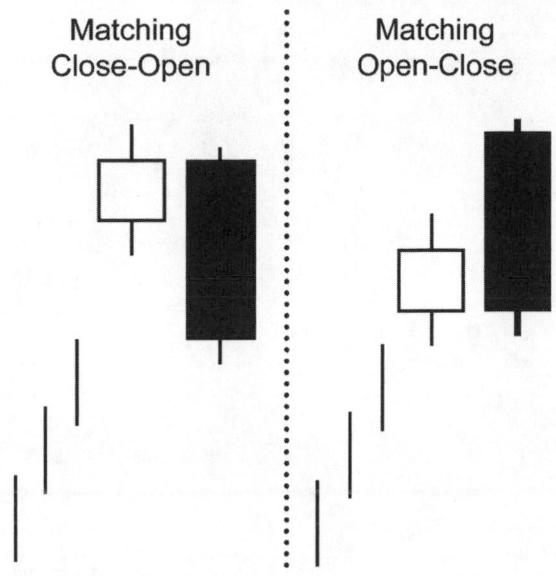

FIGURE 3.37 Acceptable bearish engulfing patterns

Pattern Psychology In a rising market, price opens in the direction of the trend but then makes an abrupt turnaround. The strong bearish engulfing session sends a clear message that the bears have overtaken the bulls. The bearish engulfing pattern is a prominent formation and will be noticed by many traders.

The bearish engulfing pattern is similar to the dark cloud cover pattern except that, rather than piercing deeply into the prior candle's white real body, it completely envelops it. In addition, the first candle's real body need not be at least average length or longer, as required by the dark cloud cover pattern. The bearish engulfing pattern is generally a stronger reversal signal than the dark cloud cover pattern.

Chart Example Figure 3.38 shows a daily chart of Bolt Technology Corp. (BTJ). A bearish engulfing pattern formed on July 9, 2007. This engulfing pattern was made stronger because: it followed a sharp upward move; the engulfing candle was significantly longer than the prior candle; and it was accompanied by heavy volume. Price declined during the session following the engulfing day, and then rallied back up from July 11 to 13 and formed a dark cloud cover pattern at resistance provided by the top of the bearish engulfing pattern. That test of resistance also set up a small bearish Western double top pattern, which was confirmed on July 25 when the stock broke down through support at the July 10 swing low (dotted line). Price gapped down the next day, then curled back up for three days and tested the prior support (dotted line) as resistance before declining further.

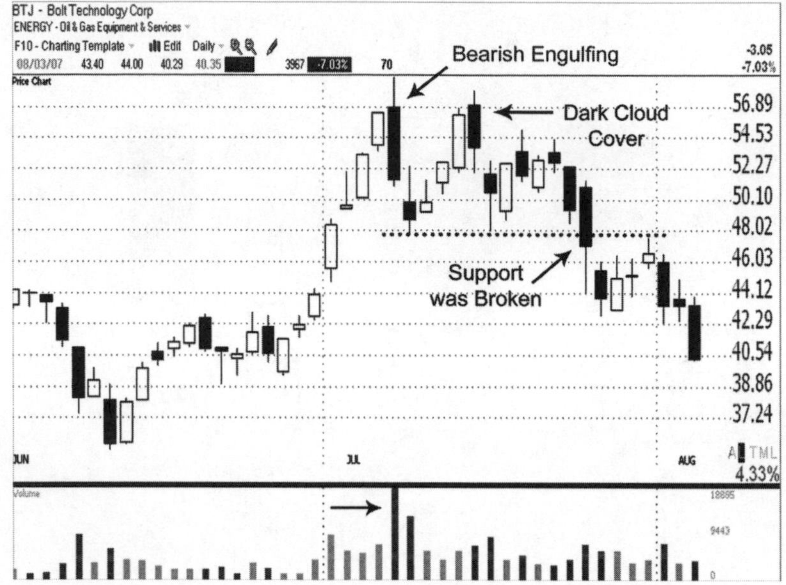

FIGURE 3.38 Bearish engulfing pattern formed after a swift move up
Source: TeleChart 2007®

Bullish Engulfing Pattern

A *bullish engulfing pattern* forms after a price decline. It is the bullish counterpart of the bearish engulfing pattern. The first candle has a bearish real body. The second candle has a longer bullish real body that completely surrounds the prior candle's black real body (Figure 3.39).

Pattern Psychology In a declining market, price opens in the direction of the trend but then makes an abrupt turnaround. The strong engulfing session sends a clear message that the bulls have overtaken the bears. Many traders will react to this prominent pattern. Concerned bears will scramble to cover their positions, providing fuel for a rally.

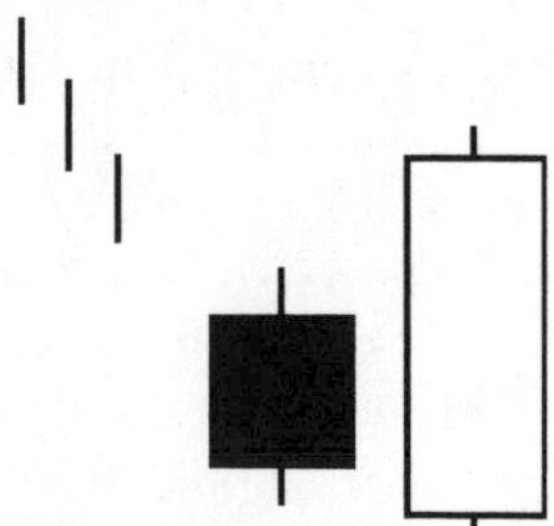

FIGURE 3.39 Bullish engulfing pattern

The bullish engulfing pattern is similar to the piercing pattern except that, rather than piercing deeply into the prior candle's black real body, it completely envelops it. In addition, the first candle's real body need not be at least average length or longer, as required by the piercing pattern. As a general rule, the bullish engulfing pattern is a stronger signal than the piercing pattern.

Chart Example Figure 3.40 shows a daily chart of Biomarin Pharmaceuticals (BMRN). A strong bullish engulfing pattern formed on May 10, 2007. This pattern was a major reversal signal for several reasons. First, it formed at prior support at the April low (dotted line), which set up the potential for a bullish Western double bottom pattern. Thus, the engulfing pattern formed a candlestick pattern within the larger bullish pattern. Second, heavy volume accompanied the engulfing session. Third, the prior day's real body was very small (a spinning top). Finally, the engulfing session was a long candle with a shaven bottom. It not only enveloped the real body of the prior candle, but also the real bodies of the three candles before it.

The Western Outside Day

In Western technical analysis there is a similar reversal bar pattern to the engulfing pattern called an *outside day* (or *outside bar* on other time frames). In both instances,

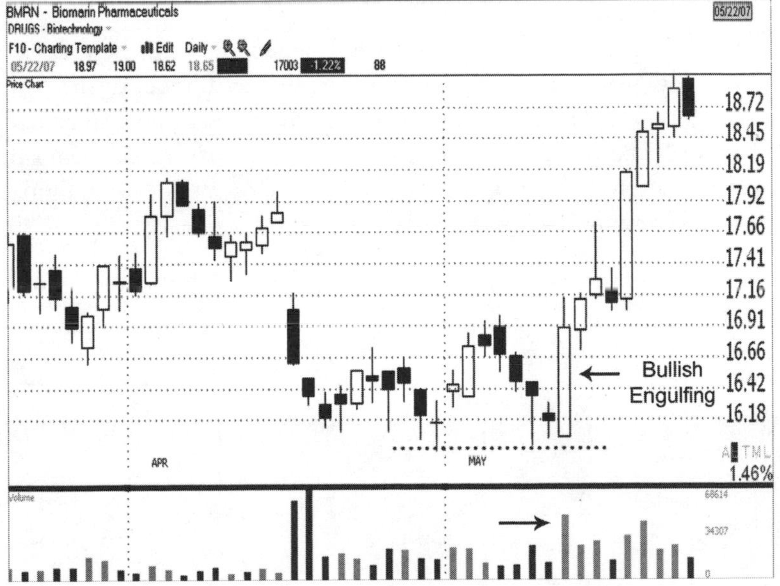

FIGURE 3.40 Strong bullish engulfing pattern formed at support
Source: TeleChart 2007®

there must be an identifiable trend to reverse. There are distinct differences, however, between the Japanese engulfing pattern and the Western outside day:

- The Japanese put the emphasis on the real bodies. The first candle of an engulfing pattern must have a smaller real body than the second candle. The upper and/or lower shadow of the first session *can* extend beyond the range of the second session.
- The focus of the Western outside day is on the bar's range from high to low. The range of the first bar must be within the range of the second bar. Therefore, the shadows of the first bar *cannot* extend beyond the second bar's range.
- The Western outside day does not indicate that the second bar must be opposite in sentiment to the first bar. The Japanese engulfing patterns must have real bodies of opposite color.

Because of the differences mentioned above, not all engulfing patterns qualify as outside days, or vice versa. Figure 3.41 is an outside day because it made a new high and its range surrounded the prior bar's range. However, it would not qualify as a bearish engulfing pattern because the smaller real body is not surrounded by the following session's long black real body. Conversely, Figure 3.42 is a bearish engulfing pattern, but would not qualify as an outside day because it did not make a new high, and therefore the range of the second bar does not surround the previous bar's entire range.

Like the engulfing patterns, a Western outside day can be a negative or positive signal, depending on whether it is preceded by a price advance (bearish) or a decline (bullish). Figures 3.41 and 3.42 both represent bearish signals after upward moves. The outside day has stricter criteria, so the engulfing pattern will draw your attention to impending reversals that may not be recognized using a standard bar chart.

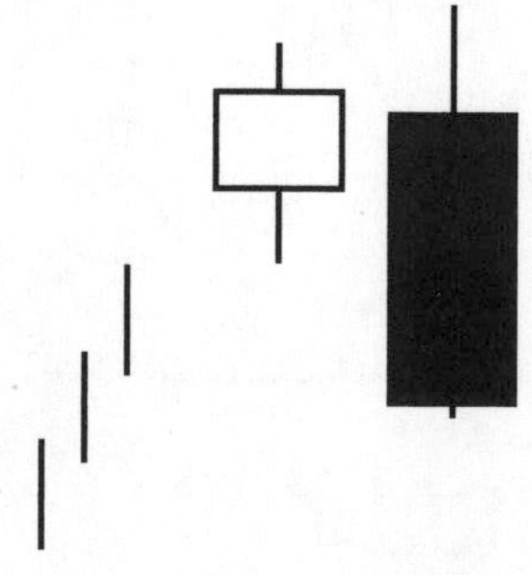

FIGURE 3.41 Western outside day

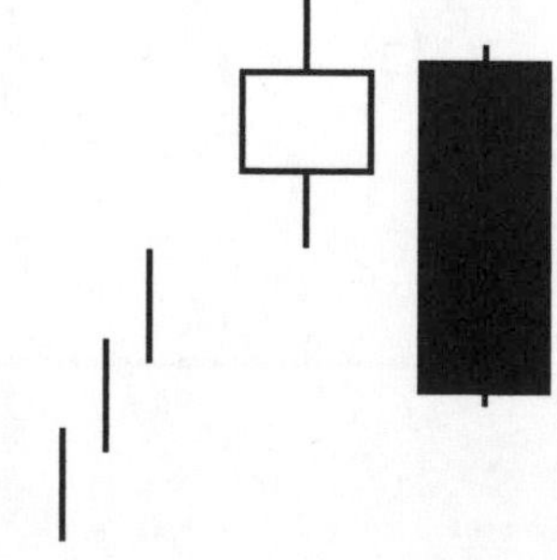

FIGURE 3.42 Bearish engulfing pattern

Harami

As mentioned previously, doji and spinning tops, while important in their own right as individual candlestick lines, are also components of other candlestick patterns. The harami is one such pattern.

The harami can have bearish or bullish implications, depending on whether it forms following a price advance (bearish) or a decline (bullish). It is a two-candle formation that is comprised of a small real body that forms within the prior candle's long real body.

Pattern Description and Criteria

The harami pattern includes the following criteria:

- The first candle has a long real body. Its color reflects the direction of the trend: black in a downtrend and white in an uptrend.
- The real body of the second candle is significantly smaller than the prior candle's real body. In many instances it will be a spinning top.
- The second candle's small real body can be either black or white. However, in most instances, it is the opposite color of the prior real body.

The following criteria will add strength to the harami pattern:

- The smaller the body of the second candle, the stronger the signal. A very small body shows hesitation.
- If the second candle is a doji, it is interpreted as even more powerful and is called a *harami cross.*
- If the small real body (or doji) forms after an unusually long candlestick line, it increases the probability of a change in direction.

The harami pattern is the opposite of the engulfing pattern. Rather than engulfing the first candle's real body, the harami's second candle forms within the prior candle's real body. Another important distinction between these patterns is that the engulfing pattern criterion requires that the two candles be of opposite colors, whereas the second session of the harami can be either black or white.

Although harami patterns may not typically be as strong as some other reversal patterns, such as the engulfing patterns or the morning or evening stars, the appearance of a harami is an indication that the market may be losing momentum and should signal caution.

Bearish Harami

A *bearish harami* forms after a price advance. The first candle's long white real body is followed the next session by a noticeably smaller real body, either black or white, that resides within the prior candle's longer body (Figure 3.43).

If the second candle is a doji, the pattern is referred to as a *bearish harami cross* (Figure 3.44) and is a stronger signal. According to Steve Nison, in his book *Japanese Candlestick Charting Techniques* (New York Institute of Finance, 2001, p. 83): "A harami cross occurring after a very long white candle is a pattern a long trader ignores at his or her own peril."

If the second candle's small body gaps up open above the prior candle's long white body, it is not a harami pattern. It may be a hanging man or a bearish star pattern.

Pattern Psychology The bearish harami represents a shift from a session where the leadership is clearly one-sided in favor of the bulls, to a session where there is no real conviction by the bulls or bears. The second candle's lower close will cause some concern for the bulls. If price continues lower following the harami, many bulls will exit their long positions, increasing the bearish sentiment.

Chart Example Figure 3.45 shows a daily chart of Corn Products International Inc. (CPO). On June 28, 2007, a long bullish candle formed. Price gapped down open during the following session and formed a doji (circled) within the prior candle's long white real body. Price stalled again the next day (a spinning top) and then continued to decline.

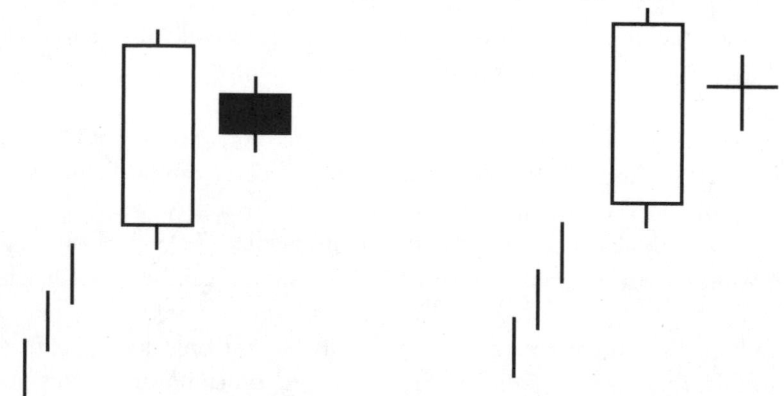

FIGURE 3.43 Bearish harami

FIGURE 3.44 Bearish harami cross

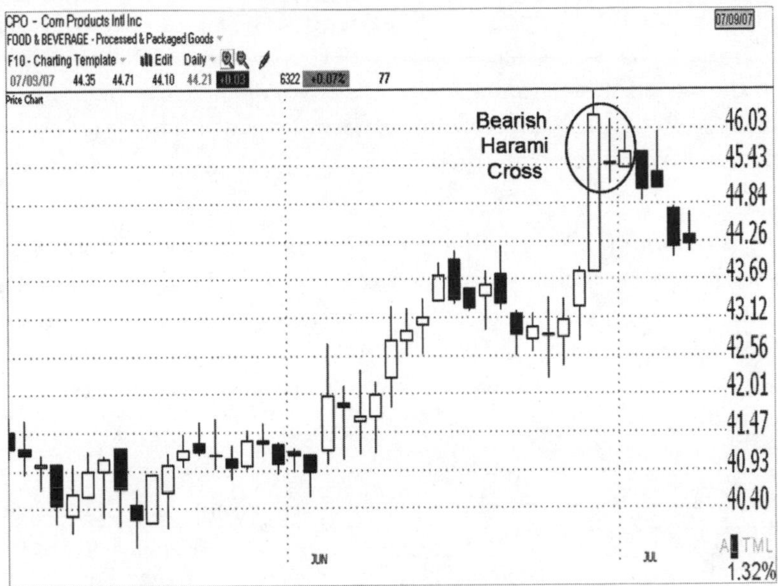

FIGURE 3.45 Bearish harami cross formed in an uptrend
Source: TeleChart 2007®

Bullish Harami

A *bullish harami* forms after a price decline. It is the bullish counterpart of the bearish harami. The first candle's long black real body is followed in the next session by a noticeably smaller real body, either black or white, that resides within the prior candle's longer body (Figure 3.46).

If the second candle is a doji, the pattern is referred to as a *bullish harami cross* (Figure 3.47) and provides a stronger signal. According to Nison, the

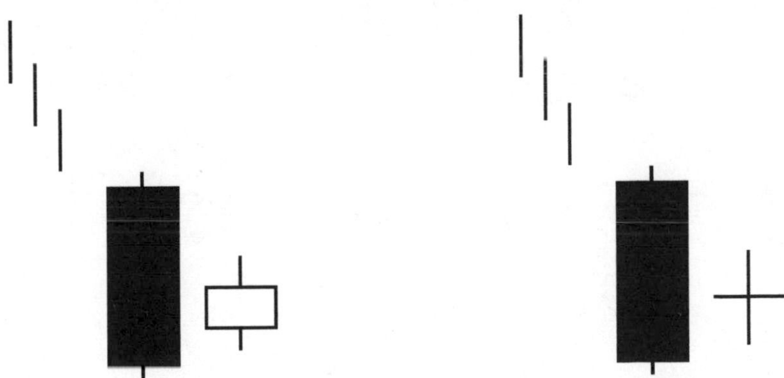

FIGURE 3.46 Bullish harami

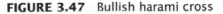

FIGURE 3.47 Bullish harami cross

harami cross can call bottoms, but they tend to be more effective at calling tops.

If the second session's small body gaps down open below the prior candle's long black real body, it is not a harami pattern. It may be a hammer or inverted hammer, or a bullish star pattern.

Pattern Psychology The bullish harami represents a shift from a session where the leadership is clearly one-sided in favor of the bears, to a session where there is no real conviction by the bulls or bears. The second candle's higher close will cause some concern for the bears and result in some short covering. If price continues higher following the harami, more bears will cover their short positions, providing fuel for a rally.

Chart Example Figure 3.48 shows a daily chart of Ship Finance International Ltd. (SFL). On June 7, 2007, price gapped down open and fell sharply, forming an unusually long bearish candle. The following session opened higher (circled) and left a spinning top by the close of market, which formed a bullish harami pattern.

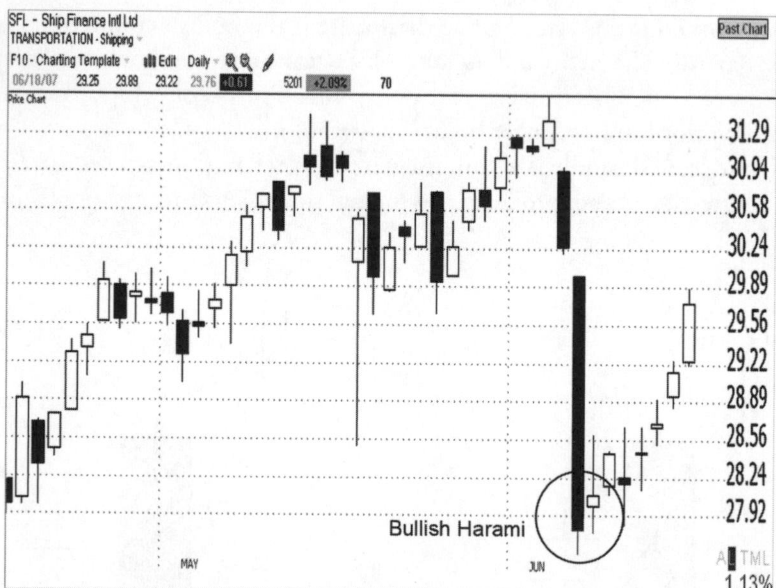

FIGURE 3.48 Bullish harami formed after a sharp decline
Source: TeleChart 2007®

The Western Inside Day

In Western technical analysis there is a bar pattern that is similar to the harami called an *inside day* (or *inside bar* on other time frames). There are distinct differences between the Japanese harami and the Western inside day:

- The Japanese put the emphasis on the real bodies. The first candle of a harami pattern must have a long real body and the second candle has a small real body. The upper and/or lower shadow of the second candle *can* extend beyond the range of the first candle.
- The focus of the Western inside day is on the bar's range from high to low. The range of the second bar must be within the range of the first bar. The shadows of the second bar *cannot* extend beyond the range of the first bar.
- The Western inside day does not indicate that the second bar must have a short distance between the opening and closing prices (a small body).

Because of the differences mentioned above, not all harami patterns qualify as inside days, and vice versa. Figure 3.49 is an inside day, but would not qualify as a harami because the small real body is not completely surrounded by the prior candle's long real body. Figure 3.50 is a harami, but would not qualify as an inside day because the upper shadow extends beyond the high of the first bar.

Like the harami patterns, a change in the direction of price may follow an inside day. However, it is not as strong a signal as an outside day.

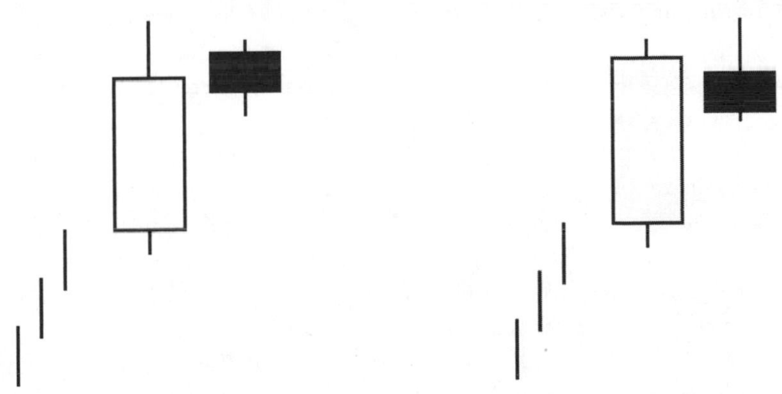

FIGURE 3.49 Western inside day

FIGURE 3.50 Bearish harami

Stars

A star is formed when a candle with a long real body is followed by a small real body, or a doji, that gaps away from the first candle. A star can be a bearish sign if it forms after a price advance, or a bullish sign if it forms after a decline.

Pattern Description and Criteria

A star includes the following criteria:

- The first candle has a long real body. Its color reflects the direction of the trend: black in a downtrend and white in an uptrend.
- The second candle gaps away from the real body of the first candle. Although this gap will sometimes leave a void on the chart (a true gap), all that is required is that there be a gap between the two consecutive real bodies that comprise the pattern; their shadows may overlap. (Gaps are covered in detail in Part II.)
- The real body of the second candle is significantly smaller than the prior candle's real body, for example, a spinning top. The second candle's small body can be either black or white.
- The second candle may form a doji, in which case it would be referred to as a *doji star.*

The description of a star pattern sounds similar to a harami, but there is an important distinction between the two. The second candle of a harami forms within the real body of the first candle. The second candle of a star gaps away from the prior candle's real body. In other words, the real bodies of the two sessions of the star don't touch, although their shadows may overlap. There may be cases where the two bodies meet, or slightly overlap, that could be acceptable variations, especially if the pattern forms at a point where price is overextended or has reached a support or resistance area.

A *bearish star* is comprised of two candlestick lines that form after a price advance. The first candle has a long bullish real body. The star is formed when price gaps up open during the next session and leaves a small real body (Figure 3.51). The small real body is the star portion of the pattern; it can be either black or white. If the session following the long candle is a doji, it is a stronger signal referred to as a *bearish doji star* (Figure 3.52).

A *bullish star* forms after a price decline. It is the bullish counterpart of the bearish star. The first candle has a long bearish real body. The star is formed when price gaps down open during the following session and leaves a small real

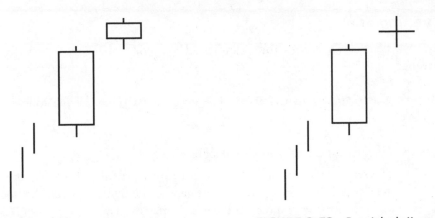

FIGURE 3.51 Bearish star

FIGURE 3.52 Bearish doji star

body (Figure 3.53). The small real body can be either black or white. If the second candle is a doji, it is a stronger signal referred to as a *bullish doji star* (Figure 3.54).

A two-candlestick star pattern can stand on its own as a potential reversal signal. However, it is best known as a component of other reversal patterns. For example, the bearish shooting star pattern was discussed earlier in this chapter. Two other well-known star patterns are the three-candle evening star and morning star formations. They both include either a star or doji star as the first two candlestick lines in the pattern.

Pattern Psychology The presence of a star signals a loss of momentum and may be followed by a change in price direction. The atmosphere changes from one in which there is clear leadership in the form of a long bullish or bearish real body, to a session in which there is a standoff between the bulls and bears.

FIGURE 3.53 Bullish star

FIGURE 3.54 Bullish doji star

Evening Star

An *evening star* is a bearish three-candlestick pattern that forms after a price advance.

Pattern Description and Criteria The evening star includes the following criteria:

- The first candle has a long bullish real body.
- The second session gaps up open and forms a small real body creating the star portion of the pattern. The gap need only be between the bodies of the first two candles; the shadows may overlap.
- The small real body can be either black or white, or a doji.
- The third candle has a bearish real body that intrudes deeply into the first candle's long bullish real body.

The deeper the intrusion of the third candle's black real body into the first candle's long white real body, the more likely a reversal, especially if the third session is accompanied by heavy volume.

An ideal pattern (Figure 3.55) would have the required gap between the bodies of the first and second candles, and a gap between the bodies of the second and third candles. However, ideal patterns are not very common. There is often some overlap between the bodies of the second and third candles (Figure 3.56). If the third candle's real body envelops the star's real body, it is also a bearish engulfing pattern (as long as the star's body is white or a doji). If the star portion of the pattern is a doji, the pattern is referred to as an *evening doji star* (Figure 3.57). The inclusion of a doji strengthens the signal.

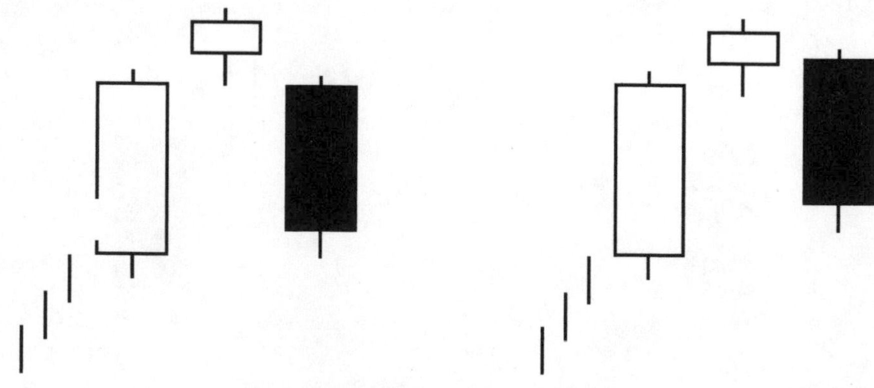

FIGURE 3.55 Evening star (ideal)

FIGURE 3.56 Evening star

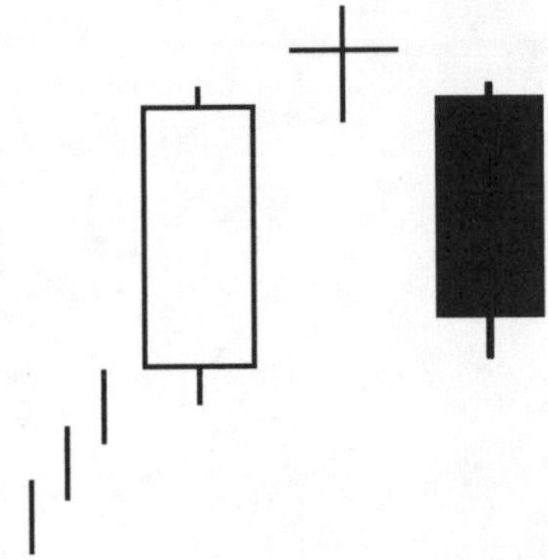

FIGURE 3.57 Evening doji star

Pattern Psychology Price has been advancing, and the formation of a long white candle shows further evidence of the bulls' dominance. That leadership comes into question during the next session with the formation of the star and the indecision that it signifies. A major shift in sentiment comes during the third session, when a sharp sell-off erases much of the gains the bulls had achieved during the first session's rally.

Chart Examples Figure 3.58 shows a daily chart of Copart Inc. (CPRT). An evening doji star formed from July 6 to 10, 2007 (circled). The pattern was very strong for a few reasons. First, it included a doji in the formation. Second, the black real body of the third candle penetrated very deeply into the first candle's white real body. In fact, it closed near the open of that candle erasing all of that session's gains. Finally, the pattern formed very near resistance at the June high (dotted line). Take a closer look at the June high. It would have been an evening star as well except that there were two candles in between the long candles rather than one. Those two candles in between were both back-to-back bearish hanging man patterns.

Figure 3.59 shows a daily chart of ConocoPhillips (COP). An evening star formed from July 12 to 16, 2007 (circled). It includes the required gap between the real bodies of the first and second sessions. The bodies of the second and third candles touch; however, that does not take away from the strength of this setup. The third session was accompanied by very heavy volume, increasing the chance that a reversal would follow, which it did.

Acceptable Variation In most texts on candlestick charting, the criterion for the third candle of the evening star indicates that it should protrude deeply into the long real body of the first session. I have never seen it written that, if the third candle's long black real body extends beyond the first candle's long white

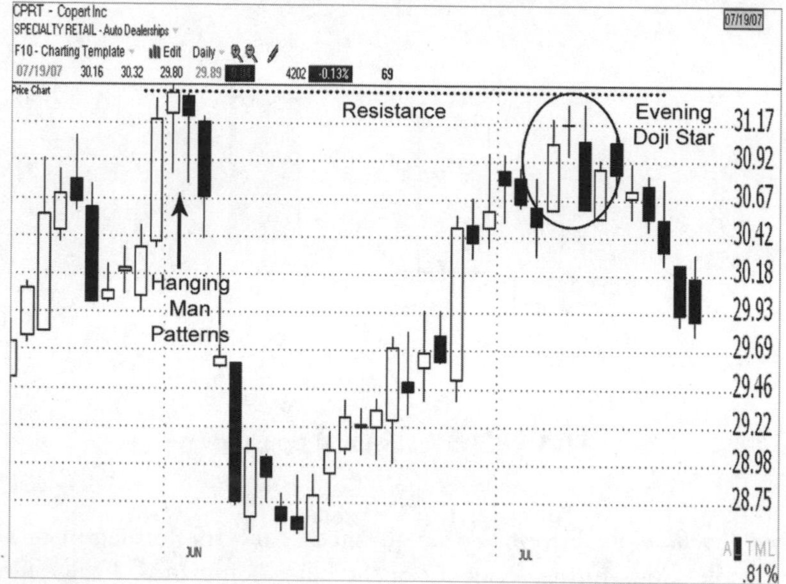

FIGURE 3.58 Bearish evening doji star formed in an uptrend near resistance at the June high

Source: TeleChart 2007®

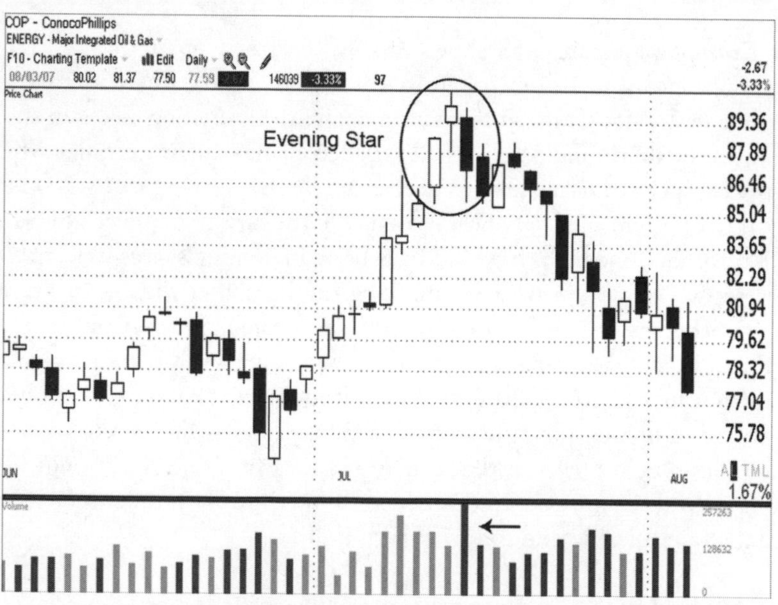

FIGURE 3.59 Bearish evening star formed after an uptrend. Heavy volume increased the likelihood of a reversal

Source: TeleChart 2007®

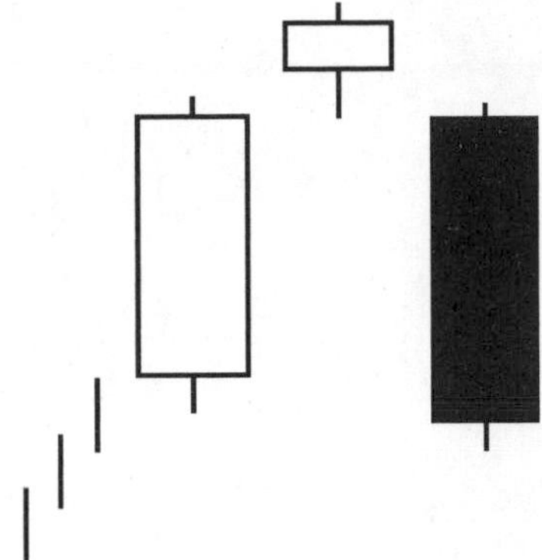

FIGURE 3.60 Evening star (variation)

real body (Figure 3.60), the signal is invalid. Thus, I consider it to be an acceptable variation of the pattern. However, it is important to note that with such a long candle on the third session, there may not be an adequate reward-to-risk ratio to enter a short position upon its completion. Reward versus risk is discussed in Part II.

reward-to-risk ratio
A ratio used by traders to determine the potential reward (profit) compared to the potential risk (loss) if a position is taken in a stock or other trading instrument. The ratio is calculated by dividing the potential reward by the potential risk.

Chart Example (Variation) Figure 3.61 shows a daily chart of McMoran Exploration Co. (MMR). The above referenced variation of an evening star formed from April 13 to 17, 2007 (circled). There was a gap between the real bodies of the first and second candles, as well as between the second and third candles. The star portion of the pattern was a hanging man. The third candle's real body extended well beyond the body of the first candle and was accompanied by heavy volume.

Helpful Hint The "evening star" is a nickname for the planet Venus, which is visible just before dark. As its appearance shows, the formation goes from light to dark. Think of the first candlestick line as daylight, the second as dusk, and the black real body of the third candle as darkness.

Morning Star

A *morning star* is a three-candle pattern that forms after a price decline. It is the bullish counterpart of the evening star.

FIGURE 3.61 Variation of the bearish evening star pattern
Source: TeleChart 2007®

Pattern Description and Criteria

The morning star includes the following criteria:

- The first candle has a long bearish real body.
- The second session gaps down open and forms a small real body creating the star portion of the pattern. The gap need only be between the bodies of the first two candles; the shadows may overlap.
- The small real body can be either black or white, or a doji.
- The third candle has a bullish real body that intrudes deeply into the first candle's long bearish real body.

The deeper the intrusion of the third candle's white real body into the first candle's black real body, the more likely a reversal, especially if the third session is accompanied by heavy volume.

An ideal pattern (Figure 3.62) would have the required gap between the bodies of the first and second candles, and a gap between the bodies of the second and third candles. However, ideal patterns are not very common. There is often some overlap between the second and third candles (Figure 3.63). If the third candle's real body envelops the star's real body, it is also a bullish engulfing pattern (as long as the star's body is black or a doji). If the star portion of the pattern is a doji, the pattern is referred to as a *morning doji star* (Figure 3.64). The inclusion of a doji strengthens the signal.

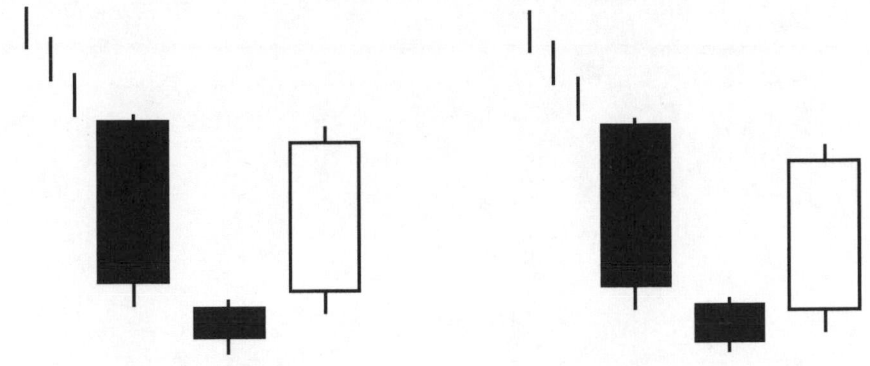

FIGURE 3.62 Morning star (ideal)

FIGURE 3.63 Morning star

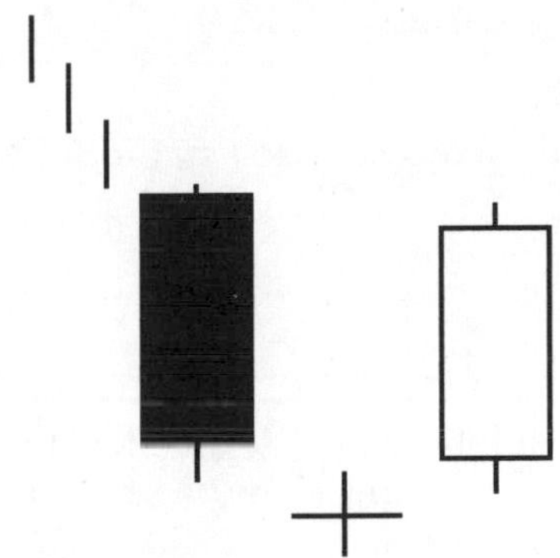

FIGURE 3.64 Morning doji star

Pattern Psychology Price has been declining when a long black candle forms, offering further evidence of the bears' dominance. That leadership comes into question during the next session with the formation of the star and the indecision that it brings. A major shift in sentiment comes during the third session when a strong rally erases much of the gains the bears had attained during the first session's sharp decline. It shows that the bulls have arrived, and many bears will cover their positions, providing fuel for a rally.

Chart Examples Figure 3.65 shows a daily chart of Knight Capital Group Inc. (NITE). A morning doji star formed from March 2 to 6, 2007 (circled). The star session was a long-legged doji. Note that there were gaps on both sides of the star, increasing its strength.

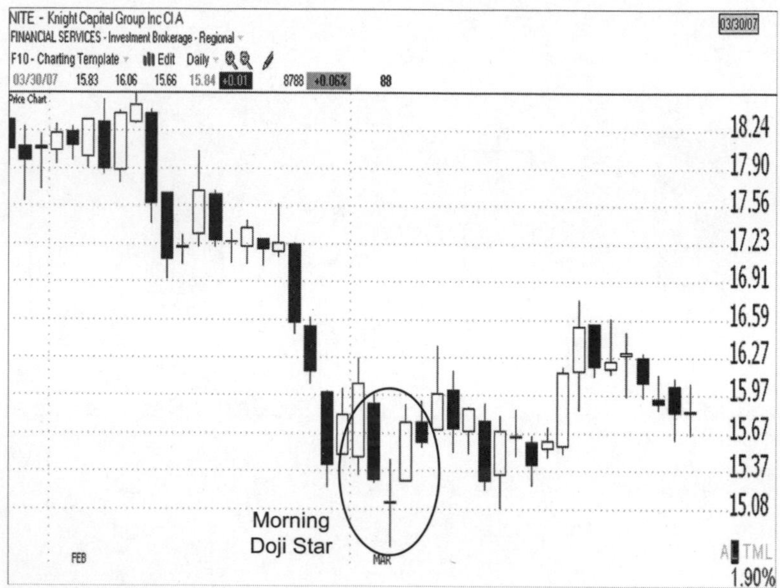

FIGURE 3.65 Bullish morning doji star formed in a downtrend
Source: TeleChart 2007®

Figure 3.66 shows a daily chart of Las Vegas Sands (LVS). A bullish morning star formed from June 26 to 28, 2007 (circled). The required gap was present between the first candle's black real body and the star. The third candle's white real body enveloped the star's smaller real body; however, this was not a bullish engulfing pattern because the two real bodies were not of opposite color. Note that the star portion was a hammer.

Acceptable Variation The criterion for the third candle of the morning star indicates that it should protrude deeply into the long real body of the first candle. I consider it an acceptable variation if the third candle's long white real body extends beyond the first candle's long black real body (Figure 3.67). However, such a long candle on the third session may not create an adequate reward-to-risk ratio to enter a long position upon completion of the pattern.

Chart Example (Variation) Figure 3.68 shows a daily chart of Under Armour Inc. (UA). The above-referenced variation of a morning star formed on the chart from March 2 to 6, 2007 (circled). There was a gap between the bodies on both sides of the star strengthening the pattern. The third candle's long white real body extended beyond the first candle's black real body.

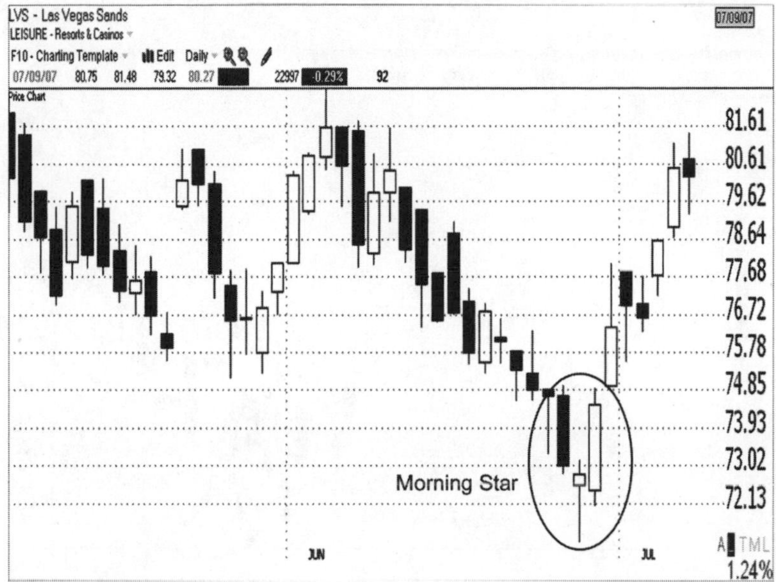

FIGURE 3.66 Bullish morning star formed after a downtrend
Source: TeleChart 2007®

Helpful Hint The "morning star" is a nickname for the planet Mercury, which appears shortly before sunrise. As its appearance shows, the formation goes from dark to light. Think of the first candlestick line as darkness, the second as dawn, and the white real body of the third candle as daylight.

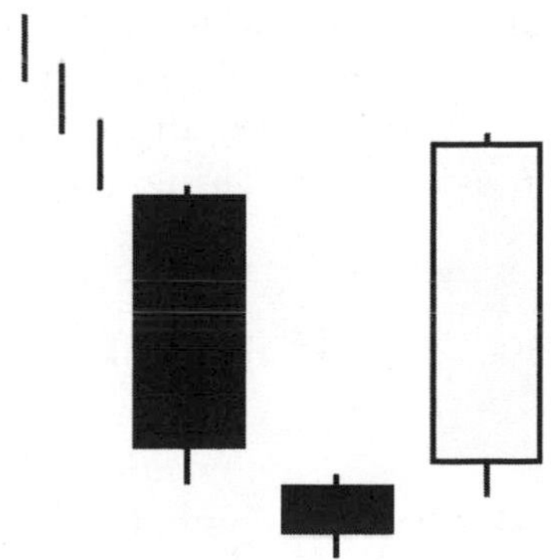

FIGURE 3.67 Morning star (variation)

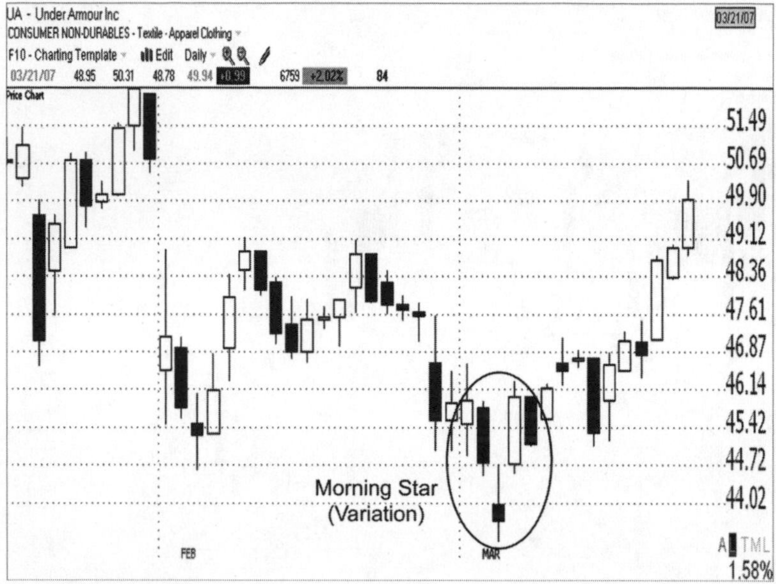

FIGURE 3.68 Variation of the bullish morning star formed after a downtrend
Source: TeleChart 2007®

Multiple Signals

It is not unusual to see one reversal pattern followed by another. For example, in Figure 3.69 a bearish harami (1-2) was followed in the next session by a bearish shooting star (3). Back-to-back bearish or bullish reversal patterns simply send a stronger warning that a change in price direction may occur.

You'll also see instances where a single line reversal pattern is part of a reversal pattern that includes two or three distinct candle lines. In Figure 3.69 the second candle of the harami (2) was a bearish hanging man. And in Figure 3.70 a hammer (2) was part of a three-candle morning star (1-2-3).

Putting the Reversal Patterns to Work

The primary focus of this chapter was to introduce you to the various reversal patterns. You have enough information now to recognize the patterns and understand the messages they provide about investor psychology.

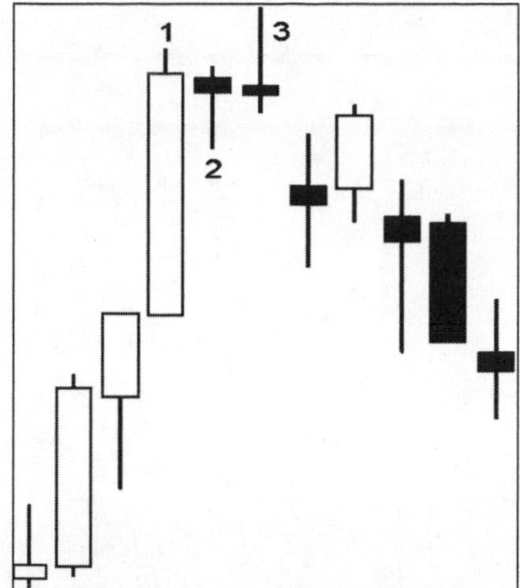

FIGURE 3.69 Back-to-back reversal patterns
Source: TeleChart 2007®

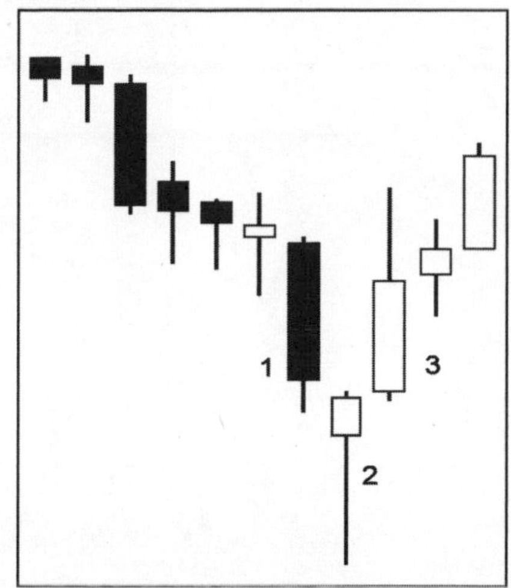

FIGURE 3.70 Reversal pattern within a reversal pattern
Source: TeleChart 2007®

Chapter 4 will provide additional information on how the patterns form and some factors that may impact their signals. These two chapters will be very helpful in your chart analysis; however, they are not enough to show you how to unlock the full potential of the reversal patterns. Each subsequent chapter will provide another rich layer of knowledge that will move you toward the ultimate goal of putting the candlestick signals to work in your chart analysis and trading strategies.

Chapter 4

More on Reversal Patterns

Now that you are familiar with the primary candlestick reversal patterns, this chapter will solidify your understanding of how they form. It will also point to some factors that may influence the occurrence and performance of the signals.

The Pattern Must Have Something to Reverse

It matters where a candlestick reversal pattern forms on a chart. In order for a reversal signal to have significance, price must be moving in a direction, either up or down, prior to the formation of the pattern. Bearish reversal patterns are relevant if they form after an upside move. Conversely, bullish reversal patterns are important if they form after a downside move. As a general rule, the reversal pattern should form at, or near, the end of the directional price move.

overbought
A condition in which a stock or market has risen too far too quickly and is likely to suffer at least a short-term decline or period of consolidation.

oversold
A condition in which a stock or market has fallen too far too quickly and is likely to experience at least a short-term rally or period of consolidation.

If price is moving sideways, referred to as *consolidation,* and a reversal pattern forms within that congestion area, it has little or no significance, especially if price has been moving sideways for several days already when the pattern forms. If the stock was in a short-term overbought or oversold condition prior to the consolidation, that overextended condition has already been alleviated by the sideways price action. In other words, there is no longer a move to reverse; price has already changed direction.

Example

Figure 4.1 shows a daily chart of OSI Pharmaceuticals Inc (OSIP). On October 29, 2007 a bearish hanging man formed during the session following a very long bullish candle. This bearish signal was meaningful because there was a price advance to reverse. Price changed direction moving sideways for several days following the hanging man. On November 7 a bearish shooting star formed. However, price had already been consolidating for several days prior to the formation of the shooting star so it had little significance as a bearish reversal signal. What the shooting star's long upper shadow did show us in this scenario was a failed breakout attempt. Price had rallied intraday above the consolidation area but the bulls were not able to sustain the rally and price closed back inside the consolidation area leaving just the upper shadow.

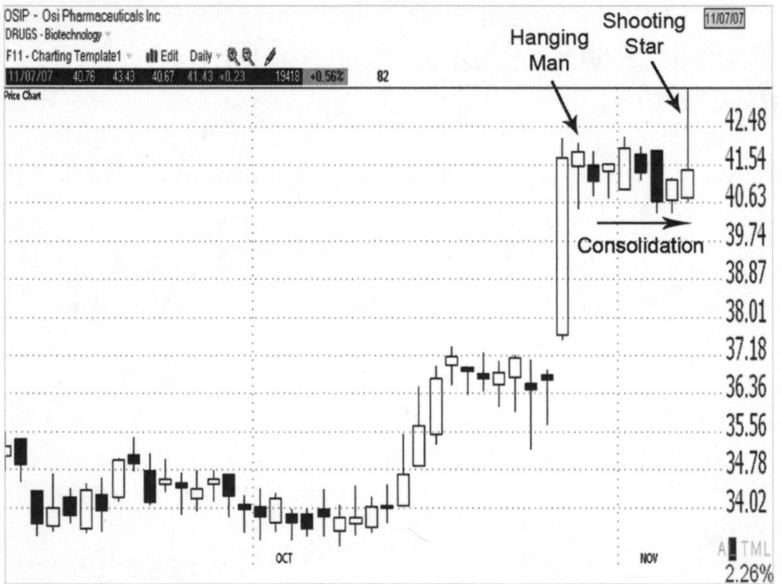

FIGURE 4.1 Reversal patterns are not significant if they form during consolidation
Source: TeleChart 2007®

rectangle
A pattern that forms on a chart when price moves sideways, swinging back and forth in a bounded range. The top of the range becomes resistance, and the bottom of the range becomes support. A rectangle represents a pause within a trend and is usually resolved with a breakout in the direction of the trend; however, at times it will precede a trend reversal.

The consolidation shown in Figure 4.1 was very tight. I refer to this type of shallow sideways movement as "basing." According to Nison, the Japanese refer to it as a "box range." Another type of consolidation occurs when price moves sideways but makes identifiable price swings across the consolidation (see Figure 4.2). This price action is called a *rectangle.* It may also be referred to as a *trading range* or a *horizontal channel.* The short-term price swings across the rectangle often find resistance near the ceiling and support near the floor. You may see candlestick reversal patterns form at those turning points because there is a short-term trend to reverse.

On the daily chart of Commercial Metals Co. (CMC) in Figure 4.2, the stock was trapped in a trading range from May through July 2007. Several of the short-term swings across the rectangle ended with candlestick reversal patterns as follows:

1. *May 9:* A bearish hanging man (1) created the first peak in what eventually evolved into a trading range.
2. *June 4:* A doji (2) formed as the May 9 swing high was tested.
3. *June 13:* A bullish hammer (3), which was also part of a bullish harami, formed as the May low was tested.
4. *June 27:* Another bullish hammer (4) formed at what is now clearly defined as support.
5. *July 16:* After breaking out just above the ceiling of the rectangle, a bearish engulfing pattern (5) pulled price back down, leaving a false breakout. False breakdowns through support may also occur. Such false moves are common and are frustrating for unsuspecting traders.

false breakout
Price closes above an identifiable resistance area, or below an identifiable support area, but does not have enough momentum to continue the move. Price reverses direction invalidating the breakout and forcing traders to exit their positions.

In summary, a key component of analyzing candlestick reversal patterns is to make sure to evaluate the price

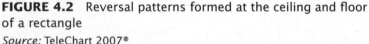

FIGURE 4.2 Reversal patterns formed at the ceiling and floor of a rectangle
Source: TeleChart 2007®

action that *preceded* the formation of the pattern. There must be at least a short-term price move to reverse in order for a reversal signal to have validity.

Factors That May Strengthen the Reversal Signal

Listed below are some factors that may increase the likelihood that a change in price direction will follow a reversal pattern:

- The stock is overbought when a bearish pattern forms or oversold when a bullish pattern forms. Oscillators are technical indicators that can measure these overextended conditions. Overextended conditions and the use of oscillators are detailed in Part II.
- The pattern follows a steep move. Significant gains can be made during a swift move, and traders will be protective of those gains. Therefore, these events are very vulnerable to profit-taking. If price starts to reverse, many stops will trigger. The result is often a fast and sharp decline after a bearish pattern or advance following a bullish pattern.

- The pattern does not occur much on the stock. If the pattern forms frequently, it may not have a significant impact on price movement unless, of course, when it does form often, it usually follows through well. Otherwise, if a pattern forms often, the emergence of yet another of the same pattern may not be very significant.
- The pattern forms at a strong support level (bullish pattern) or resistance level (bearish pattern). Several such chart examples were provided in Chapter 3 and more discussion on support and resistance is included in Part II.

Broad Market Environment

It is important to pay attention to the broader market. If a broad market rally or sell-off occurs, many stocks will rise or fall in kind, at least for the short term. This can have an influence on the success or failure of reversal patterns. It can also impact how stocks respond to support and resistance levels. When the broad market rallies strongly, you'll see many stocks break up through resistance. Conversely, when the broad market melts down, many stocks will break down through previously strong support levels.

The market environment may also influence the type and number of reversal patterns that form on the charts of stocks. At the time of this writing (July–August 2007), the broad market was experiencing a correction. One of the primary drivers was the problems in the subprime mortgage market, which hit many financial stocks hard. It sent a ripple through the markets. The result was a dramatic increase in volatility. Day after day the Dow Jones Industrial Average experienced triple-digit advances or declines (see Figure 4.3). On many days, the intraday action resembled a roller coaster ride. The S&P 500 Index fared even worse since its component list includes many financial stocks.

stock index
An indicator used to track the composite value for a particular group of stocks. The S&P 500 is a very well known large-cap index that is commonly used as a benchmark for the stock market.

During that volatile period, many candlestick lines and patterns formed on charts, which echoed the market's instability. Long shadows were common, highlighting the wide price swings intraday. Although reversal formations were prevalent, their signals were very short term and not always reliable given the unsettling environment. It was an exasperating time for investors as they worried over their portfolios; however, it was a profitable time for experienced day traders and swing traders who understood how to benefit from the volatility.

Example

On August 16, 2007 a hammer with a very long lower shadow formed on the daily chart of the Dow Jones Industrial Average (Figure 4.3). The body was so small that some chartists would have interpreted it as a dragonfly doji; regardless, it was a bullish signal. In fact, the three days from August 15 to 17 formed a variation of a bullish morning star. Hammers also formed on the S&P 500 and Nasdaq Composite index charts on August 16. Given that, just imagine how many hammers, dragonfly and long-legged doji, and other bullish reversal patterns formed on the charts of individual stocks.

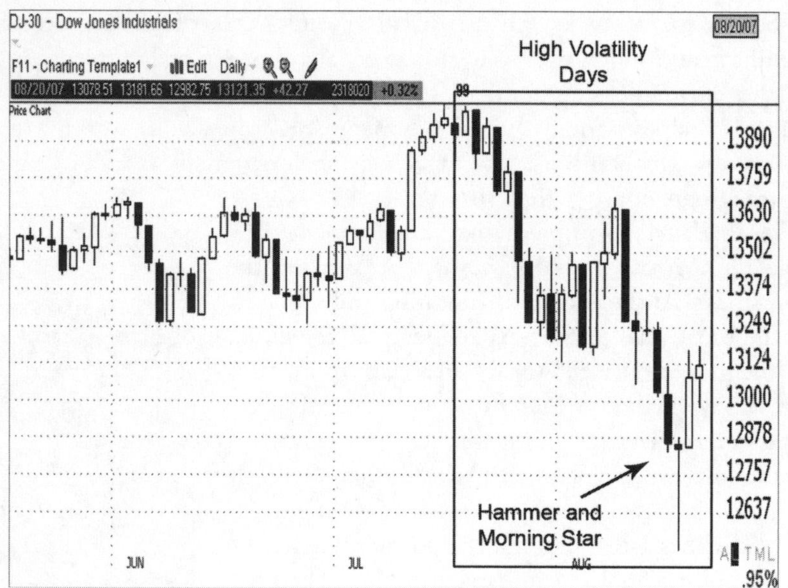

FIGURE 4.3 Volatile days for the Dow
Source: TeleChart 2007®

Remember that this broad market decline was largely spurred by credit concerns. Therefore, many financial stocks declined sharply. The long candles and long shadows that formed on their charts illustrated the increased volatility.

Example

Figure 4.4 shows a daily chart of Morgan Stanley (MS), a brokerage stock. Note the dramatic increase in volatility (circled) that reflected the troubles in the financial sector.

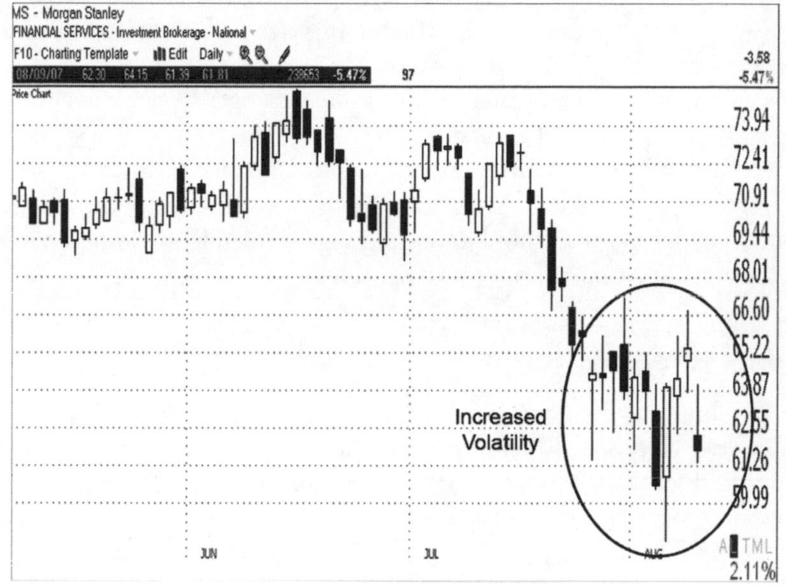

FIGURE 4.4 Increased volatility in a financial stock
Source: TeleChart 2007®

Reversal Patterns May Not Reverse a Trend

Traders should be cautious of the word *reversal.* Although the candlestick patterns introduced in Chapter 3 are referred to as reversal patterns, and they do have the tendency to be followed by a change in the direction of price, it does not mean the patterns will be followed by a *trend reversal.* A trend reversal is a significant event. Price would have to retrace at least two thirds of the prior trend before it technically would be deemed a trend reversal. Moreover, these patterns warn that price may reverse the current direction, at least temporarily.

When a bearish reversal pattern forms after an upward move, it signals that price may change direction from up to down, or sideways, and vice versa for a bullish signal after a downward move. If a significant reversal does not follow a candlestick signal, it does not mean that the candlestick pattern failed.

price target
A projected price level where, if it is reached, a trader intends to exit an open position.

Candlestick reversal patterns provide primarily short-term signals. If a pattern is followed only by a pullback or period of minor consolidation, the signal was still successful at calling a change in price direction.

No matter how strong a reversal signal, or how ominous its name or appearance, it does not dictate how significant the change in price will be (the magnitude). Candlestick patterns do not provide price targets. Nor do they predict how long a change in price direction will last (the duration).

An entire chapter in Part II is devoted to the discussion of trend analysis. Once you've completed that segment, you'll have a better understanding of the role of candlestick patterns within the bigger picture of price movement.

Failed Reversal Patterns

Traders should not expect that every reversal signal will be successful at calling a change in price direction. Reversal patterns can and do fail. To my knowledge, nothing in technical analysis works 100 percent of the time. However, it is better to respond to a signal that turns out to be false than to ignore a valid one.

Price should change direction shortly after the emergence of a reversal pattern. If, instead, price immediately moves again in the direction of the trend, the signal has been negated. For example, if a bearish hanging man forms and price fails to close below the hanging man's real body, and instead moves higher, the hanging man's signal is no longer valid. If price is still overextended, though, the stock is vulnerable and additional reversal signals may follow. Refer back to Figure 3.27 in Chapter 3 for an example. On that chart, a hammer formed during a sharp decline, but price continued lower in the next session, negating its bullish signal. Two days after the hammer's failed signal, a long-legged doji formed at support. Buyers stepped in at that level and many shorts covered stopping the stock's fall.

The probability of follow-through can be enhanced by combining the reversal signals with classic Western technical analysis, which is the focus of Part II.

Reversal Pattern Psychology

One of the most important aspects to absorb when studying the reversal patterns is the psychology behind their formations. Rather than just memorizing the look of the pattern and its name, try to really understand how the price action unfolded during the session(s) that formed the pattern. At the close of market, the daily bar provides a snapshot of the day's battle; but if you view the intraday time frames, you'll see the *details* of the battle. Reference was made several times in Chapter 3 to the bulls taking control from the bears intraday, or vice versa. The discussion that follows demonstrates how that transfer of power might occur.

Example

Figure 4.5 shows a daily chart of Peabody Energy (BTU). On August 6, 2007, a bullish hammer formed after a price decline. A short-covering rally occurred in the days following the reversal pattern. However, that rally actually began intraday on the day the hammer formed, as you'll see on the 5-minute chart in Figure 4.6.

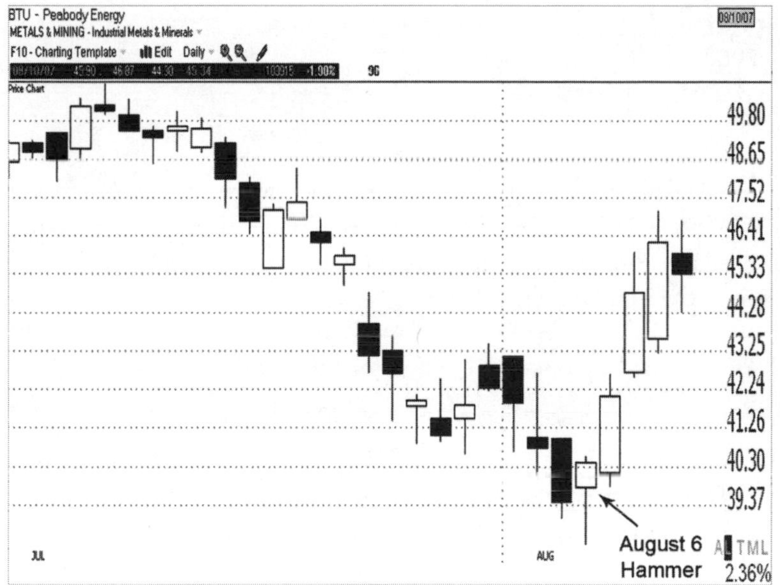

FIGURE 4.5 Daily chart of Peabody Energy (BTU). A bullish hammer formed on August 6, 2007
Source: TeleChart 2007®

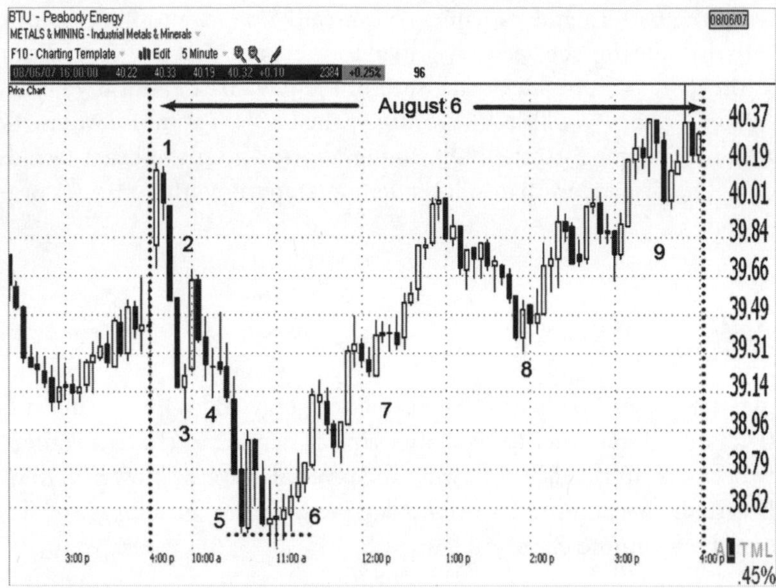

FIGURE 4.6 5-minute chart of Peabody Energy (BTU) on August 6, 2007
Source: TeleChart 2007®

Figure 4.6 shows the August 6 intraday price action that created the bullish hammer on BTU's daily chart. The following commentary steps you through the day's price action as it appeared on a 5-minute chart. The numbers correspond to the numbers on the chart:

1. Price gapped up open and rallied for the first 5 minutes of trading.
2. Price reversed direction and declined for 15 minutes.
3. Some buying pressure occurred over the next two bars, temporarily stopping the fall and putting in the first bottom.
4. Price turned down again and tested the bottom (at 3), which did not hold.
5. The decline continued for several more bars. Price turned up again for 5 minutes. That bounce put in the second prominent bottom of the day.
6. Price turned back down and tested the new low (at 5). This time the bottom provided support and price rallied.
7. After each swing up , price pulled back some before moving higher.
8. Price pulled back deeper this time, correcting part of the uptrend before continuing higher.

9. Price continued its series of upward intraday swings, followed by minor pullbacks until the end of the day.

From this intraday price action you can see where the bulls were successful at taking control from the bears. The bears dominated most of the price action between numbers 1 and 5. This is obvious from the price direction, but also by the fact that most of the price bars during that time were bearish candles. Between numbers 6 and 9 the bulls were in charge and were able to push price back up to close slightly higher than it opened. The intraday decline that was followed by a reversal is what created the hammer's long lower shadow that you see on the daily chart. If you were to press all those intraday price bars together, you'd see how they translate into a hammer with a white real body on the daily chart.

You can learn a lot by examining the daily candle and then shifting down to a lower intraday time frame to see how that daily candle was created from the intraday price movement. If your intention is to swing trade the markets or become a day trader, understanding these concepts will help you develop your trading strategies. It may make a significant difference on your profitability. Even if you intend to hold most of your positions longer-term, the weekly and monthly charts break down to lower time frames as well, so the lesson is still applicable.

Beware of Thin Markets

Caution! Beware of thinly traded stocks or markets. Candlestick signals are much more reliable on stocks that trade adequate volume than they are on illiquid issues. Volume will be discussed in Chapter 6.

Chapter 5

Tails

A candlestick line's upper and lower shadows represent the price extremes (the high and low) of the trading session. Although the Japanese do put a lot of emphasis on the candlestick's real body, the shadows can also tell us a lot about the psychology of market participants. Therefore, shadows play an important role in chart analysis. The following discussion specifically addresses the formation and implications of long shadows.

Long shadows are often called *tails*. As you learned in Chapter 3, there are several reversal patterns that include tails in their formation, for example, the hanging man and the shooting star. Not every candlestick line that forms a long shadow will meet the criteria of a specific candlestick pattern. Regardless of whether the formation has a name or not, it is important to understand the message behind a tail.

Long upper shadows are *bearish shadows* (Figure 5.1). The presence of one or more bearish shadows after a price advance demonstrates that the market is reaching for a top. There is not enough demand at higher prices to continue to propel the stock upward, at least for the short term. This is especially evident near a resistance area or in an overbought condition. The tail(s) indicates that the bulls are taking profits and bears are stepping into short positions.

The presence of long upper shadows on a standard bar chart can be deceiving. They might come across as bullish since price may still be making higher highs and, in some cases, higher closes. The candlestick line makes it easy to see, though, that price has closed well off its high. The inability of the bulls to sustain the intraday rally and close nearer the high is actually a bearish sign if it occurs after a price advance.

Long lower shadows are *bullish shadows* (Figure 5.2). The formation of one or more bullish shadows after a price decline, especially near support or in an oversold condition, shows us visually that the market is reaching for a bottom. In this case, the tail(s) indicates that lower prices are being rejected.

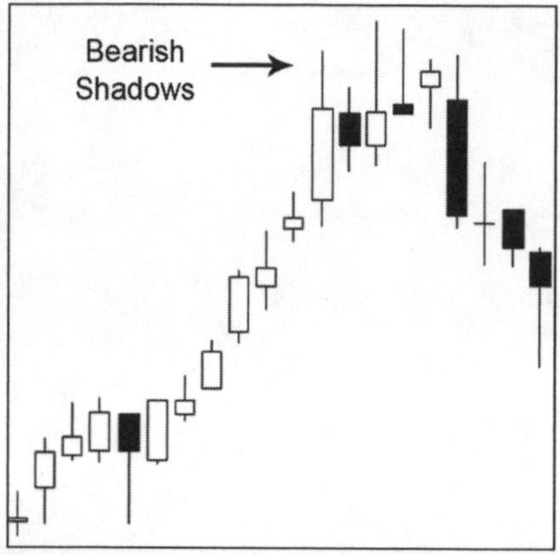

FIGURE 5.1 Bearish shadows
Source: TeleChart 2007®

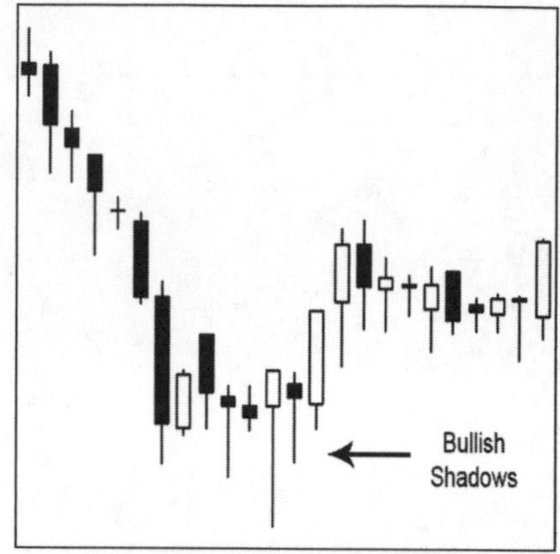

FIGURE 5.2 Bullish Shadows
Source: TeleChart 2007®

The bears are covering their short positions and bulls are stepping into long positions.

Smart Investor Tip

Beware of bad data! The presence of an unusually long shadow on a chart may be the result of bad data. When you observe such a shadow, it is advisable to check the intraday data to see if the lower time frames show the same extreme price level shown on the daily bar. Also consider consulting a second charting source to make sure the long shadow is not bad data. For example, if you use TeleChart or MetaStock for charting, you may consult Stockcharts.com (a free online service) to verify that the data appears the same in their platform. Charting services are not infallible, and periodically a bad bar will slip through.

Tails at Support and Resistance

The presence of one or more tails at, or near, an area of support (bullish shadows) or resistance (bearish shadows) is fairly common. Experienced traders pay close attention to visible barriers on the chart and often execute trades near those points. Support and resistance is discussed briefly here and is covered in more detail in Part II.

When a stock that is rising encounters resistance, many traders use that barrier as a target to exit long positions. In addition, bearish traders may enter short positions near a resistance area in anticipation of a downside move. (Once a decline begins, it may be more difficult for them to borrow the shares to sell short.)

Price may retreat from resistance, leaving a single tail, or there may be two or more tests of resistance in a short period of time. The tail indicates that the bulls were able to rally price, pushing it up to resistance or even above it during the session. However, they were not able to sustain the rally and the stock closed well off its high.

Example

Figure 5.3 shows a daily chart of Con-Way Inc. (CNW). On April 25, 2007, a gravestone doji formed the April high (1). Price retreated and then settled into a horizontal trading range for several weeks during May. Price rallied up again at the end of May and tested the April high. A bearish shadow formed on May 31, a shooting star (2a), and another on June 1, a doji (2b), as resistance was tested. Higher highs were made on those two days, which might appear to be bullish if you were viewing a standard bar chart, and if you were not aware that a prior peak (the April high) may act as resistance. On June 1 (2b) price actually broke out just slightly above the April high intraday, but *closed* below it, resulting in a failed breakout attempt. Price declined for several weeks during June. Another uptrend in July took price back up to that visible resistance area where, once again, bearish shadows formed. On July 16 a bearish shadow formed (3a), and back-to-back long-legged doji formed on July 18–19 (3b and 3c). On July 18 (3b), price broke out above the resistance area intraday, but again the bulls could not sustain the breakout and price closed well off its high. These long-legged candles show the violent tug-of-war that occurred intraday between the bulls and bears. The bulls finally gave up, and price turned back down. A very strong and visible ceiling (dotted line) is now seen on the chart. At some point in the future it may be broken, but until that time, you can bet that traders will react every time price approaches that area.

(*continues*)

Example *(continued)*

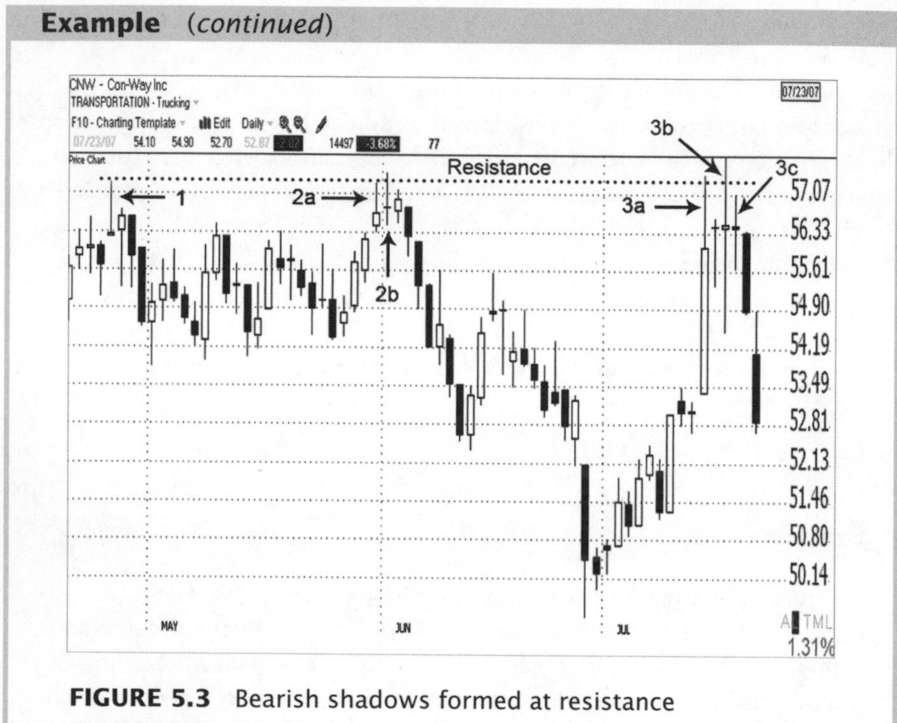

FIGURE 5.3 Bearish shadows formed at resistance
Source: TeleChart 2007®

triple top
A bearish reversal pattern that occurs when three prominent, parallel (or nearly parallel) peaks form in an uptrend. It is a valid reversal pattern when price closes below the lowest point between the three peaks.

The three parallel peaks that formed the April, June, and July tops on the chart of CNW in Figure 5.3 sets up a larger bearish Western triple top pattern. Long before the triple top was known in the Western hemisphere, the Japanese had recognized it and named it the *three mountain top.* If the center peak is noticeably higher than the peaks on either side of it, the pattern is called a *head-and-shoulders top* in Western analysis. The Japanese name for a head-and-shoulders top is a *three Buddha top.*

Whereas the candlestick reversal patterns discussed in Chapter 3 provide primarily short-term signals, these larger triple and head-and-shoulders tops have more significant implications and may be followed by a trend reversal.

Example

Figure 5.4 shows a daily chart of Coherent Inc. (COHR). An intermediate-term uptrend that started from the March 2007 low ended on April 17 with a bearish dark cloud cover pattern. Price then declined back to the March low (dotted line) reversing the entire uptrend that occurred during March–April. On May 16, as the March low was tested, a bullish hammer formed. The hammer's long tail shows us that the bears used that visible support area to cover short positions, and the bulls were willing to step into long positions. The bears were able to drive price down intraday to near that support area again during the three trading sessions following the hammer; however, the support held up and a rally ensued.

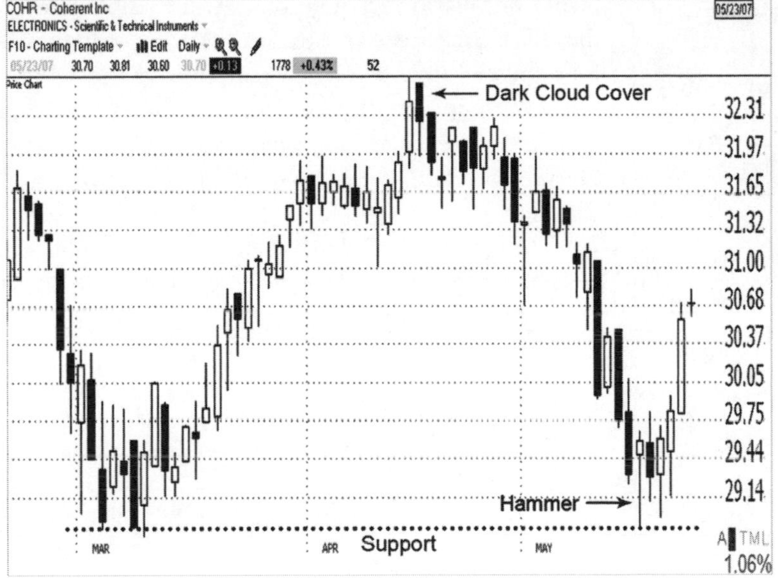

FIGURE 5.4 Bullish shadows formed at support
Source: TeleChart 2007®

A single test of support may occur, leaving one bullish shadow, or there may be more than one test of support. If there are several bullish shadows, it shows that the bears are able to push the stock lower during the day but the bulls step in each day at, or near, the support level and push the price back up.

head-and-shoulders top

A variation of a triple top pattern in which the center peak is noticeably higher than the two peaks on either side. It is a valid reversal pattern when price closes below the neckline. The neckline is a support line that connects the swing lows on both sides of the head. Head-and-shoulders tops are fairly reliable patterns, and they form more frequently than triple tops.

Summary: At the end of a price advance or decline, the emergence of one or more bearish shadows (advance) or bullish shadows (decline) is an indication that the stock is attempting to put in a top or a bottom. This action is often followed by a price reversal or a period of consolidation.

Tails in Overbought or Oversold Conditions

Although it is common to see tails form when price approaches visible support and resistance areas, you'll see plenty of tails form where there is no visible barrier on the chart. Price need not be near a strong ceiling or floor for a tail to form. Price may simply have moved too far too quickly in one direction, causing a short-term overbought (uptrend) or oversold (downtrend) condition. Overbought and oversold conditions are discussed in Part II.

Just remember that when you see a tail(s) form, you should be prepared for price to move in the opposite direction of the tail. Price may reverse the direction of the trend or at least consolidate for a period of time.

East Meets West

Chapter 6

Price, Volume, and Volatility

Learning to recognize and interpret the candlestick lines and patterns is the first step, albeit an important one, on the path to putting candlesticks to work. The knowledge you have already acquired in Part I should serve to dramatically improve your chart analysis skills. There is plenty more to be learned, though, in order to really master the power of candlestick charting. It is time to blend them with Western technical analysis. After you finish reading the next few chapters, you will have the additional tools you'll need to evaluate candlesticks in the context of the broader chart landscape, which can dramatically enhance their effectiveness.

In the introduction it was suggested that once you learn candlesticks, you may look at a standard bar chart and feel that it is incomplete. The same is true of combining Eastern candlestick charting with Western technical analysis. Once you learn how to put the two together, you may find that trying to analyze candlesticks without the aid of the bigger picture feels incomplete.

An introduction to Western technical analysis begins with learning about the roles of price, volume, and volatility. Understanding these elements is crucial to successful chart analysis, stock selection, and trade management. Advanced traders who are already familiar with these concepts may elect to skim through this chapter or bypass it. However, traders who are developing their Western technical analysis skills should be aware that each chapter in this book builds upon the prior chapters, so it is best to read them in order and to spend adequate time digesting each one.

Price

Price is the king of the chart. It is the purest measure of market sentiment. Price action is a manifestation of the combined psychology of all market participants. It tells us the perceived value of a security at a given time.

setup
An identifiable price formation that presents a potentially profitable trading opportunity.

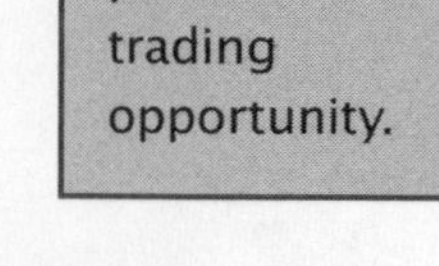

Price action provides the setups that we trade. There are numerous price setups for traders to choose from. For example, candlestick patterns provide setups, as do classic Western bar and chart patterns such as key reversals and head-and-shoulders patterns.

A setup by itself cannot make you money; however, a strategy for trading it can. A trader may achieve consistent success by learning to recognize one or more price setups and devising a profitable strategy to trade the setup(s). A strategy should seek to enhance profits while limiting risk.

strategy
A set of rules and conditions that determine such factors as what generates a signal and how to enter, manage, and exit the trade.

Many novice traders get caught up in looking for the perfect technical indicator and neglect to put sufficient emphasis on price. It is more effective to learn how to evaluate the price action and use indicators as complementary analysis tools. When an aspiring trader points out an indicator signal to me, such as an overbought or oversold oscillator, and asks if I would execute a trade, I respond, "It depends on what is happening with *price.*" I do not enter or exit a trade based solely on a signal from an indicator. Think of technical analysis as a big toolbox. Just as candlestick charting is one tool, indicators are another type of tool. Successful trading results from employing a set of tools rather than using each one in isolation.

Many technical indicators are derived from price. Moving averages are calculated by averaging the price of a stock over a designated period of time, for example, 20 days. Oscillators are a group of indicators that measure the momentum of price. These indicators are discussed later in this book. Technical indicators can be very useful; however, it is still the price action itself that confirms or invalidates an indicator's signal.

Part I of this book was devoted almost entirely to the discussion of price. The candlestick lines and patterns are formed from the open, high, low, and closing prices during a trading period. The candlestick reversal patterns must follow a directional price move in order for their signals to have significance.

There is still plenty more discussion to come on price movement as you'll see in chapters 7 through 9, which cover trend analysis, gaps, support, and resistance. But, first, let's bring volume and volatility into the mix.

Volume

Volume is second in importance only to price as a technical analysis tool. Volume's role in chart analysis will be referenced many times throughout this book. So far, you have seen how it may play a role in the formation of certain candlestick patterns, as discussed in Chapter 3.

Volume provides a measure of the level of activity by market participants in a specific stock or trading instrument. Every share of stock that changes hands between buyers and sellers serves to increase the volume for that trading period. The most commonly quoted time period for volume is daily; but it is also tracked for higher time frames, such as weekly, as well as for each intraday time frame.

volume
The number of shares or contracts that are traded during a specified period of time.

In addition to being tallied for individual stocks, volume is also measured for entire markets, such as the New York Stock Exchange (NYSE). In the futures and options markets, volume is represented in the number of contracts traded rather than in shares.

Displaying Volume on the Chart

In addition to price data, vendors of charting software also supply volume, and they may offer various ways to display it. I use the following displays of volume in the TeleChart platform (see Figure 6.1).

Volume in Shares A field that displays the bar volume is inserted in the data line above the chart. The bar volume indicates the number of shares traded for a given period of time, for instance, during a daily trading session. In most charting programs, volume is displayed in hundreds, so you'll need to mentally add two zeros to the end of the number.

Example

Figure 6.1 shows 2,807 shares traded on August 21, 2007, for Advent Software Inc. (ADVS). Add two zeros to the end and you can see that 280,700 shares were traded that day.

Average Daily Volume A field is also inserted in the data line showing a percentile ranking for average daily volume over the last 90 days. This ranking

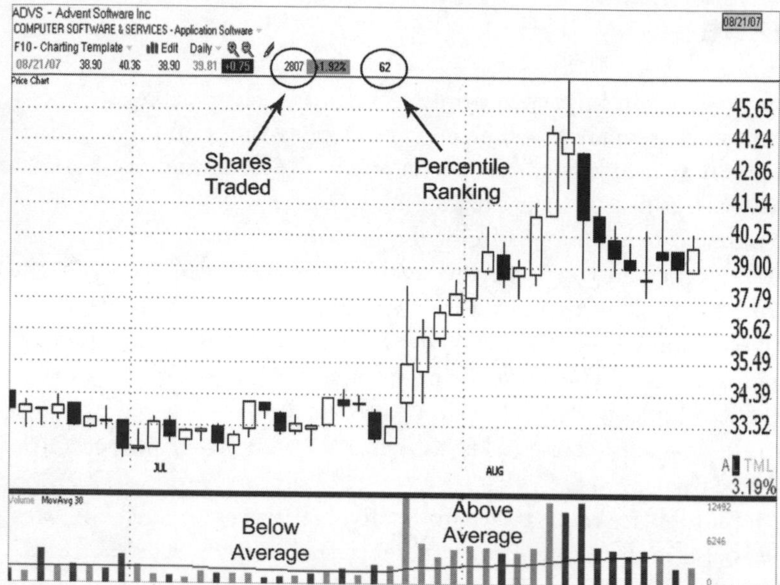

FIGURE 6.1 Volume may be displayed in various ways
Source: TeleChart 2007®

provides a quick gauge of the stock's liquidity over the past few months by indicating how heavily the stock is traded compared to all other stocks listed on the major U.S. exchanges. The lower the average daily volume, the more thinly traded the stock.

Example

In Figure 6.1, the number 62 in the data line indicates that Advent Software currently trades more volume than 62 percent of stocks. Most of the stocks that I trade rank in the 50 to 99 percentile, which equates to about 125,000 shares per day or higher. Novice traders may elect to start with more heavily traded stocks to avoid problems with order fills and excessive slippage. For instance, stocks in the 70 to 99 percentile trade a minimum of about half a million shares per day.

Volume Bars Volume can be plotted as a histogram (a bar graph) that provides a visual representation of each trading period's volume. The histogram allows a trader to quickly analyze the pattern or trend of volume. The volume bars are colored red or green, which corresponds to the current time period's closing price. A red volume bar indicates a lower close than the prior trading period, and a green bar indicates a higher close. Figure 6.1 shows the volume bars plotted in the panel below the chart window.

Smart Investor Tip

It is a common practice to plot a moving average over an indicator in order to smooth the data. I was first introduced to the idea of plotting a moving average of volume in John Bollinger's book *Bollinger on Bollinger Bands* (McGraw-Hill, 2002). Mr. Bollinger referenced using a 50-period simple moving average, but I prefer a shorter 30-period as demonstrated in Figure 6.1. The moving average is overlaid on the volume histogram in the panel below the chart window. This technique makes it very easy to see when volume is above or below average compared to the last 30 days. Experiment with different settings if you'd like; however, I would not suggest using a length of fewer than 20 periods for this purpose.

Analyzing Volume Patterns and Trends

The amount of volume that transpires during one or more trading periods can tell a story about the force behind the price movement. Consider the following examples:

- If heavy volume accompanies the formation of a bullish candlestick pattern, such as a hammer or a bullish engulfing pattern, it helps confirm that the stock may be putting in a bottom.
- An upside breakout after a period of consolidation is usually accompanied by heavy volume. In fact, the breakout is suspect if not and may be a false breakout. Volume attracts more buyers and is needed to propel the stock higher. Heavy volume may also accompany a downside break; however, it is not as significant because the market can continue to fall under its own weight.
- After an upward move, if price pulls back or consolidates on diminishing volume, it is usually an indication that short-term traders are taking profits after a directional move rather than a large number of market participants exiting the stock. Another upside move often follows in such cases.

These are just a few of the many instances where utilizing volume can provide insight into the psychology of traders. Incorporating volume in the examination of price movement can dramatically improve your stock selection and chart analysis skills.

The preceding examples are instances where fairly short-term events are analyzed. It is important to distinguish between analyzing a *short-term* volume pattern and a *longer-term* volume pattern or trend. If you are examining the volume pattern over the past several trading periods, volume can be analyzed from one bar to the next, providing a short-term picture. For instance, if after an upward move price pulls back on diminishing volume, in such a case you are looking at the price-volume relationship from one bar to the next as price pulls back. By my definition, diminishing volume occurs when most of the volume bars during the period being analyzed either drop below the moving average of volume or decline in a downward stepping pattern (see Figure 6.2, left).

There may also be times when you wish to evaluate the volume pattern over a longer period of time. For example, you may need to gauge the strength of the longer trend, or analyze the price-volume relationship of a large chart pattern. In cases where the bigger picture of volume is to be evaluated, look beyond the past few volume bars and instead look at the volume peaks (see Figure 6.2, right).

Short-Term Analysis Figure 6.3 shows a daily chart of Calgon Carbon Corp. (CCC). Price was in an uptrend for several weeks during May–June 2007. The dotted lines correspond to the volume patterns during pullbacks within the trend. Each time price pulled back for a few days, volume declined with it. After a directional move, when price pulls back or consolidates accompanied by diminishing volume, it may offer traders an opportunity to get aboard a

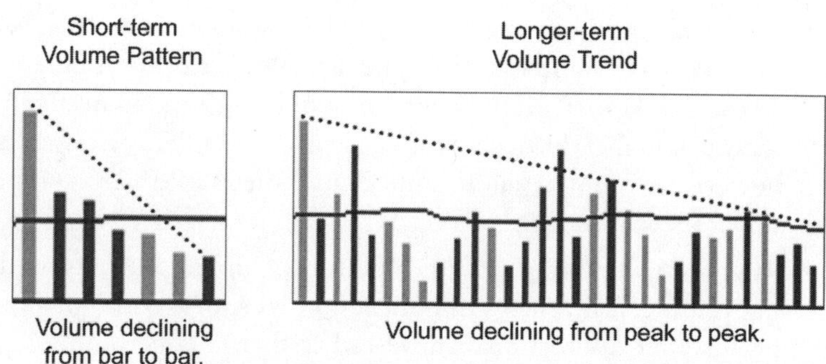

FIGURE 6.2 Analysis of volume bars vs. volume peaks

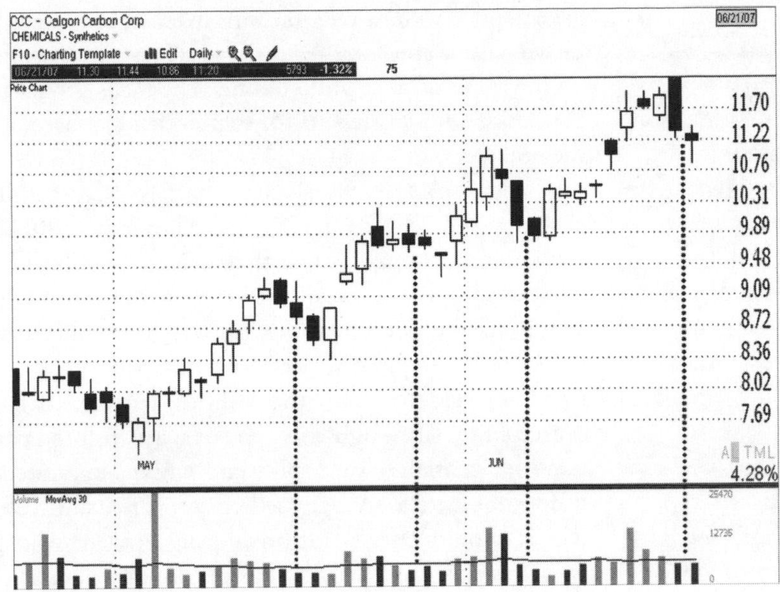

FIGURE 6.3 Volume declined as price pulled back
Source: TeleChart 2007®

trending stock. Rather than chasing the stock as it is rallying (or declining in a downtrend), the trader can use the interruption of the trend to enter at a point where an initial protective stop can be placed closer to the entry price.

Longer-Term Analysis When analyzed in conjunction with price action, volume can help us gauge the strength (or weakness) of a trend. Table 6.1 summarizes the

Table 6.1 Price-Volume Relationships

Price-Volume Relationship	*Implication for the Trend*
Price is rising Volume is rising	Strong Uptrend
Price is rising Volume is declining	Uptrend Weakening
Price is declining Volume is rising	Strong Downtrend
Price is declining Volume is declining	Downtrend Weakening

divergence
A scenario where the price of an asset moves in the opposite direction of an indicator. When price continues to form higher peaks in an uptrend, while the peaks in an indicator begin to decline, it signals a *negative divergence*, and the uptrend may be weakening. When price is making lower bottoms in a downtrend, but the indicator bottoms are rising, it indicates a *positive divergence* and an early warning that the downtrend may be weakening.

general price-volume relationships that can be gleaned from intermediate- and long-term trends. The emphasis here is on the trend of price and volume. The focus should be on the peaks, with less regard for each individual bar between the peaks.

Figure 6.4 shows a daily chart of Riverbed Technologies Inc. (RVBD). During May–July 2007 price was in an uptrend. Notice that volume was heavy during the rallies that occurred early in the trend. As the trend matured, even though price was still forming higher peaks, the level of market participation had diminished, as evidenced by the volume pattern (declining dotted line). Although this type of price-volume pattern does not guarantee that the trend will change direction, it does indicate a divergence between price and volume, which should elicit caution among traders who hold long positions. On July 24, price closed below a strong up trendline accompanied by heavy volume, which sent a stronger message that the trend direction may be changing.

If you choose to expand your study of Western technical analysis, you'll inevitably be introduced to many Western continuation and reversal patterns. There are some small Western bar patterns, such as key reversals and the inside and outside days referenced in Chapter 3. Flags and pennants also form in a short amount of time. Many of the Western patterns, though, are larger patterns that form over a period of several weeks or months. It is helpful to study the trend of volume as those large patterns form. For instance, a head-and shoulders is a fairly reliable top reversal pattern. An ideal head-and-shoulders has the following volume pattern: volume is strong as the left shoulder is formed; volume is usually still strong as the head is formed; volume declines noticeably as price pushes up to form the peak of the right shoulder.

Technical analysis is a broad field of study, one area of which includes Western chart patterns, such as head-and-shoulders, triangles, and wedges, just to name a few. Many technical analysis books touch on this topic, but none that I have found delve into this area as thoroughly as

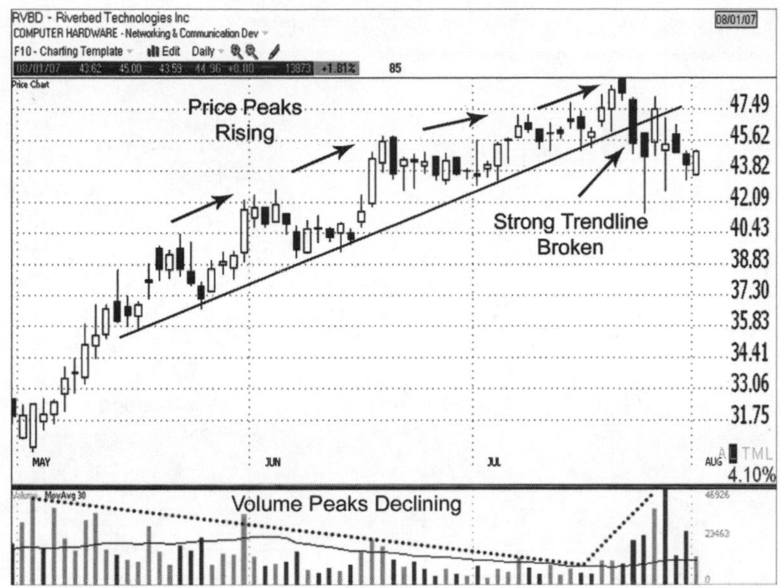

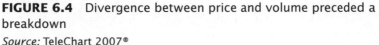

FIGURE 6.4 Divergence between price and volume preceded a breakdown
Source: TeleChart 2007®

Thomas Bulkowski does in his books. His latest book *Getting Started in Chart Patterns* (John Wiley & Sons, 2006) is an excellent resource for those who wish to add an understanding of chart patterns to their knowledge base.

Example

Figure 6.5 shows a head-and-shoulders top on the daily chart of Continental Airlines (CAL). Volume was above average as a peak formed the left shoulder (this pattern actually had a double left shoulder). Price pulled back and then rallied again on above-average volume to form the head. As price rose up to form the right shoulder, volume remained below average. There was not enough momentum to push price to a new high.

(*continues*)

Example *(continued)*

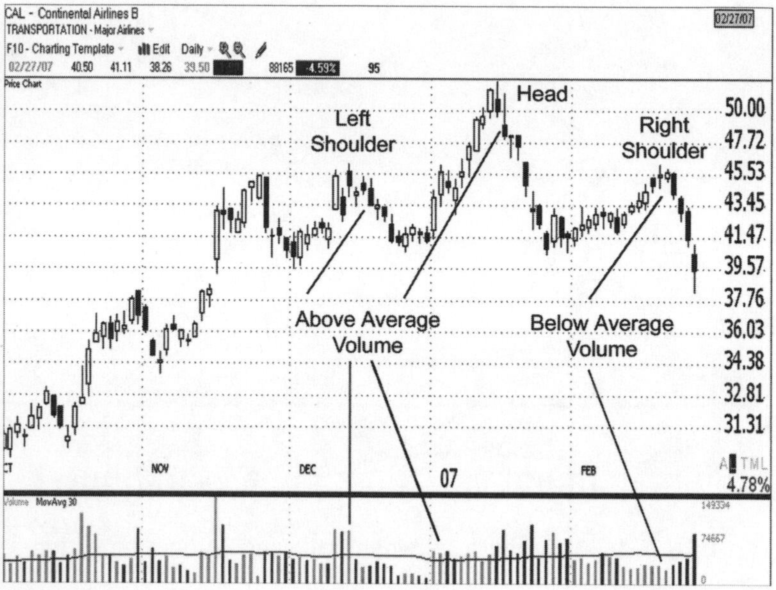

FIGURE 6.5 Volume may provide confirmation of a chart pattern
Source: TeleChart 2007®

Volatility

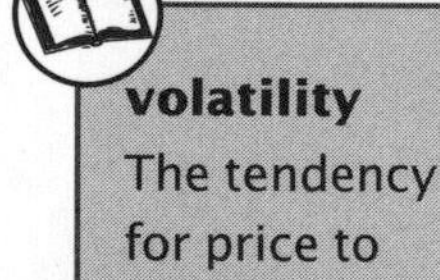

volatility
The tendency for price to fluctuate.

High volatility means that a stock's price can change dramatically over a short period of time in either direction. Low volatility means that a stock's price does not fluctuate dramatically. Volatility does not just apply to stock prices, but to other trading instruments and markets as well.

Volatility is not static—it may be highly variable over time. There is typically an ebb and flow that can be seen on a chart. Periods of low volatility are often followed by periods of high volatility, and vice versa. Traders must learn to recognize when volatility moves to one extreme or the other. Great trading opportunities can be found by implementing adequate focus on volatility.

Smart Investor Tip

Bollinger Bands can be effective for drawing attention to periods of low or high volatility. The setting I use for this indicator is that which is recommended by its creator, John Bollinger: a 20-period simple moving average of price with the bands plotted at two standard deviations from the moving average.

Example

When price makes a directional move, the Bollinger Bands will diverge (expand), indicating a period of higher volatility. When price pulls back or moves sideways, the bands will converge (contract). If price moves sideways long enough, the bands will constrict around price, sometimes very tightly. This is referred to as a *Bollinger squeeze.* This contraction-expansion phenomenon can be seen on the daily chart of Immersion Corp. (IMMR) shown in Figure 6.6.

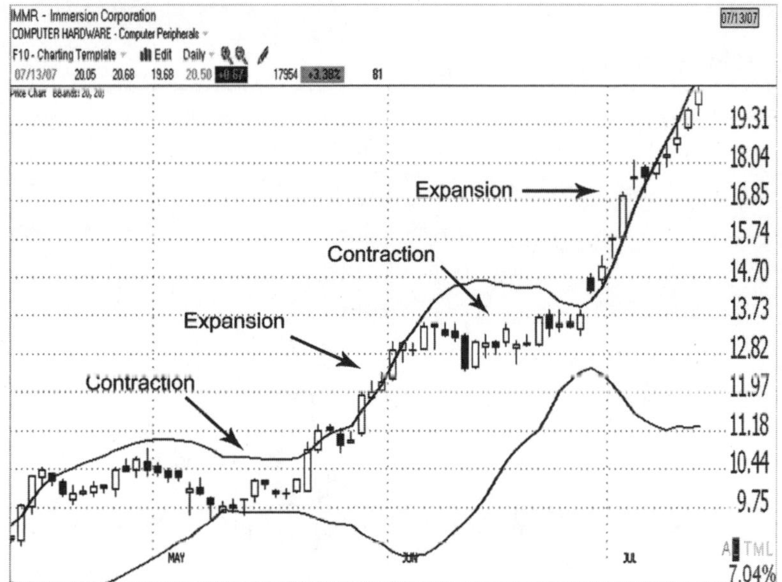

FIGURE 6.6 Contraction is followed by expansion and vice versa
Source: TeleChart 2007®

The term *volatility* may conjure up negative thoughts for those who do not understand or respect its role. A certain amount of volatility is necessary in order for stocks, and markets, to survive. And yet too much volatility can be frustrating and treacherous for traders, especially for those who do not yet have a lot of experience trading a volatile stock or market. As is the case with most trading-related concepts, it is usually not so much the volatility itself that is dangerous or risky, but rather the trader!

Measures of Volatility

There are various methods of measuring volatility. One measure is *standard deviation*, which measures the dispersion of data from the mean. In other words, it compares a stock's current volatility to its average. Bollinger Bands are constructed using standard deviation. *Beta* is another commonly used measure, which compares a stock's volatility to that of the market. The S&P 500 large-cap index is commonly used as a market benchmark.

After you have developed a strong foundation in charting, you may wish to expand your study of beta and standard deviation, or other measures of volatility, in order to further your understanding of this important concept. For now, though, consider using the logarithmic scale as a quick and easy method of gauging a stock's volatility.

Logarithmic Scale

Prices are displayed on the vertical axis (y-axis) on a chart. In most charting programs, horizontal division lines called gridlines are displayed in the chart window. They line up with the price scale (see Figure 6.7).

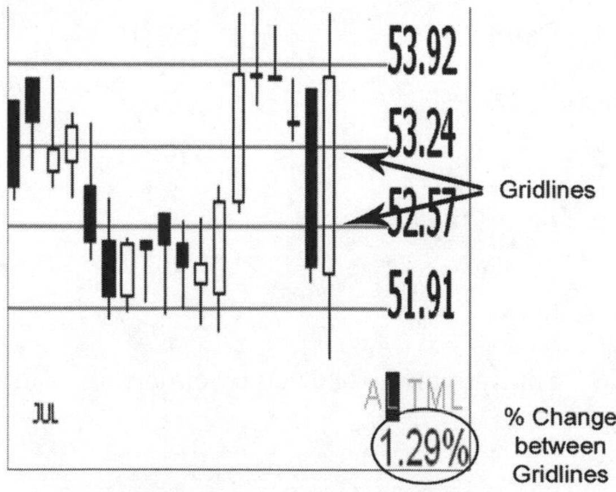

FIGURE 6.7 Logarithmic scale
Source: TeleChart 2007®

There are two commonly used methods of scaling: arithmetic and logarithmic. The arithmetic scale displays the price change from one horizontal division line to the next in equal increments (points). The logarithmic scale displays the price change as a percentage. The scaling method you choose is up to you. Many seasoned traders use logarithmic for charting stocks, which is also my preference.

When the logarithmic scale is selected, the percentage change between each gridline should be displayed in the chart window of your charting program, for example, below the price column as shown in Figure 6.7. That percentage indicates that if price moves up or down one gridline, it is a move of approximately *x* percent for that stock, with *x* being the percentage indicated, for instance, 1.29 percent. The percentage shown is not static; it indicates the current volatility. That percentage can change over time as volatility increases or decreases.

The percentage between the gridlines can provide a gauge of a stock's current volatility. It can also be used to compare the stock's volatility to other stocks. Generally speaking, the higher the percentage displayed, the higher the current volatility of the stock, and vice versa.

Smart Investor Tip

In order to ensure that you are making a proper comparison, be sure to use a consistent horizontal compression (zoom) for all the stocks being analyzed. In TeleChart, zoom 5 shows about five months of data on a daily chart. Don't compare one stock using zoom 5 to another using zoom 3, which shows about 10 months of data, because the percentage adjusts as the stock is compressed. If your charting program allows for vertical compression, that can also impact the scale.

Looks can be deceiving. What may appear *visually* to be about the same distance move on the chart of two different stocks can actually be significantly different from a *percentage* standpoint. If you have ever been shocked by the change in your unrealized profit or loss on a trade after what appeared to be a small move on the chart, it was a volatile stock—or at least a volatile period for that stock.

Example

Figure 6.8 shows a daily chart of Western Digital Corp. (WDC) from April through mid-July 2007. The stock gained about 40 percent during that time. The daily chart of Hoku Scientific (HOKU) in Figure 6.9 looks like it had a similar run up; however, it gained almost 250 percent during that uptrend. Clearly, HOKU, at approximately 11 percent between gridlines, was a much more volatile stock than WDC, at approximately 3 percent between gridlines.

(*continues*)

Example *(continued)*

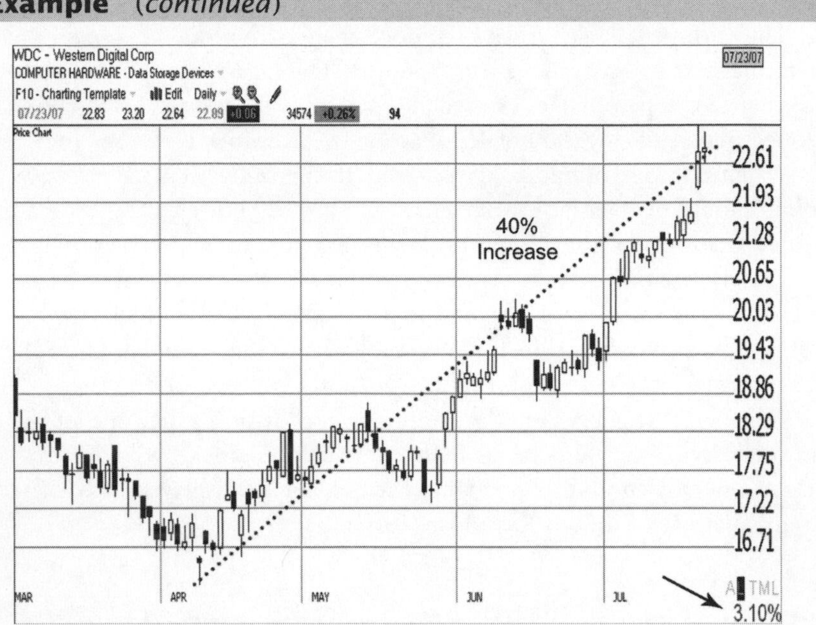

FIGURE 6.8 Stock gained approximately 40 percent in about four months
Source: TeleChart 2007®

FIGURE 6.9 Stock gained approximately 250% in about two months
Source: TeleChart 2007®

Smart Investor Tip

There are times when it is helpful to view the arithmetic scale, though, for example, when viewing market indicators such as the McClellan Summation Index where the index has a baseline of zero. Additionally, in some cases when checking for a price retracement, it is best to view the arithmetic scale. Thus, it is wise to become familiar with the method in your charting program for shifting from logarithmic to arithmetic and back, so you can quickly change the scale if needed.

As you continue your review of the remaining chapters, reference will be made several times to a stock's volatility, for example, when determining whether the reward of a trade outweighs the risk, or when determining if a stock is better suited for swing trading or for a long-term position.

Chapter 7

Trend Analysis

The primary role of technical analysis is the study of trends. You may be familiar with some of the well known axioms that have arisen over the decades regarding trends, such as: "The trend is your friend" and "Don't fight the trend." The phenomenon of trends is one of the major organizing principles of technical analysis. In order to become a skilled chartist, it is essential to learn how to identify and evaluate trends.

Numerous trading strategies have been developed around the fact that markets tend to move in trends. Trend followers strive to identify a new trend as early as possible in its formation and ride that trend until it runs out of steam and changes direction. Therefore, much of technical analysis is devoted to the identification of trends and gauging their strength or weakness so traders can implement the appropriate trading strategies.

trend
The direction of a price move. A trend may move up or down and is often classified by its duration as either short, intermediate, or long term.

A trend signifies the direction that the market is moving. In addition to the trend direction, traders also attempt to measure the duration, magnitude, and momentum of the trend. These concepts will be covered in this chapter.

Trend Direction

Markets move in trends. A stock or market may trend up or it may trend down. There may also be periods in which price moves sideways. While it might seem as if the direction of the trend should be quite obvious, that is not always the case, since trends do not develop in a linear fashion. The following discussion addresses some technical tools and methods to help determine the direction of a trend.

Moving Averages

The moving average is one of the oldest and most widely used technical indicators. Moving averages are trend-following indicators designed to catch major price moves. They are most effective when used in trending markets and fairly ineffective when price moves into a prolonged trading range. Moving averages are not precise timing indicators. While they do a good job of pointing out the direction of the trend, moving averages "lag" price, so they will be late at calling the turning points when a trend changes direction.

moving average
A trend-following indicator that smoothes out price action by averaging price over a designated period of time.

There are various ways to utilize moving averages. For the purposes of this discussion, we'll focus on the role of moving averages in helping determine the direction of the trend. In Chapter 9, you'll learn how they also play a role as support and resistance. Novice traders are encouraged to pursue additional study of moving averages, as well as other technical indicators that are beyond the scope of this book.

A trend does not develop in a straight line. Price typically zigs and zags its way across the chart's landscape. Plotting a moving average over price helps to smooth out those fluctuations and distortions that are inherent in most trends. It provides a clearer picture of the primary direction of the trend (see Figure 7.1).

Smart Investor Tip

As a general rule, a rising moving average indicates an uptrend, and a declining moving average indicates a downtrend. Think of a moving average as sort of a moving trend line.

In order to construct a simple moving average of price, the first step is to calculate the average. An *average* (or mean) of a set of values is determined by summing the values and dividing the result by the total number of values in the set. For stocks, the closing price is most often used in the calculation. To produce a *moving average*, the average is recalculated each new period. The newest bar's closing price is added to the calculation, and the oldest bar's closing price is dropped. The process is repeated with each new bar resulting in a line that represents a moving average of price.

Example

To compute a 20-period simple moving average, the closing prices of the last 20 bars are added together and divided by 20. When a new bar forms, the closing price of the 20th bar is dropped from the calculation and the closing price of the new bar is added.

Fortunately, modern charting programs do all the calculating for us. Traders need only to select the length for the moving average, and it will be plotted in the chart window, as shown in Figure 7.1.

One or more moving averages may be plotted in the chart window. The 10- and 20-period are popular short-term moving averages. Longer moving

FIGURE 7.1 20-period simple moving average smoothes out the fluctuations in price
Source: TeleChart 2007®

averages will lag farther behind the current price, since there are more values included in their calculations. The 50-period is a popular intermediate-term moving average. Price often finds support at or near this moving average on a deep pullback in an uptrend, and vice versa in a downtrend. The 200-period is a long-term moving average that is watched closely by traders. Price often finds support (or resistance) at or near this moving average during a correction of a trend.

Smart Investor Tip

At a minimum, I suggest plotting a 20-period simple moving average of price to help determine the direction of the current trend. The 20-period moving average represents approximately one month of trading on a daily chart and has proven to be a robust setting. It also tends to perform well on other time frames. As a general rule, price will stay above the 20-period moving average most of the time during an uptrend, and below it most of the time while in a downtrend.

Peaks and Bottoms

As price moves up and down in the general direction of the trend, a series of peaks and bottoms is formed on the chart. A peak is formed after a price advance when price stops making higher highs and makes a lower high. A peak includes three bars, with the middle bar's *high* being higher than those of the two bars on either side of it (Figure 7.2). A bottom is formed after a price decline when price stops making lower lows and makes a higher low. It includes three bars, with the middle bar's *low* being lower than the bars on either side of it (Figure 7.3). Peaks and bottoms show where price turned, resulting in at least a temporary change in direction.

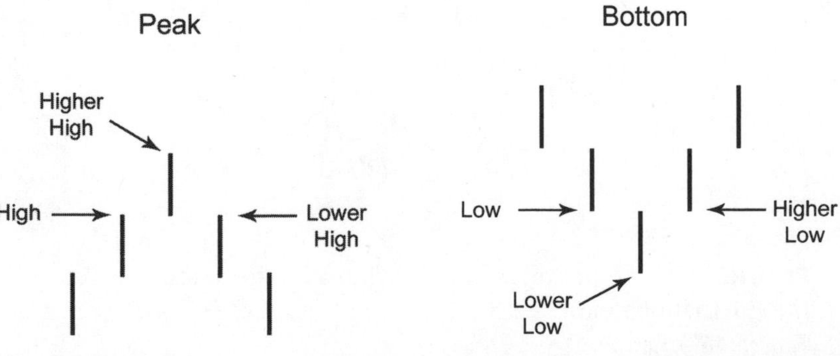

FIGURE 7.2 Peak (swing high) **FIGURE 7.3** Bottom (swing low)

A peak is often referred to as a *swing high* and a bottom as a *swing low*. These events show us the turning points of price moves. Some of the swing points will be prominent, while others will be minor. The prominent formations will draw your attention to the direction of the trend, as shown in Figure 7.4. An uptrend is comprised of a series of higher swing highs and higher swing lows. Conversely, in a downtrend, lower swing highs and lower swing lows are evident. You'll see several examples of peaks and bottoms on the charts shown in Figures 7.6 through 7.11.

Candlesticks are excellent for short-term timing signals. After a directional price move, it is fairly common to see a candlestick reversal pattern form at the swing high or the swing low. Even if no reversal pattern forms, you'll often see other indications that the move is running out of steam, such as spinning tops or long shadows.

Trend Lines

A trend line is one of the simplest charting tools available; but don't let its simplicity take away from its value. Trend lines can be very helpful for determining the trend direction. Most charting programs provide a trend line–drawing feature, allowing users to draw lines in the chart window.

Classic trend lines are drawn on the chart connecting the turning points of the peaks or bottoms. The trend line should touch as close as possible to the

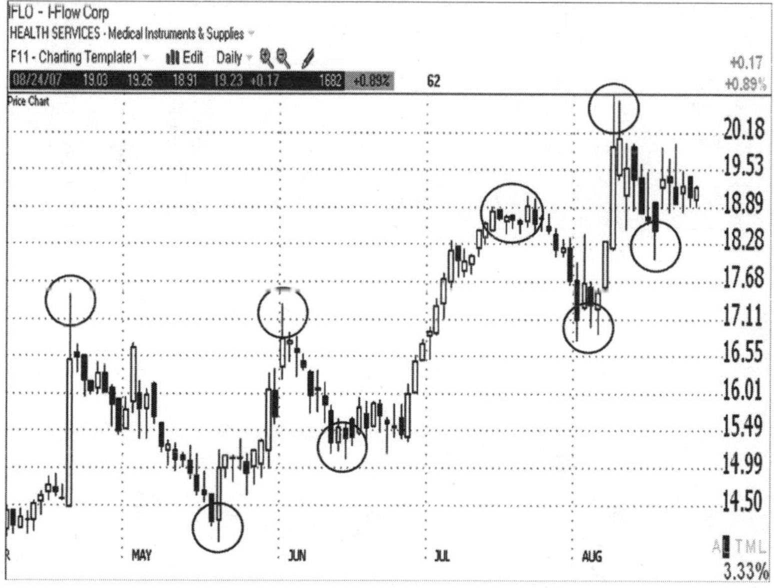

FIGURE 7.4 Prominent peaks and bottoms (circled) help define the uptrend

Source: TeleChart 2007®

trend line
A straight line drawn on a chart to determine the direction and slope of the current trend, or to identify the boundaries of a consolidation area.

actual turning point (the high of a peak bar or the low of a bottom bar). There will be times when the trend line will not quite touch the pivot, or will breach one or more bars. It is okay to clip one or more shadows if it means touching the trend line to more turning points; however, be careful about drawing the line through one or more real bodies as doing so may result in an invalid trend line.

There must be at least two turning points (touches) to draw a valid trend line. Ideally, there are three or more touches on the line. Trend lines with three or more touches are more significant than those with only two.

A common mistake traders make is attempting to draw a trend line across the highs or lows of individual price bars and neglecting to touch the line to two or more peaks or bottoms. The result is in an invalid trend line.

Example

Figure 7.5 shows two trend lines. The lower trend line is valid because it connects the turning points of three rising bottoms. It was necessary and acceptable to clip the lower shadow of the second bottom in order to touch the third bottom. The steeper trend line is not valid because it touches rising *lows*, not rising *bottoms*.

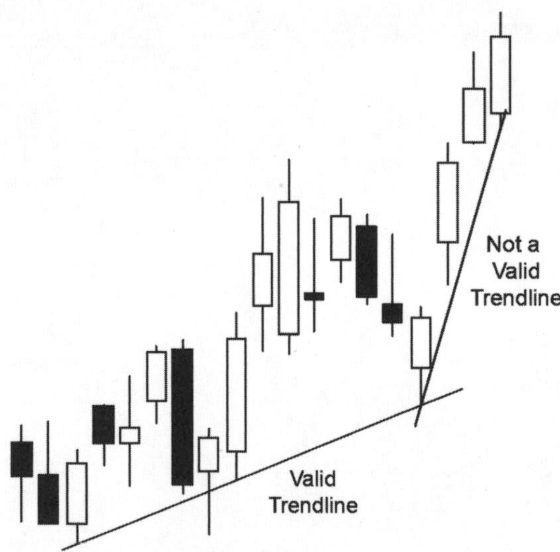

FIGURE 7.5 Valid versus invalid trend line

In an uptrend, the primary trend line is a rising support line drawn below, and connecting, the rising bottoms (see Figure 7.6). Once an uptrend starts to emerge, there must be two bottoms formed on the chart before a support trend line can be drawn. You may also be able to draw a parallel, rising resistance line above the rising peaks. It is common for price to rise in a channel.

In a downtrend, the primary trend line is a declining resistance line drawn above and connecting the declining peaks (see Figure 7.7). You may also be able to draw a parallel, declining support trend line below the declining bottoms if the stock is descending in a channel.

As the trend progresses, the primary trend line (and the parallel channel line if applicable) can be adjusted slightly and extended. Sometimes there will be more than one strong support or resistance trend line. In the example of Immucor Inc. (BLUD) shown in Figure 7.7, the downtrend accelerated in June 2007, resulting in a sharper angle of the declining peaks. Both resistance lines shown are valid. The tighter line is more indicative of the most recent price action and will be broken more quickly if the trend changes direction.

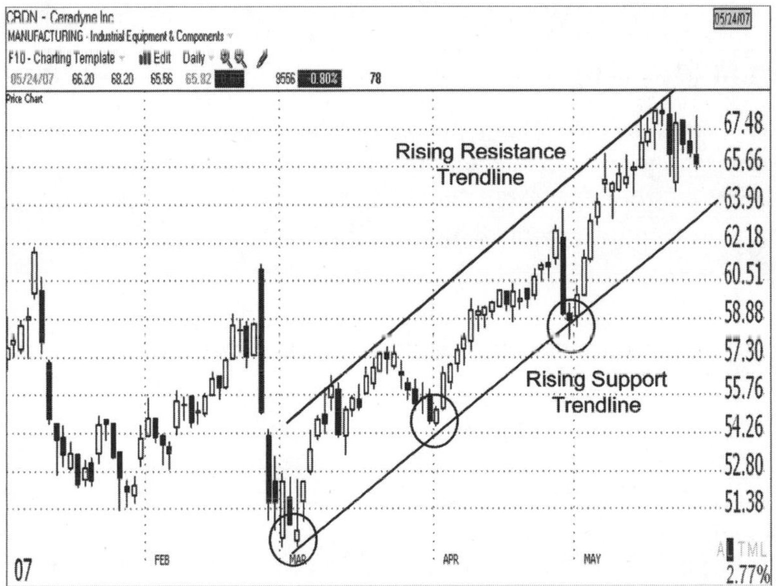

FIGURE 7.6 In an uptrend, the primary trendline connects the rising bottoms (circled)
Source: TeleChart 2007®

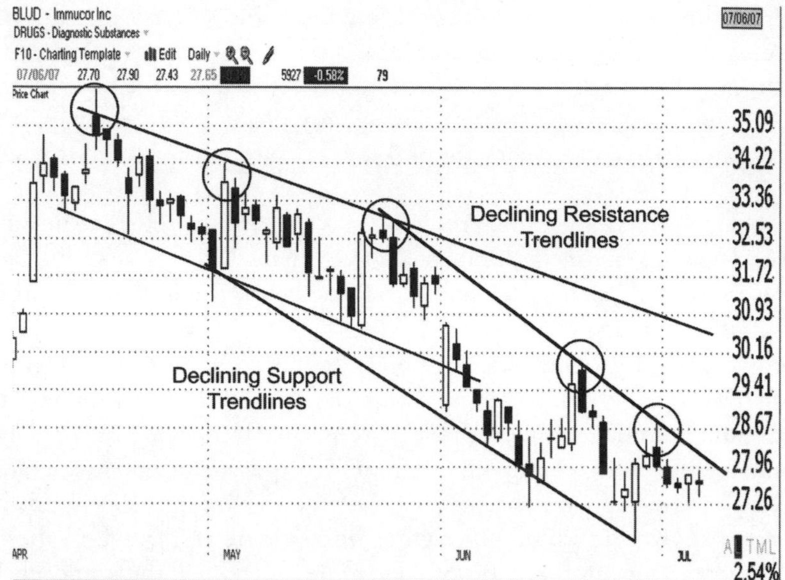

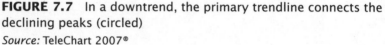

FIGURE 7.7 In a downtrend, the primary trendline connects the declining peaks (circled)
Source: TeleChart 2007®

Uptrend (Bullish)

Now let's combine the three methods mentioned previously for determining trend direction: moving averages, peaks and bottoms, and trend lines. The daily chart of Shaw Group Inc. (SGR) in Figure 7.8 illustrates a stock in an uptrend, which can be identified by the following criteria:

- It consists primarily of rising peaks and rising bottoms.
- Price remains above the 20-period simple moving average throughout most of the uptrend.
- A rising support trend line can be drawn below the prominent rising bottoms.

In an uptrend, the magnitude of the upward swings is usually more than that of the pullbacks. The upswings typically consist of predominantly bullish candles. Therefore, once an uptrend has been established, it is usually best to trade in the direction of the trend, which means trading primarily long positions. In this type of environment, look for opportunities to buy on pullbacks (dips) or corrections in the trend.

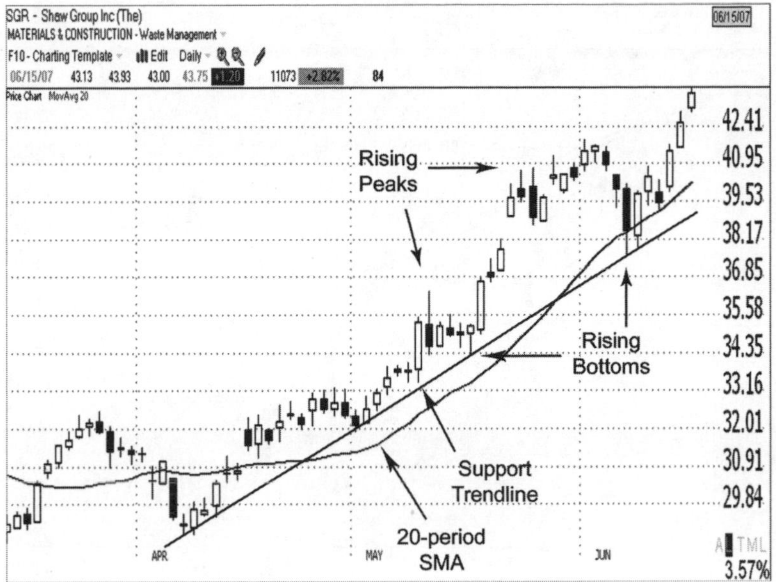

FIGURE 7.8 Stock in an uptrend
Source: TeleChart 2007®

Smart Investor Tip

Be careful trading against a strong uptrend. You'll probably do much better taking long positions than you would trying to sell short off the rallies. The momentum is upward and such price action will attract more buying. Selling short in this environment is like swimming against the tide, and if done at all, it is a practice best left to experienced traders.

Downtrend (Bearish)

The daily chart of Retail Ventures Inc. (RVI) in Figure 7.9 shows a stock in a downtrend, which can be identified by the following criteria:

- It consists primarily of declining peaks and declining bottoms.
- Price remains below the 20-period simple moving average throughout most of the downtrend.
- A declining resistance trend line can be drawn above the prominent declining peaks.

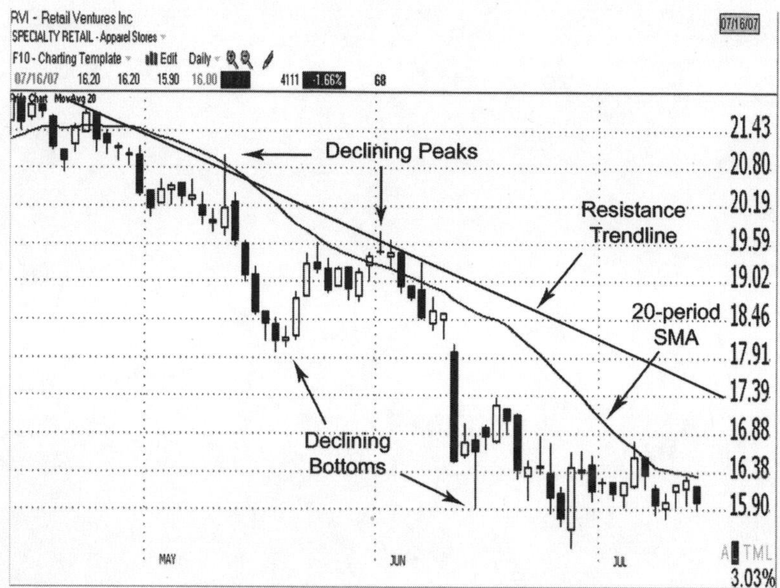

FIGURE 7.9 Stock in a downtrend
Source: TeleChart 2007®

Once a downtrend has been established, it is usually best to trade in the direction of the trend, which means trading primarily on the short side. In this type of environment, look for opportunities to sell the rallies. Many novice traders get burned attempting to "nail the bottom" of a downtrend. They take long positions when they see a single bottom form in the downtrend, thinking it will be the one that finally reverses the trend. Often, it does not, and the result is a losing trade. Countertrend trading is a practice best left to experienced traders.

Example

The daily chart of Investools Inc. (SWIM) in Figure 7.10 shows how several single bottoms that formed in May–June 2007 (identified by the short horizontal lines) were unsuccessful at reversing the downtrend. Finally, in July, a double bottom formed (dotted line), setting up a stronger reversal pattern.

(*continues*)

Example *(continued)*

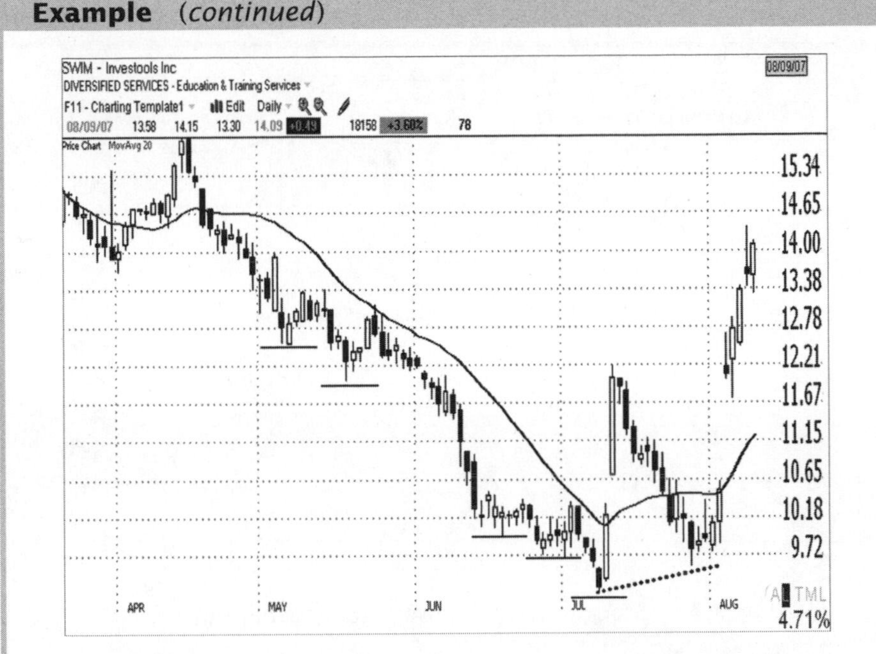

FIGURE 7.10 Trying to nail a single bottom in a downtrend can be a frustrating and costly endeavor

Source: TeleChart 2007®

Smart Investor Tip

Traders who do not sell short should wait for a downtrend to show signs of solid bottoming action to trade the long side. For example, watch for the appearance of a double, head-and-shoulders, or rounded bottom to form. An alternative to shorting that allows traders and investors to profit during a down market (the ProShares exchange-traded funds) will be discussed in Chapter 10.

Sideways (No Trend)

When a stock moves sideways, it is a condition referred to as *consolidation*. The daily chart of Dryships (DRYS) in Figure 7.11 illustrates a stock that is consolidating, which can be identified by the following criteria:

- Price is confined within a trading range. There is no clear direction indicated by the peaks and bottoms.

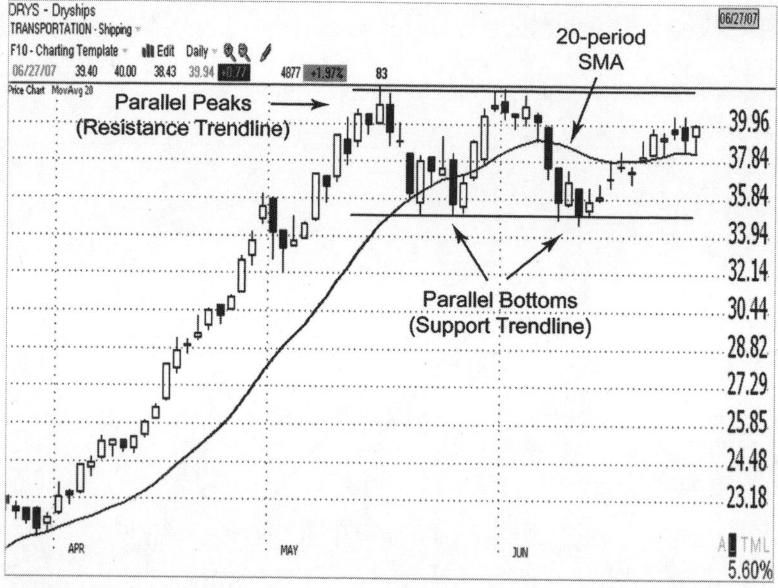

FIGURE 7.11 Stock moving sideways (consolidating)
Source: TeleChart 2007®

- The 20-period simple moving average flattens out and may whipsaw. Price may cross above and below the moving average several times.
- The sideways price action can often be trapped between support and resistance trend lines. The trend lines may be parallel, as shown in Figure 7.11, or they may converge in the form of a triangle (refer to Figure 7.13).

Smart Investor Tip

It is usually easier to trade in a trending market than while the market is confined to a trading range, which can be a frustrating and costly time for traders using trend-following strategies. For some traders it is best to stand aside during these phases. Others are able to adapt by shifting to strategies that work in a trendless environment rather than trying to pursue a trend-following method and getting whipsawed.

Trend Duration

There are three classifications of trend duration that have been widely accepted in Western technical analysis: long, intermediate, and short term. Traders should understand the definition of these trends and be able to identify them on a chart.

Most of the examples shown in the following discussion represent an uptrending market. However, these technical events also occur in downtrending markets.

Long-Term Trend

The long-term trend may also be referred to as the *major* or *primary* trend. Some sources state that a long-term trend is one that is in effect for at least a year. However, many traders, myself included, consider a trend of six to eight months or longer to fall under the category of long term.

A long-term trend may be strung together by a series of shorter, intermediate-term trends. Price may move in the direction of the long-term trend for several weeks or months at a time, followed by an interruption of the trend that may also last for weeks or months. Those interruptions may be in the form of consolidation (sideways movement) or a correction in which price moves against the long-term trend.

Example

Figure 7.12 shows a daily chart of O2 Micro International Ltd. (OIIM). The chart is compressed so that over a year of price data can be observed. It is clear that the stock is in a long-term uptrend. Price consolidated for about four months from December 2006 through early April 2007. Price swung back and forth, forming the ceiling (resistance) and floor (support) of a trading range. Parallel, horizontal trend lines can be drawn to define the consolidation area. The 20-period simple moving average (SMA) flattened out during those months. Price broke out from the trading range on April 5, resuming the long-term uptrend. The stock consolidated again from May through June. That consolidation was tighter than the prior consolidation. The 20-period SMA flattened out again until price broke out above the ceiling of the trading range on June 29, once again resuming the long-term uptrend.

(*continues*)

Example *(continued)*

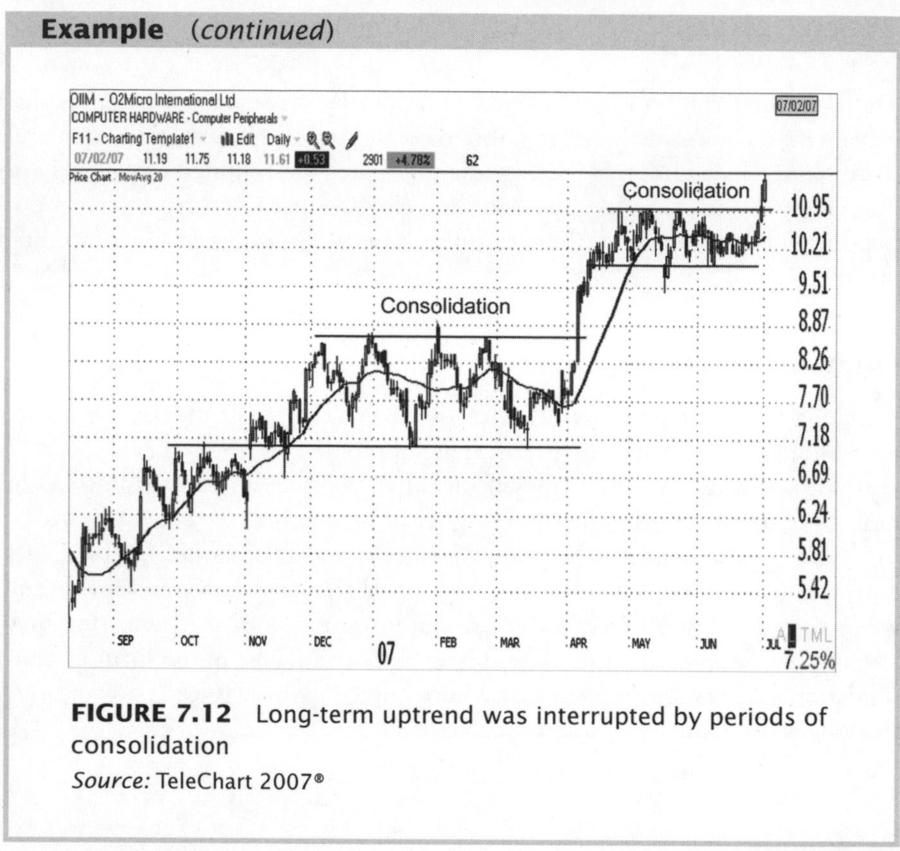

FIGURE 7.12 Long-term uptrend was interrupted by periods of consolidation

Source: TeleChart 2007®

In some cases, the consolidation takes the form of a triangle. Instead of parallel lines, converging support and resistance trend lines can be drawn to define the price action.

Example

Figure 7.13 shows a daily chart of Honeywell International (HON). A long-term uptrend was interrupted for several weeks during March–April 2007. Price consolidated in the form of a symmetrical triangle swinging back and forth for weeks and making no headway in the direction of the long-term trend. The 20-period SMA flattened out as price coiled into the apex of the triangle. Finally, price broke out from the triangle in mid-April 2007 and accelerated with a continuation gap on April 20 (gaps are discussed in Chapter 8).

(continues)

Example *(continued)*

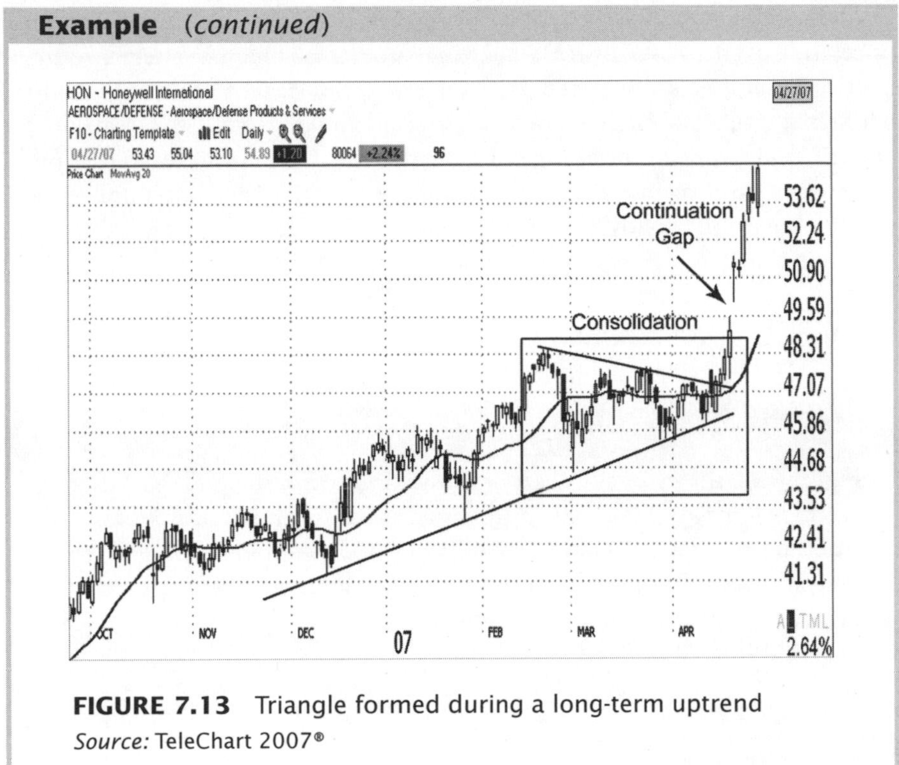

FIGURE 7.13 Triangle formed during a long-term uptrend
Source: TeleChart 2007®

The trend will not always resume after a period of consolidation. In some cases, what appears to be consolidation when it forms at the right edge of the chart will turn out to be topping (uptrend) or bottoming (downtrend) action that precedes a trend reversal. If a stock in an uptrend closes below the floor of a trading range rather than breaking out above it, the trend may be changing direction, and vice versa in a downtrend.

In addition to periods of consolidation, as a long-term trend develops there may also be times when price turns back against the trend correcting a portion of the prior move. A correction may also be referred to as a *retracement*. Price retracements of one third to one half of the prior trend are common. A retracement of two thirds of the prior trend may also be seen. If price corrects beyond two thirds of the prior trend, it is considered to be a trend reversal, and the prior trend is unlikely to resume.

triangle
A chart pattern that forms when price moves sideways. The swings across the consolidation area tighten as price moves toward the apex of the triangle. There are three types of triangles: ascending, descending, and symmetrical.

The use of *Fibonacci* retracement levels has become increasingly popular since the advent of mainstream charting programs. Fibonacci refers to a sequence of numbers discovered by Leonardo Fibonacci, a thirteenth-century mathematician. Common Fibonacci retracement levels are 38.2 percent, 50 percent, and 61.8 percent of the prior trend. The 38.2 percent number is often rounded to 38 percent and corresponds fairly closely to the one-third retracement discussed previously; 61.8 percent is often rounded to 62 percent and corresponds closely to the two-thirds retracement.

Example

Figure 7.14 shows a daily chart of Trinity Industries Inc. (TRN). After advancing for a few months, price retraced part of the prior uptrend, stopping at the 61.8 percent Fibonacci level. The uptrend resumed for several more weeks until late February 2007. Price corrected again before resuming the long-term uptrend.

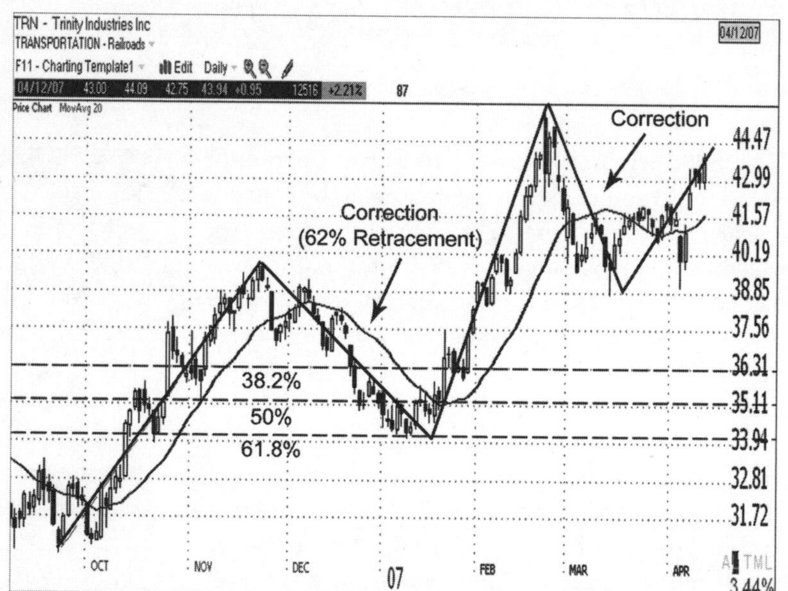

FIGURE 7.14 Long-term uptrend was interrupted by price corrections

Source: TeleChart 2007®

Smart Investor Tip

Many of the mainstream charting programs now include a Fibonacci retracement grid, making it quick and easy to measure the magnitude of a retracement.

The long-term trend resumes after interruptions of the trend until it finally tops out (uptrend) or bottoms out (downtrend) and reverses direction. Always assume that the prevailing trend is in force until there is clear evidence to the contrary.

Intermediate-Term Trend

An intermediate-term trend may also be called the *secondary* trend. It typically lasts from several weeks to several months. An intermediate-term trend is usually strung together by a series of shorter-term price swings that are separated by brief pauses, pullbacks, or periods of minor consolidation.

Recall from discussion in Chapters 3 and 4 that the candlestick line tells a story of investor psychology. When you look at a candlestick line on the daily chart after the session has ended, you see the end result of the intraday battle between the bulls and bears. But if you wish to see the precise details of how that battle unfolded throughout the trading session, you need to shift down to an intraday time frame to see more price data. Take that same concept and apply it to trends. The long-term trend gives a big picture view of price action. But if you wish to see how that trend is developing, you'll need to analyze the smaller trends within the larger trend.

There will be times when you'll observe a smooth long-term trend that only has minor interruptions; but that will be more the exception than the rule. More often, when you take a closer look, you'll see that the long term trend zigs and zags its way up or down. If you analyze a typical long-term trend, you'll usually find that it is really several intermediate-term trends and periods of consolidation strung together. An intermediate-term trend can move in the direction of the long-term trend, or it can move against it. Look again at Figure 7.14. The upward moves each lasted for several weeks (intermediate-term uptrends) separated by corrections that also lasted for several weeks (intermediate-term downtrends).

Short-Term Trend

If you take the analysis a level lower, you'll find that there are yet shorter trends. A short-term trend may also be called a *minor trend* or a *price swing*. It typically lasts from a few days to a couple of weeks, but not usually more than about three weeks. There may be several such swings within a larger up- or downtrend. The short-term trend may move in the direction of the larger trend, or against the trend (countertrend).

Example

Figure 7.15 provides a closer look at one of the intermediate-term uptrends that formed on the Trinity Industries Inc. (TRN) chart (October–November 2006). A closer look at that uptrend shows that it is actually comprised of several short upward and downward price swings.

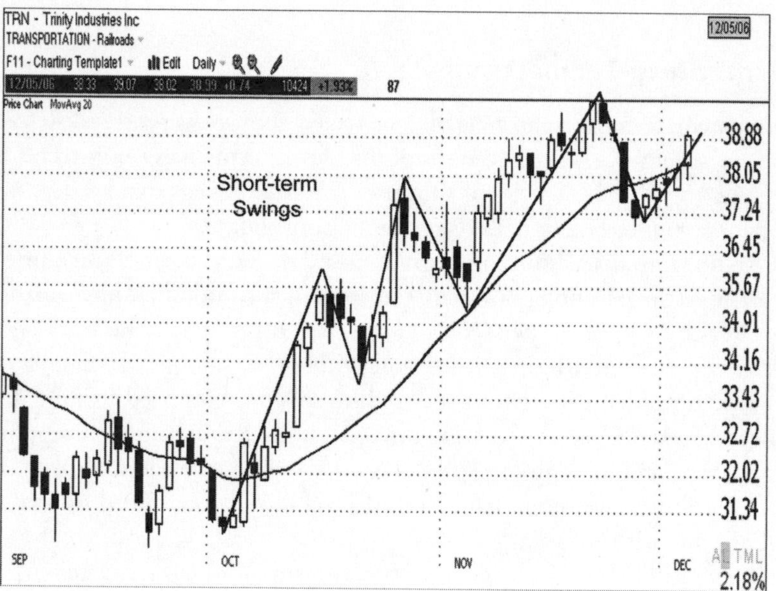

FIGURE 7.15 Short-term trends within an intermediate-term trend

Source: TeleChart 2007®

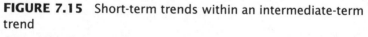

Smart Investor Tip

Swing trading is a trading style that has become increasingly popular over the years. Swing traders take advantage of the short-term moves to buy the dips and sell the rallies, or vice versa.

Pay Attention to the Major Market Averages

Traders should not only analyze the charts of the individual stocks they trade, but they should be aware of the long-, intermediate- and short-term trends of the major market averages. The tone of the broad market can have a strong impact on individual stocks. In the United States, the three best-known averages include: the Dow Jones Industrial Average, the S&P 500 Index, and the Nasdaq Composite Index.

While the direction of short- and intermediate-term trends of the averages can be influenced by rumor, news, and the sentiment of market participants, the long-term trend of the market is driven primarily by fundamental factors. The major trend reflects the condition of the U.S. economy and may also be impacted by global markets.

A long-term uptrend that occurs on an index chart is referred to as *bull market* and a long-term downtrend is called a *bear market*. As of this writing, the broad market was still in a long-term uptrend (see Figure 7.16). During July–August 2007, however, the major averages experienced a *bull market correction* (see Figure 7.17) of about 10 percent (many individual stocks declined much more).

Multiple Time Frames

Whether evaluating the charts of individual stocks or market averages, take advantage of different time frames to analyze trends. The long-term trend is usually quite obvious on a weekly or monthly chart. The higher time frame provides a bigger picture view and eliminates much of the "noise" of the lower time frames. When analyzing the intermediate- and short-term trends you'll want to see more detail so use the daily chart. At times you may even wish to consult the hourly chart to get a good feel for the short-term trend.

Example

Figure 7.16 shows a monthly chart of the S&P 500 large-cap Index as of August 2007. You can see the historical bull market that ended in 2000, followed by the bear market of 2000–2002. Note that it took only two years to wipe out about four years of gains during that bear market, and it took the current bull market of almost five years to return to the prior bull market's high. In the markets, it usually takes longer to build up than it does to tear down.

(*continues*)

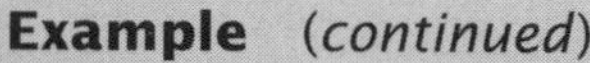

Example *(continued)*

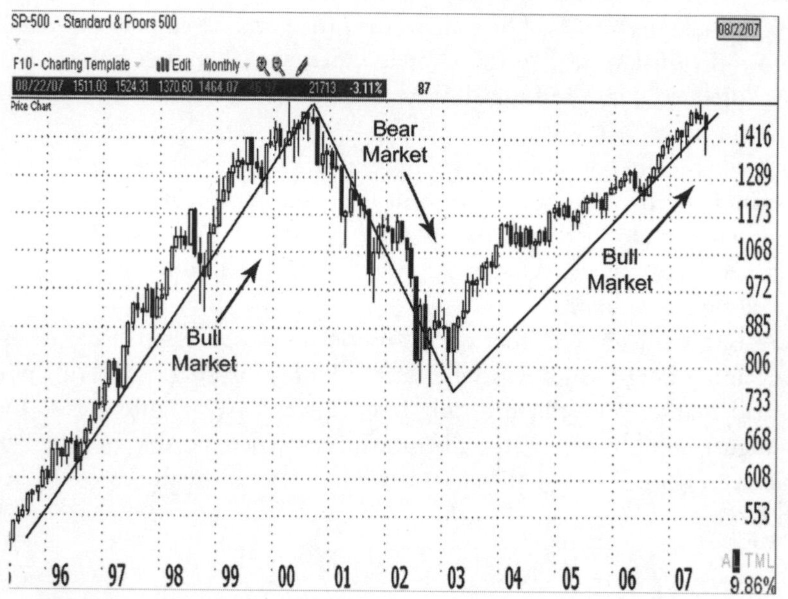

FIGURE 7.16 Long-term trends (bull and bear markets) on the S&P 500 Index

Source: TeleChart 2007®

Example

Figure 7.17 shows a daily chart of the S&P 500 Index. The intermediate-term trend on the S&P 500 chart is down and the short-term trend is up. The current short-term uptrend actually began intraday on August 16, as evidenced by the long tail of the hammer. At the time the low was made during that session, the candle was very bearish. The long tail shows us that there was a dramatic turnaround intraday as the bulls took control from the bears. It was a very volatile trading session!

(continues)

Example *(continued)*

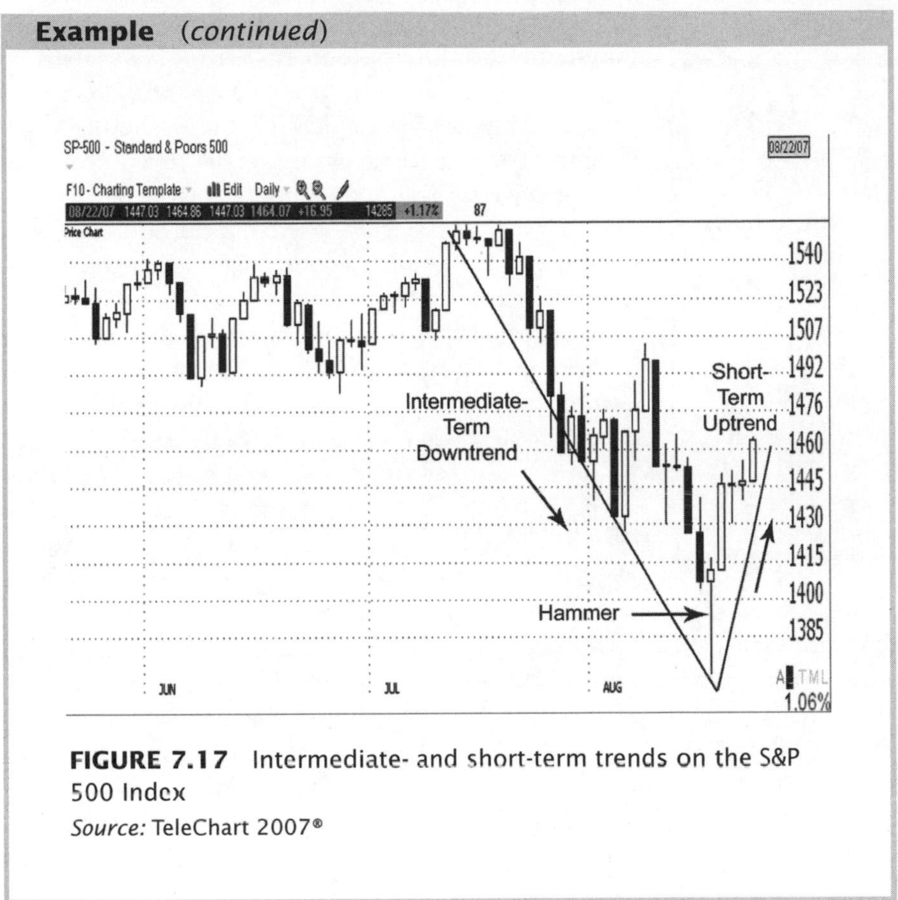

FIGURE 7.17 Intermediate- and short-term trends on the S&P 500 Index

Source: TeleChart 2007®

Probability and Reversion to the Mean

Don't worry, you won't have to attend a statistics class in order to learn how to trade successfully (although it sure wouldn't hurt). It is important, though, that traders understand some basics about averages and probability because it can have a direct and potentially dramatic impact on their trading.

Reversion to the Mean

As a general rule, price does not deviate far from the average (or mean), and when it does, it becomes vulnerable to a change in direction. When price moves

mean reversion
A statistical concept that suggests that a value eventually moves back toward the mean, or average. For price, the mean can be a historical average of the price.

away from the average, it has a tendency to move back toward it, which is referred to as *reverting to the mean.*

I pay attention to the proximity of price to the 20-period moving average. When price moves too far away from that strong moving average, I refer to it as "catching air." Granted, that is not an impressive technical description, but it seems effective at getting the point across to traders who are learning about price movement. When price has moved too far from the average, the stock may be overextended. That condition can be alleviated either by price pulling back toward the average (Figure 7.18, left), or by a period of sideways movement that allows the average to catch up (Figure 7.18, right).

In an uptrend, after price swings up, it is often followed by a decline back toward the average, called a *pullback* or a *dip.* Price may also pull back upward after a swing down in a downtrend. Pullbacks are quite common within a trend. They are primarily the result of traders taking profits on short-term price moves. Traders exiting their positions cause the minor retracements, which are often followed by another swing in the direction of the longer trend.

When price moves sideways instead of pulling back, allowing the moving average to catch up, I refer to it as *minor consolidation* or *basing action.* The Japanese refer to this type of basing action as a *box range.* Basing action is a period of tight sideways movement after a directional price move (not to be confused with "base building" after a long downtrend that you'll see referenced in

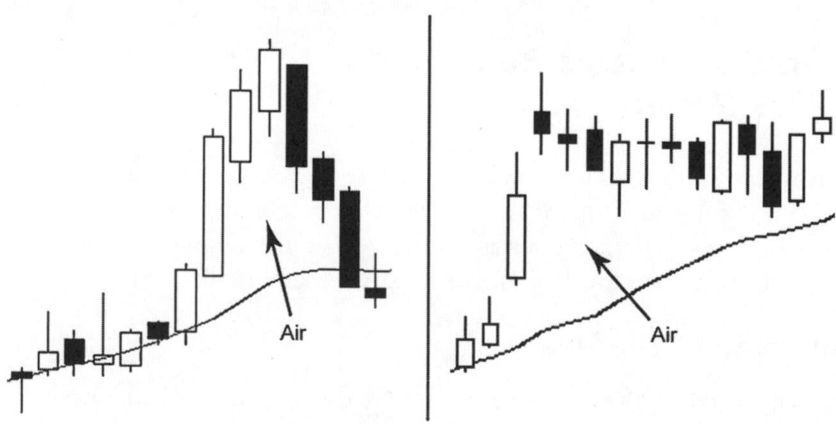

FIGURE 7.18 Mean reversion

some technical analysis texts). A tight base may last from a few days to a few weeks. It is a less significant event than a prolonged period of consolidation that interrupts a long trend, such as a horizontal trading range or triangle shown previously. In a strongly trending environment, basing action is often followed by a resumption of the prior trend.

The difference between a pullback and basing action is that a pullback turns *against* the trend (a countertrend move), whereas a base is a *sideways* move (refer to Figure 7.19). Both of these setups have the effect of allowing the trend to rest up for another move. Such interruptions are healthy for a trend's development. Without them, price would move too quickly to extreme, unsustainable levels. The fact that the stock is able to consolidate the gains and then move again in the direction of the longer trend is a testament to the trend's strength. *Note:* If a pullback or a period of basing action is preceded by a sharp upward move (or a sharp decline in a downtrend), it may be referred to as a pennant or a flag.

When price has moved away from the average it becomes vulnerable to profit-taking by swing traders so be alert for candlestick reversal patterns. Reversal patterns often give short-term reversal signals at, or near, the end of price swings. Figure 7.20 shows a daily chart of Cal Dive International Inc. (DVR).

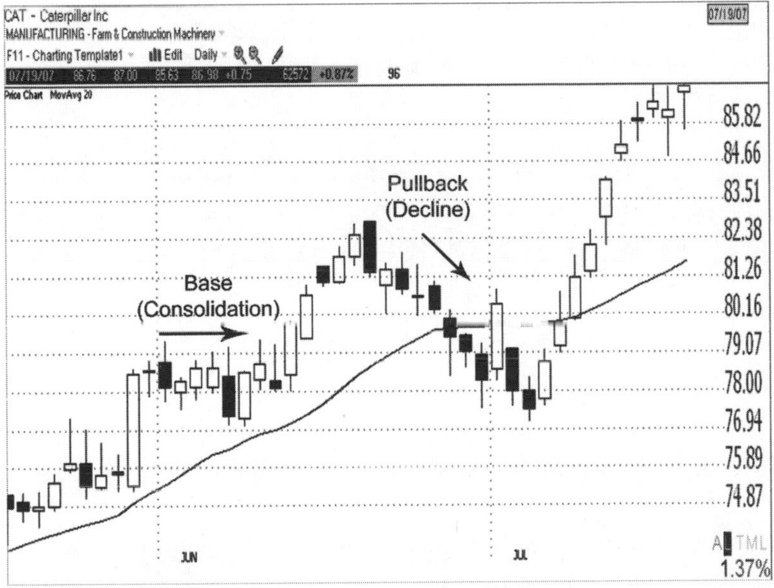

FIGURE 7.19 Pullbacks and periods of minor consolidation are common during the development of a longer trend
Source: TeleChart 2007®

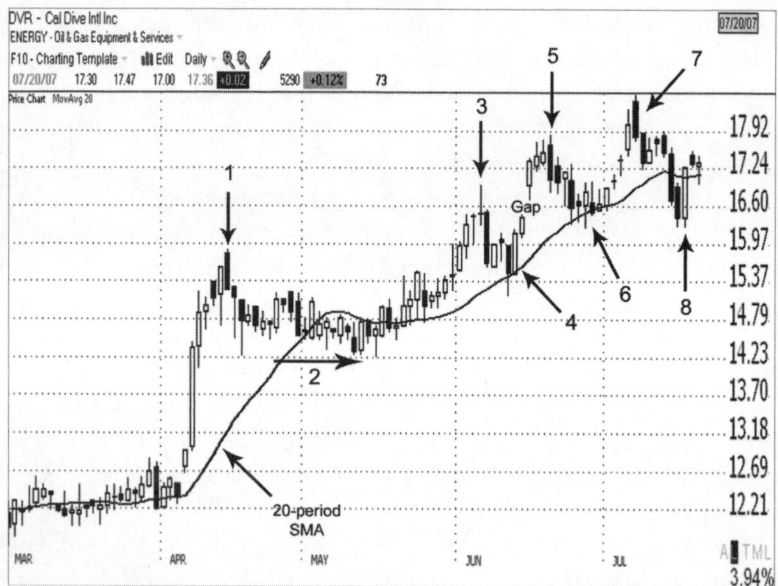

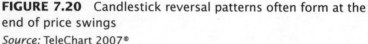

FIGURE 7.20 Candlestick reversal patterns often form at the end of price swings
Source: TeleChart 2007®

Price was in an uptrend from April through July 2007. The following discussion corresponds to numbers 1 through 8 on the chart:

1. A strong rally moved price far above the 20-period simple moving average (SMA). Notice how much "air" there was between price and the moving average. That was not just air, it was Air Jordan! On April 16 a bearish dark cloud cover pattern formed (1).
2. Price pulled back to the 20-period moving average and consolidated for several weeks. It is not unusual for a stock to consolidate the gains after a strong move.
3. Price rose up again away from the moving average. On June 5 a dragonfly doji formed, followed by a near gravestone doji (3) the following session.
4. Price pulled back to the moving average, offering buyers another entry opportunity. The next swing up began with a bullish engulfing pattern (4) on June 13.
5. Price lifted up from the average and gapped up on June 15. Two spinning tops followed signaling a loss of momentum of the move. On

June 20 a bearish engulfing pattern formed (5), starting another pullback toward the moving average.

6. Price stopped declining at the 20-period SMA and consolidated there for a few days.
7. Price caught air again, ending with another dark cloud cover pattern (7) on July 9.
8. Price pulled back below the moving average. On July 18 a bullish engulfing pattern formed (8).

If a candlestick reversal signal calls the end of a price swing, and then price resumes the longer trend after pulling back or consolidating, it does not mean that the candlestick pattern failed. The presence of a reversal pattern does not imply that an entire intermediate- or long-term trend will reverse. When price pulls back or consolidates after an upward move, it does change direction for a period of time; either from up to down or from up to sideways, respectively. Candlestick reversal signals serve as warnings that a change in price direction may occur. They do not tell us how significant the change will be, or how long it will last.

Reversion to the mean does not only occur in an uptrend; watch for the same phenomenon in a downtrend. There will always be sellers covering short positions, and "bottom fishers" looking for buying opportunities, whose trading actions will drive price back toward the mean.

Figure 7.21 shows DVR again, but this time a few months later. The stock topped out in July 2007, forming a bearish Western head-and-shoulders top. Price closed below the neckline (dotted line) of the head-and-shoulders pattern on July 26, confirming the bearish pattern. Price curled back up a few days later and tested the neckline as resistance. It is very common for prior support to be tested as resistance after a breakdown, and vice versa after an upside breakout. The price action that occurred during the subsequent decline corresponds to numbers 1 through 4 on the chart:

1. Price declined for a couple of weeks, moving far away from the 20-period SMA. The decline ended with a gap down and intraday sell-off on August 6. By the close of that session, the stock had recovered much of the intraday decline, as evidenced by the long tail, and formed a bullish hammer (1) on the daily chart. During the following session a bullish engulfing pattern formed around the hammer's real body and the prior session's gap was filled. Price closed well off its high on the engulfing day leaving a long upper shadow and evidence that there were still sellers around.
2. The next day price traded up to near the 20-period SMA (2) intraday; here you see the reversion to the mean. The stock then closed well off its high leaving another long upper shadow.

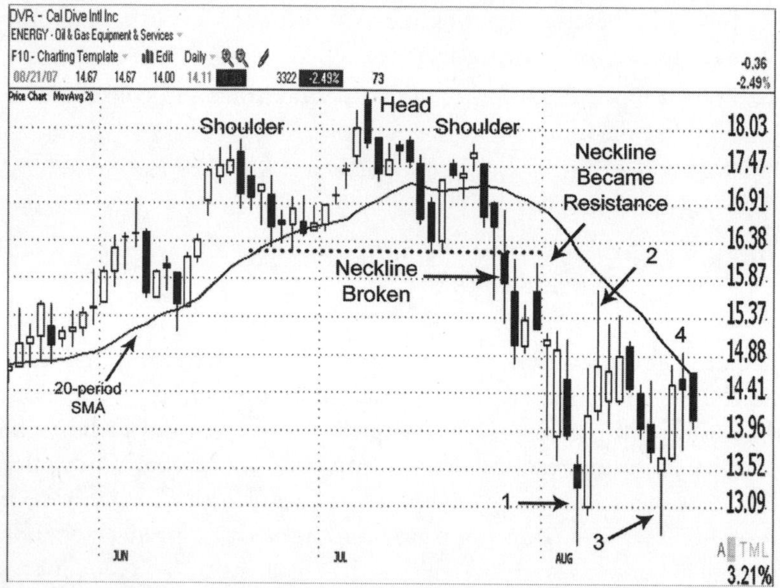

FIGURE 7.21 When price declines too far from the average, it tends to move back toward it
Source: TeleChart 2007®

3. Price declined again and tested the August low (at 1), setting up the potential for a Western bullish double bottom pattern. A bullish hammer (3) formed on August 16, creating a smaller candlestick pattern within the larger double bottom. I call this a *pattern inside a pattern* and interpret it as strengthening the larger setup.
4. Price moved back up to the 20-period SMA.

The phenomenon of reversion to the mean offers traders opportunities to enter positions at lower-risk areas than when price has moved away from the average where it is vulnerable to a setback. Reward and risk will be addressed later in this book.

The Importance of Probability

Trading successfully is not a matter of chance; it is a result of trading in a manner that puts the odds of winning on your side. For example, when price moves too far away from the average, it is more likely to revert to the average than to continue moving farther away from it. That is not to say that when price moves away from the average and moves back toward it, a long trend is likely to reverse. Remember that price tends to swing back and forth while still moving in the general direction of the trend (see Figure 7.20).

Since the probability is good that price will revert to the mean, that factor should influence the way traders select and manage their trades, especially swing traders. If a swing trader holds a long position in a stock and does not wish to hold it through a pullback, once price catches air it may be time to exit, or start scaling out of the position, or at least be very watchful for a warning, such as a candlestick reversal signal. If a stock that he does not yet hold a position in, but would be interested in purchasing, has moved far away from the average, he can watch for a dip back toward the average for a lower-risk entry opportunity. If an entry is taken while the stock is far away from the average, chances are good that the trader is setting himself up to hold through a pullback or sideways move.

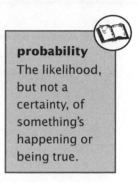

probability The likelihood, but not a certainty, of something's happening or being true.

Even traders who hold long-term positions should evaluate each stock individually. An investor may plan on holding through pullbacks as the trend develops. However, looks can be deceiving. Don't forget to consider the stock's current volatility. What may appear to be a small move on the chart may actually be a significant percentage move.

Example

Figure 7.22 shows a daily chart of Echelon Corp. (ELON). Price pulled back to the 20-period SMA in late July 2007. Price consolidated for a few days followed by a strong swing up. At that point price had moved away from the average, leaving a pocket of air below and the stochastic oscillator provided an overbought reading, indicating the move was overextended. (The stochastic oscillator is discussed later in this chapter.) Price then turned down for several days, finally stopping at the 50-period SMA. Recall that you can quickly look at the logarithmic scale to get a gauge of the stock's current volatility. To find out exactly how far this stock fell, calculate the distance from the high of the upswing ($32.49) to the low of the downswing ($19.92). The difference was $12.57, or a decline of approximately 39 percent from the swing high to the swing low. Notice that a long lower shadow formed the swing low indicating that bulls were willing to step into long positions at the 50-period moving average.

(*continues*)

Example *(continued)*

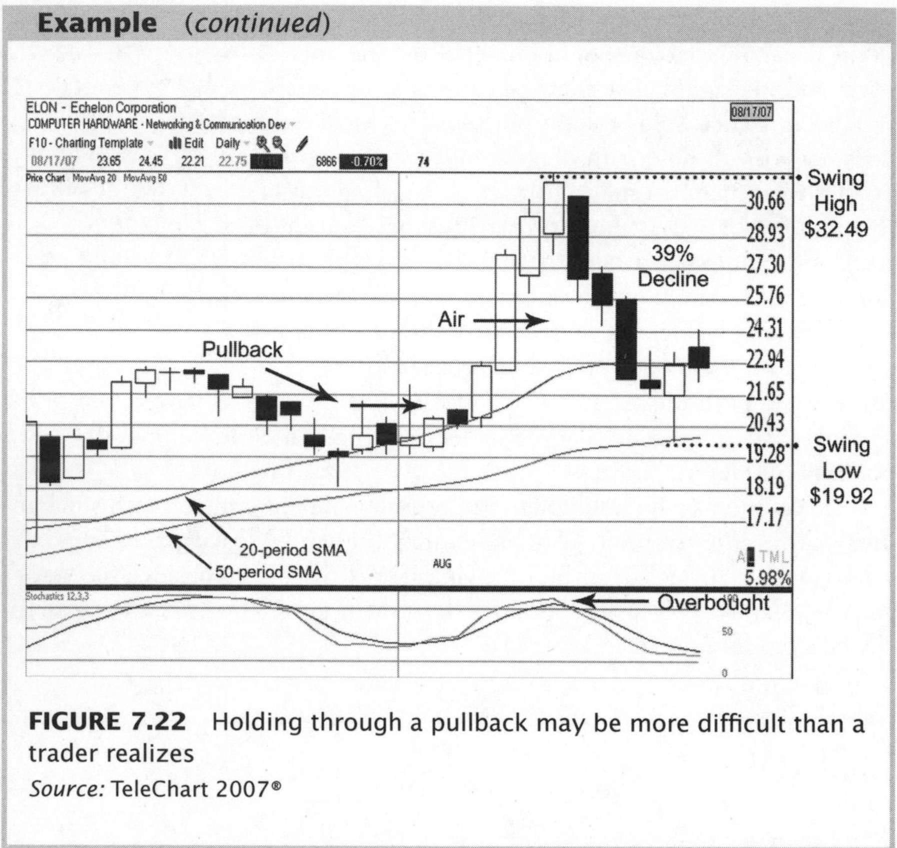

FIGURE 7.22 Holding through a pullback may be more difficult than a trader realizes
Source: TeleChart 2007®

The example in Figure 7.22 was chosen in order to point out the following:

- Short-term traders who held long positions during the swing up would have no desire to watch all of their gains disappear.
- Even long-term traders would have to question whether they would wish to watch a stock decline so far.
- If a protective stop were utilized (recommended) that did not exceed the trader's maximum risk tolerance, for example, 10 percent for a swing trader and 15 percent for an investor, the stop would not have held up through the decline.
- Once price caught air, the probability of a pullback was high. A trader who chased this stock and entered a long position near the swing high watched the trade immediately turn negative and had a very painful experience due to a poorly timed entry.

Be careful not to fall into the "wishful thinking" trap. When looking back from the right edge of the chart at a stock that trended for a long period of time, you may think you could have just held on through all the pullbacks and periods of consolidation. Looking at a past chart of a stock in which you held no position is a quite different situation than monitoring a live trade in which real profits are at stake. In some cases a trader can hold on for much of the trend using a trailing stop. However, in many cases a trader may get stopped out one or more times as the trend evolves. And if a stock is volatile, what might look like it was a minor pullback on the chart may have equated to a significant percentage decline.

Although holding through a decline may not sound like a big deal, that's where experience, with real money invested, is needed in order to determine psychologically what you can handle. Short-term traders typically do not plan to hold through pullbacks. If a short-term trader finds himself holding through a lot of pullbacks, it may be an indication of poor trade selection and management. Lack of discipline will lead to failure in this business. Plan your trades in advance and know what justifies an entry, where to exit with a profit if the trade goes as expected, and where to exit with a protective stop in case it goes against you.

Beware of Chasing Overextended Stocks

A common mistake made by inexperienced traders is to chase after a stock entering a position when price has become overextended. Unfortunately, new traders often are not aware of the concept of reversion to the mean. Even those who are aware may choose to take the gamble, hoping that price will continue to move unabated. They let their emotions get the best of them. Emotional decisions typically lead to sloppy trade execution and losses that could have been avoided.

Experienced traders do not generally buy the swing high (or sell the swing low) and then hold on trying to ride out a pullback. More often, it is the experienced traders who are gladly selling their shares near the swing highs to the novice traders who shouldn't be buying at such overextended levels. The traders who buy the swing highs are sometimes called the "greater fools," because there is no greater fool willing to pay higher prices, so they are left holding the bag, so to speak, as the stock turns against them.

The experienced traders are also the ones who are waiting to take the shares off the hands of the novices who bail out because the pain of entering too high, and then having to hold through the subsequent pullback, becomes too much for them. In other words, experienced traders look to enter on weakness (pullbacks or consolidation) and exit into strength as price gets overextended.

Smart Investor Tip

In order to thrive as a trader, you must first survive. Trading is not about gambling or wishful thinking. Traders must learn to control their emotions and trade based on what is likely to happen rather than on what they "hope" will happen. Seasoned traders do not use hope as a strategy!

Momentum of the Trend

In addition to determining the direction and duration of a trend, there are also methods of measuring its momentum. In his book *Technical Analysis of the Financial Markets* (New York Institute of Finance, 1999, p. 228), John Murphy defines momentum as follows: "Momentum measures the velocity of price changes as opposed to the actual price levels themselves."

Oscillators are a group of indicators that measure the momentum of price (the rate of its ascent or descent). Price often loses momentum before it actually changes direction; thus, oscillators may act as "leading" indicators of price. While there are many different oscillators with different methods used to calculate them, their interpretation doesn't vary much. Be careful using too many oscillators because they basically measure the same thing.

There are usually at least a few oscillators to choose from in most charting programs. Stochastics and Wilder's Relative Strength Index (RSI) are among the best known.

oscillator
A technical indicator that signifies when a stock or market is in an overbought or oversold condition.

Unlike moving averages, which tend to whipsaw when price moves sideways, oscillators are effective in a nontrending environment. They can help catch the turning points when price swings back and forth across a trading range. The oscillator's fluctuations tend to correspond to the peaks and troughs in price. Oscillators are not limited to nontrending environments. They can also be helpful in a trending market. Oscillators have several uses in this regard:

- *Overextended conditions.* When price is rising and an oscillator reaches an extreme high level, it sends a signal that price may be overextended to the upside or *overbought*. When an oscillator reaches an extreme low level, it indicates that price may be overextended to the downside or *oversold.* Overbought and oversold readings warn that price is vulnerable to at least a short-term change in direction.

- *Divergence analysis.* When higher peaks are forming in an uptrending market, but the peaks of the oscillator are declining, a negative (bearish) divergence exists. In a downtrending market, if price is forming declining bottoms, but the oscillator bottoms are rising, it signals a positive (bullish) divergence. A divergence between price and the oscillator is a sign that the trend may be weakening.
- *Relationship to the midpoint.* Many oscillators have a midpoint. For some oscillators that point is zero; others that move along a scale of 0 and 100 have midpoints of 50. When price turns up after a downtrend, the oscillator will cross the midpoint and remain above it for most of the uptrend, and vice versa when price reverses from up to down. Traders may use the crossing of the midpoint as a buy or sell signal.

For now, we'll focus on using an oscillator, namely stochastics, to help determine when price may be overextended.

Stochastic Oscillator

The stochastic oscillator is a very popular momentum indicator developed by George Lane. It is based on the premise that when price is trending up, the closing prices will tend to be near the high of the price range. In a downtrend, the closing prices will be nearer the low of the price range.

The indicator includes two lines: the faster %K line and the slower %D line. The %K line is the stochastic. The %D line is a moving average of %K, which smoothes the stochastic and acts as a signal line. The result is two lines that oscillate between fixed lower and upper boundaries of 0 and 100 percent, respectively (Figure 7.23).

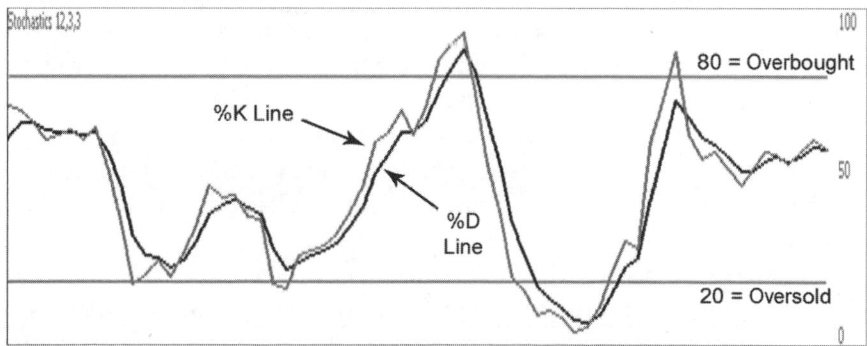

FIGURE 7.23 Stochastic oscillator
Source: TeleChart 2007®

The calculation compares the most recent closing price (on a percentage basis) to the total range of price over a designated period of time. Time periods must be chosen for the stochastic and the moving average.

Example

Two commonly used lengths are 14 periods for the stochastic with a 5-period moving average (14-5-5) and 12 periods with a 3-period moving average (12-3-3). As is usually the case with technical indicators, if you opt for speed, you give up some accuracy, and vice versa. A stochastic length of 14 will produce slightly slower signals, but they may be more accurate. A length of 12 will produce faster signals, although there may be more false signals.

Within the boundaries of 0 and 100 lie the overbought line (80) and the oversold line (20). A reading of over 80 is considered to be high; it indicates that the current closing price is near the top of the designated range. Conversely, a reading of below 20 is considered to be low; the current closing price is near the low end of the designated range.

Overbought and Oversold Conditions

The stochastic oscillator can be used to alert traders of short-term price extremes. At times, price moves for too long, or too far too quickly, in one direction. The result is an overbought (uptrend) or oversold (downtrend) condition. These conditions are generally short term in nature and can be alleviated by a pullback, correction, or a period of consolidation. In a strong trending market, confident bulls (uptrend) or bears (downtrend) will often step back into trades once the short-term overextended condition has been alleviated. There will certainly be cases when the trend will reverse after such conditions arise; however, it takes a consensus by many market participants to reverse a strong trend. Therefore, overbought and oversold signals should generally be interpreted to be short term in nature unless there is additional evidence that a trend reversal is in the making.

If a bearish candlestick reversal pattern forms while stochastic is in overbought territory, or if a bullish reversal pattern forms while stochastic is in oversold territory, it strengthens the candlestick signal. In these cases, a candlestick pattern forms when the stock is already vulnerable to a change in the direction of price.

Example

Figure 7.24 shows a daily chart of Advanced Micro Devices (AMD). In mid-July 2007, the price advance showed signs of trouble with the formation of three doji within four trading sessions. A strong bearish engulfing pattern formed on July 20. Price had moved up away from the moving average and the stochastic oscillator was in overbought territory, adding more evidence that a change in the direction of price was likely to occur.

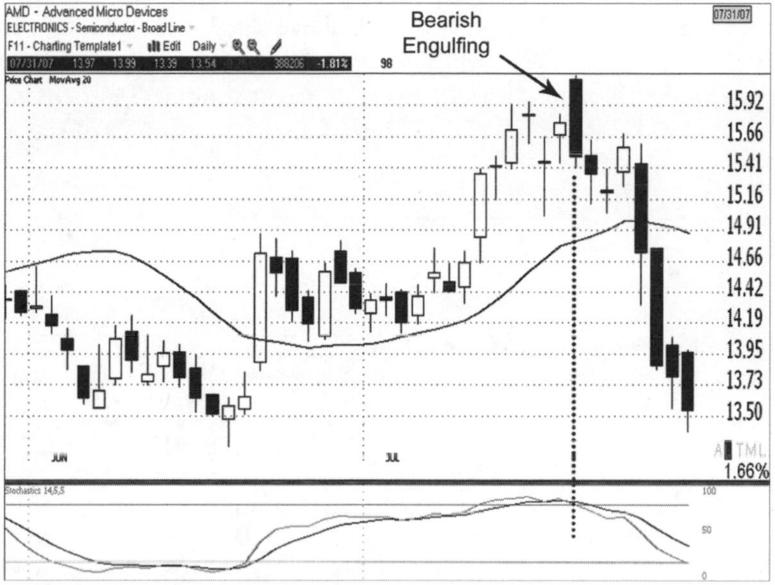

FIGURE 7.24 Bearish engulfing pattern formed while the stochastic oscillator was in overbought territory
Source: TeleChart 2007®

Enhanced Candlestick Signals

Now you know that when price moves far from the average it tends to revert to the mean. In addition, when the stochastic oscillator signals overbought or oversold, price is vulnerable to a change in direction. These two scenarios will often occur in sync, but not always, so I don't recommend that you require that price be far from the average *and* the stochastic oscillator be at an extreme in order to justify acting on a candlestick signal. However, if either or both conditions are present, the odds are good that a change in the direction of price will occur.

Example

Figure 7.25 shows a daily chart of DTS Inc. (DTSI). Price made a strong swing up in early August 2007, ending with a bearish shooting star on August 8. Follow the dotted line down from the shooting star to below the chart window and you'll see that the stochastic oscillator with a setting of 14-5-5 (middle panel) did not provide an overbought reading. Even with a shorter setting of 12-3-3 (lower panel), the indicator did not move above the overbought line. However, notice how far the two long bullish candles that formed prior to the shooting star pushed price above the 20-period SMA. In this case, in spite of the absence of confirmation from the oscillator, a change in the direction of the short-term trend should be anticipated. Price consolidated for a period of time after the appearance of the shooting star.

FIGURE 7.25 In spite of the lack of confirmation from the stochastic oscillator, price had moved away from the average when a bearish shooting star formed

Source: TeleChart 2007®

Example

Figure 7.26 shows a daily chart of Cohu Inc. (COHU). Price declined far below the 20-period SMA by early August 2007. On August 7, the stock gapped down open but closed deeply into the prior bearish candle's real body, forming a bullish piercing pattern. In this example, not only was price far below the moving average, but the stochastic was in oversold territory. Price then rallied back up to the average.

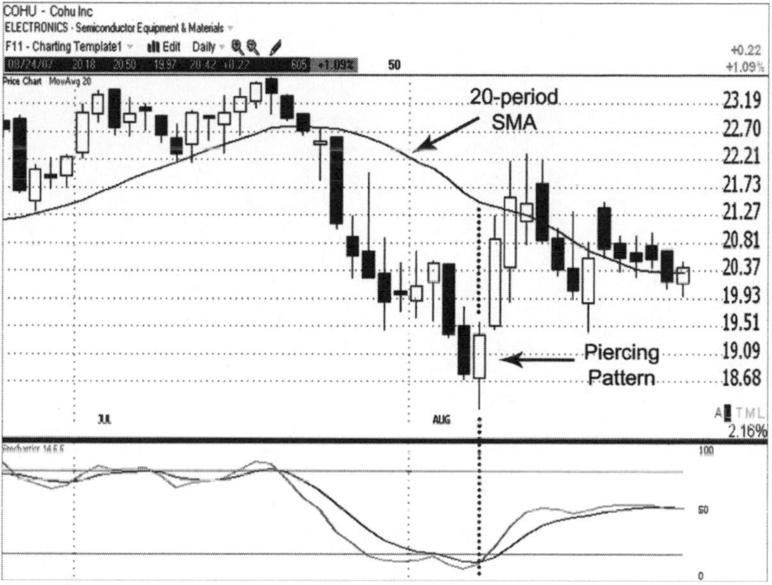

FIGURE 7.26 Bullish piercing pattern formed while price was far below the average and was confirmed by stochastics
Source: TeleChart 2007®

There will certainly be candlestick reversal signals that follow through when neither of the preceding conditions is present. The likelihood of a successful signal increases, though, if there is more evidence that price is overextended and vulnerable to a change in direction.

Chapter 8

Gaps

No instruction on charting would be complete without a discussion of gaps. It is important for traders to be able to identify gaps and understand their implications. For decades, gaps have been recognized in Western technical analysis. However, the identification and analysis of gaps did not originate in the West. The Japanese utilized gaps in their analysis long before they became known in the Western hemisphere. In Japanese candlestick charting, price gaps are referred to as *windows.*

In this chapter, you will be introduced to price gaps and a very common event called the *morning gap.* Since the term *gap* is so well known, for consistency, *gap* will be used throughout most of this discussion rather than the Japanese term *windows.*

Price Gaps

A price gap is also called a *true gap* because it leaves a void on the chart. The gap is still open by the end of the daily trading session, leaving empty space where no trading took place. Neither the real bodies nor shadows of the two consecutive bars that form the gap can overlap.

In order for an upside gap to form, the low of the current bar must be above the high of the previous bar (Figure 8.1). The Japanese refer to an upside gap as a *rising window.* For a downside gap to occur, the high of the current bar must be below the low of the prior bar (Figure 8.2). The Japanese call a downside gap a *falling window.*

> **gap**
> Empty space on a chart where no trading has occurred.

Even if a gap is very small, it is still valid. And remember that looks can be deceiving. If the stock is volatile, what looks like a small gap may be bigger

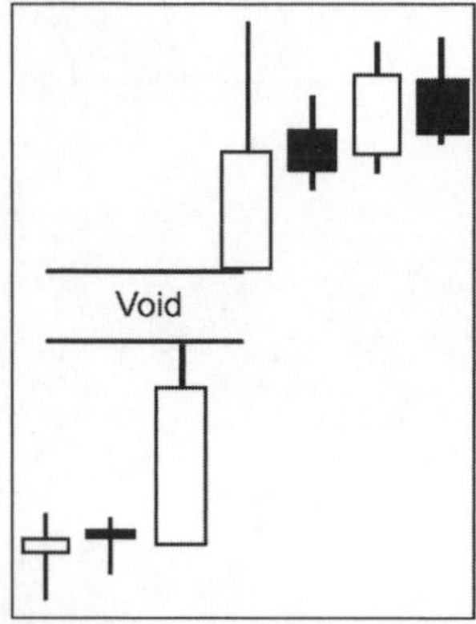

FIGURE 8.1 Upside gap (rising window)

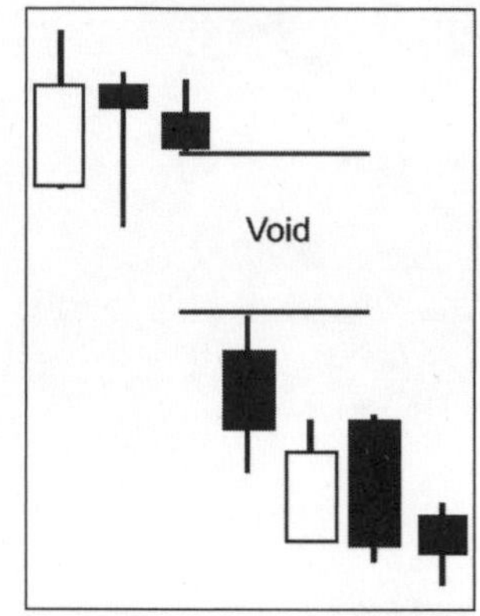

FIGURE 8.2 Downside gap (falling window)

percentage-wise than you realize. (Refer to the discussion on volatility in Chapter 6.)

Most price gaps are emotionally driven events that occur largely because of news that is released and disseminated between the close of one day's trading session and the open of the following session. The news need not be related directly to the stock in question. Stocks may be impacted by the news of other companies, sectors, industry groups, and global events. If there is no news, and no significant demand that has built up for a stock, it should open at or near the prior session's close. However, if there is news or enough demand, the market maker will fill the pending market orders accordingly, resulting in the stock's gapping up or down at the open.

Price gaps are most commonly seen on daily charts. Other than at the open, you won't often see true gaps (voids) on intraday charts. There are some exceptions, of course. For instance, if a stock is not very heavily traded, gaps may occur intraday. If news is released on a stock during trading hours, it may result in one or more price gaps intraday. If a stock's trading is halted temporarily, price may gap once the stock opens again for trading or in a fast-moving market gaps may occur. Otherwise, most of the gaps that you'll see on intraday charts are fairly small gaps between the real bodies. The real bodies or shadows overlap, so no void is visible on the chart. Gaps do occur frequently at the open. They are called *morning gaps* and are discussed in detail later in this chapter.

True gaps are fairly rare on weekly charts, and even rarer on monthly charts. Each weekly bar includes 5 days of data, and each monthly bar includes about 20 days of data. Many gaps are filled during the week or month before the next bar begins.

Types of Price Gaps

The Japanese refer to gaps simply as *rising* (bullish) or *falling* (bearish) *windows.* Western technical analysis takes the definition of gaps further. Rather than identifying gaps based strictly on the direction of the gap, either upside or downside, they are also defined by the price action that precedes and follows the gap. There are several different types of gaps observed in Western technical analysis.

An *area gap* occurs when price gaps either up or down within a trading range. An area gap may also be called a *common gap* or a *pattern gap.* Figure 8.3 shows two area gaps that formed while price was consolidating. These gaps have very little technical significance. They are usually filled quickly as price moves up and down between the boundaries of the trading range (the dotted lines in Figure 8.3).

area gap
A gap that occurs within a period of consolidation.

A *breakaway gap* is a technically significant gap. It often marks the beginning of a strong price move. An upside breakaway gap is a bullish signal that occurs when price gaps above and closes above resistance. It should be accompanied by heavy volume. A downside breakaway gap is a bearish signal that occurs when price gaps below and closes below support. A downside breakaway gap may be accompanied by heavy volume, but if it is not, it does not take away from the signal like the upside gap. It usually takes more force to propel price higher than for a stock to decline.

breakaway gap
A gap that forms when price breaks out above resistance or below support. Breakaway gaps are typically accompanied by heavy volume.

A *continuation gap* occurs when a stock is trending and price leaps forward, accelerating the move. A continuation gap may also be called a *runaway gap.* This type of gap may occur in an uptrending market (bullish) or a

continuation gap
A gap that forms while price is trending up or down.

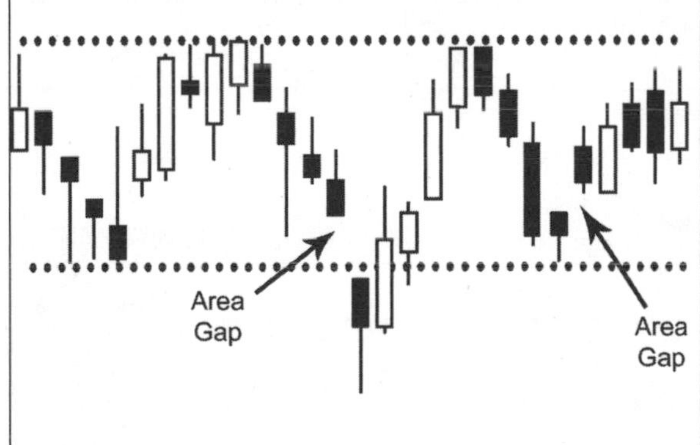

FIGURE 8.3 Area Gaps

exhaustion gap
A gap that forms at the end of a trend. Exhaustion gaps are typically accompanied by heavy volume.

downtrending market (bearish). It is said to mark the halfway point of a trend, which is why it is sometimes referred to as a *measuring gap*. A continuation gap is often filled weeks or months later during a correction or reversal of the trend.

An *exhaustion gap* occurs after a sharp move or a long trend. This gap may follow one or more prior gaps, for example, a continuation gap; however, that will not always be the case. Sometimes an exhaustion gap is not preceded by other gaps. As its name implies, this type of gap represents a climax or exhaustion move. It is often a last blast of buying in an uptrend, or capitulation in a downtrend, followed by a sharp reversal, or at least a shift to a period of consolidation. Exhaustion gaps are typically accompanied by heavy volume, and they are usually filled quickly.

Example

Figure 8.4 shows a daily chart of Foster Wheeler Ltd. (FWLT). On April 3, 2007, price gapped up above the ceiling of a horizontal trading range (dotted line), completing a bullish breakaway gap. Several weeks later, on May 9, price gapped again, forming a bullish continuation gap. Both the breakaway gap and the continuation gap were accompanied by heavy volume.

FIGURE 8.4 Breakaway gap was followed by a continuation gap
Source: TeleChart 2007®

Smart Investor Tip

The volume bars in the panel below the chart window will be rescaled as new, higher levels of volume occur. That makes past volume bars appear to be smaller than they actually were when they formed at the right edge of the chart. Therefore, when analyzing a historical chart, make sure to back up the chart to the date(s) being analyzed instead of just looking back from the right edge. Unusually high volume days leave volume spikes that make it difficult to accurately gauge the volume of other days. Some charting programs allow the volume to be truncated to reduce this effect.

Example

Figure 8.5 shows a daily chart of TransOcean Inc. (RIG). After trending up for several months, price gapped up on July 23, 2007. The gap was accompanied by heavy volume. Price reversed direction immediately and filled the gap, making it clear that it was an exhaustion gap.

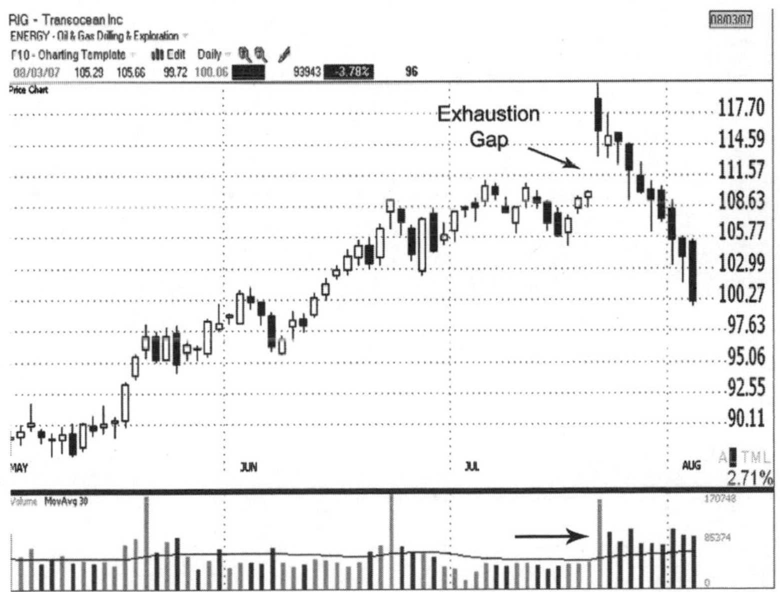

FIGURE 8.5 Exhaustion gap was accompanied by heavy volume
Source: TeleChart 2007®

island reversal
An exhaustion gap is followed soon after by another gap in the opposite direction.

When analyzing a gap at the right edge of the chart, you cannot always identify the type of gap at the time it forms. If price is consolidating and gaps, but does not break out, it is fairly easy to identify it as an area gap. Likewise, the breakaway gap is obvious because it gaps away from consolidation. However, with a continuation or exhaustion gap, you won't know for sure at the time it forms which gap it will turn out to be. It takes at least one more bar, and sometimes several more, before it is evident whether it is a continuation or exhaustion gap. Keep this idea in mind when you develop the rules of your trading strategies and outline how you'll respond to a gap should one occur.

Example

Figure 8.6 shows a daily chart of Canadian National Railway (CNI). After a steep run up, price gapped up on July 18, 2007, accompanied by very heavy volume. Price consolidated within the long bullish candle for three days. On July 24, price gapped down, forming a bearish island top (circled). By early August, price had retraced much of the prior uptrend.

FIGURE 8.6 Swift uptrend ended with a bearish island top
Source: TeleChart 2007®

An *island reversal* pattern is formed when price gaps in the direction of the trend and then gaps in the opposite direction, leaving one or more bars with a void on both sides. In an uptrend, this price action is called a bearish island top. If it occurs in a downtrend, it is a bullish island bottom.

When Has a Price Gap Been Filled?

The market does not like voids on a chart so there is a strong tendency for gaps to be filled. Most gaps are eventually closed. Some gaps are filled quickly, for example, most area gaps and exhaustion gaps. Others may take weeks, months, or even years to close. A breakaway gap, or a gap that occurs at the beginning of a long trend, may not be filled for a long time. There are occasions, although they are infrequent, when a gap is never filled.

After an upside gap forms on a chart, at some time in the future, price may fall back through that void. If price declines back to or near the bottom of the void, the gap has been closed (Figure 8.7). The reverse may occur with a downside gap. In Western technical analysis, this price action is referred to as filling or closing the gap. The Japanese would say, "The window has been closed."

Price will not always fill the gap entirely. In some instances, much of the gap will be filled, but price changes direction again before filling the entire gap. If most of the void has been filled, traders generally consider the gap to be closed.

Gaps as Support or Resistance

The phenomenon of support and resistance is a very important tenet of Western technical analysis. It is so essential that Chapter 9 is devoted to it. As you'll learn in that discussion, there are several types of support and resistance, including gaps.

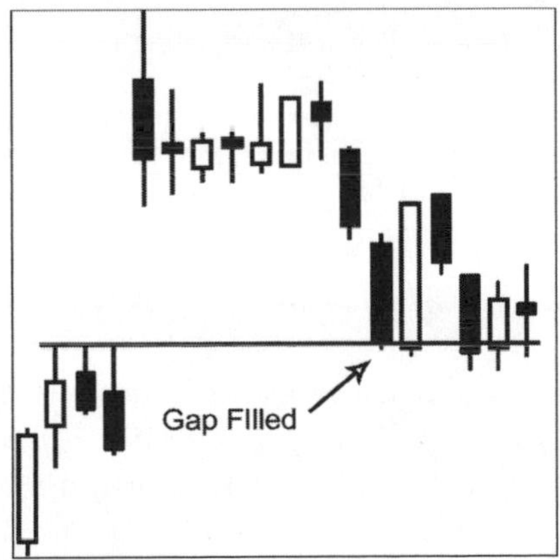

FIGURE 8.7 Closed gap

When an upside gap is filled, the bottom of the void should provide support. If price closes below the gap, support has been broken and the message turns bearish. Conversely, when a downside gap is filled, the top of the void should act as resistance. If price closes above the gap, resistance has been broken, which is a bullish sign.

Interpreting Price Gaps

The Japanese refer to a gap as a continuation pattern. An upside gap is interpreted as bullish, and a downside gap is bearish. This is only a general concept, though. Be careful about trying to employ a "one size fits all" rule in technical analysis. Just because an upside gap is considered bullish does not mean price may not decline first or move sideways before resuming the uptrend, and vice versa for a downside gap. In addition, don't expect price to always move again in the direction of the gap. Sometimes price reverses direction, trades back through the gap, and just keeps going, resulting in a reversal rather than a continuation of the trend.

The context in which the gap forms should be considered. Each price gap should be analyzed individually when determining how to respond to it. Following are some factors to consider:

- *Size of the gap.*
- *Price action that preceded the gap.* Did the stock gap out of consolidation? How far had price already moved prior to the gap? Is price overextended and vulnerable to a change in direction?
- *Surrounding chart landscape.* Is there resistance nearby that may cause an upward price move to stall or reverse (or support below that may stop a downside move)?
- *Style of trading utilized.* Is this a short-term trade or a longer-term trade that may be held for weeks or months?
- *Trader's temperament.* What is the trader's risk tolerance and risk and money management rules?
- *Current volatility of the stock.*
- *Current environment of the broader market.*

The discussion that follows addresses these factors and is intended to provoke thought on how you might interpret and react to an upside gap. The same thought processes should be considered when analyzing a bearish gap, except that the gap is to the downside.

Figure 8.8 shows a daily chart of Checkpoint Systems Inc. (CKP). The upside gap that occurred on August 2, 2007, was a large gap driven by news.

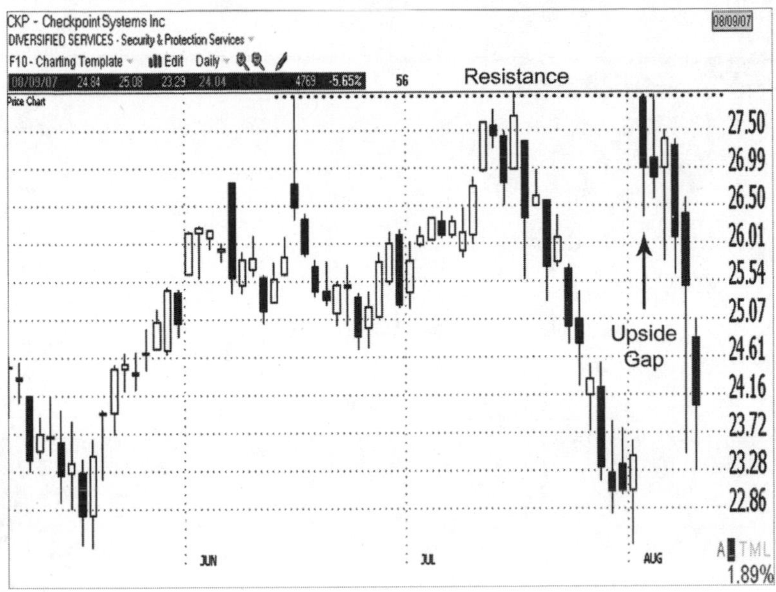

FIGURE 8.8 Large upside gap failed to break up through strong resistance
Source: TeleChart 2007®

This gap encountered a strong resistance area at the June–July Western double top (dotted line). After such a move, it is not unusual to see price turn immediately back down and at least partially fill the gap. Additionally, the major averages had sold off in late July, so the broad market environment was volatile. The stock reversed direction and filled the gap within the next few days. This example illustrates the importance of evaluating each gap individually. I certainly would not advocate entering a new long position on the gap-up day in a scenario like this one. The stock may move higher; however, the probability is high in such a situation that price will decline, or at least move sideways, before it will break out to a new high. If instead of reversing at the double top resistance area price had gapped over it and closed above it, the signal would have been a bullish one.

Figure 8.9 shows a daily chart of Fremont General Corp. (FMT). Regarding the style of trading, consider the following two scenarios: Trader A is a swing trader, which is a shorter-term style where positions are typically held from a few days to a couple of weeks. He entered a long position in FMT in early April 2007 near support provided by the March low. After price advanced for a few days, the gap-up open on April 16 was a big bonus. Trader A used the gap to exit the trade with a sizable gain. Trader B is an investor who typically holds positions longer term. She also entered a long position at the same area as Trader A, but she intends to hold the position for

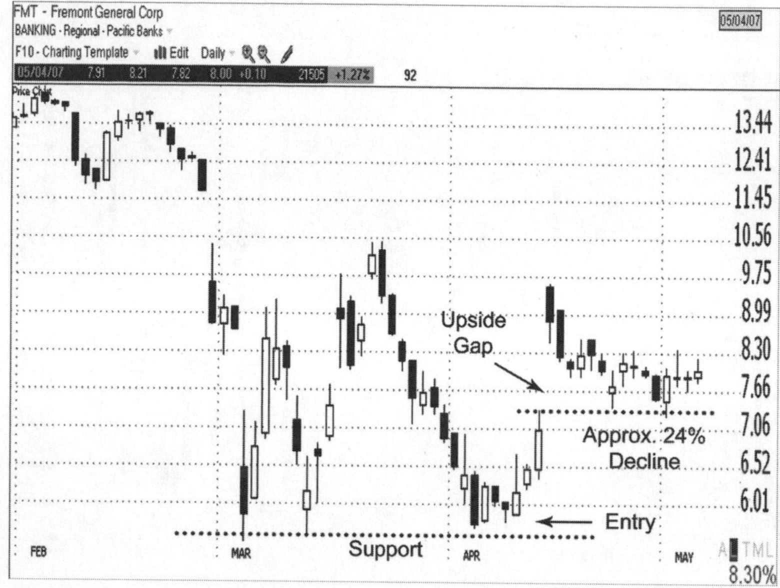

FIGURE 8.9 High percentage decline back to the bottom of the gap
Source: TeleChart 2007®

several weeks or even months. She may have no reaction to the gap other than to raise the protective stop to preserve much of the gains in the event price breaks down.

Now consider the question of the stock's current volatility. This stock had already risen approximately 23 percent from the support area *before* it gapped up. Then on April 16, the stock gapped open approximately 35 percent higher than the prior session's close. After such a strong move up, profit-taking by short-term traders may force the stock down and fill the gap. In the case of FMT, the distance from the open of the April 16 gap day back to the bottom of the void (the high of the bar prior to the gap day) was about 24 percent. The swing trader would not wish to hold through such a decline. And, in fact, is the investor willing to allow the stock that much room to pull back? Even for longer-term trades the volatility should be considered. Say that Trader B has a risk management rule (recommended) that she will not allow a long-term position to reverse more than 15 percent from the *current* price or the stock will be exited. That is not to say that a stop should be placed an arbitrary 15 percent away from the current price, but rather it should be placed at a technical level not to exceed the maximum allowed reversal of 15 percent. In that case, Trader B's stop is likely to be triggered. If FMT pulls back and fills the gap, the distance to the bottom of the void is almost 10 percent further than Trader B's maximum stop level would allow.

Smart Investor Tip

The maximum stop level may vary from one trader to the next depending on risk tolerance and trading style. For example, a maximum of 10 percent may be employed for a swing trade versus 15 percent for a longer-term trade. A day trader may have a much lower maximum, such as 3 to 4 percent, or even less. *Note:* The maximum stop loss for an individual trade should not exceed 2 percent of the total account equity. For example, a $50,000 account × .02 = $1,000.

It need not be an "all or nothing" decision. The investor may elect to sell some shares on the gap and raise the stop on the remaining shares. As such, if price continues higher, she will still hold a partial position. However, less of the gains would be exposed to a potential pullback that may be enough to trigger the protective stop.

In summary, an upside gap may ultimately turn out to be a bullish event. However, whether it is a gap, a candlestick signal, or some other technical event, it is prudent to look beyond just that particular event. Trading successfully means considering other factors that can impact your trades.

The Morning Gap

A *morning gap* is also called an *opening gap* because it occurs at the open of a daily trading session. Morning gaps are very common on daily charts; much more so than true gaps. They occur due to order imbalances that are managed by market makers at the open. (Morning gaps occur on stocks but not on the charts of continuous 24-hour futures.)

All gaps actually start out as opening gaps. A true gap must open beyond the prior day's range: above the prior high for an upside gap and below the prior low for a downside gap. By the close of market that gap has not been filled, which leaves a void on the daily chart. A morning gap also gaps up or down at the open; however, *it does not leave a void on the daily chart.* The gap is closed during the trading session. Figure 8.10 shows the contrast between a true gap and a morning gap.

morning gap
A gap that occurs at the open of a daily trading session and is filled before the close of the session.

A morning gap is defined by the opening and closing prices of two consecutive daily bars. In order to form an upside morning gap, price must open above the prior

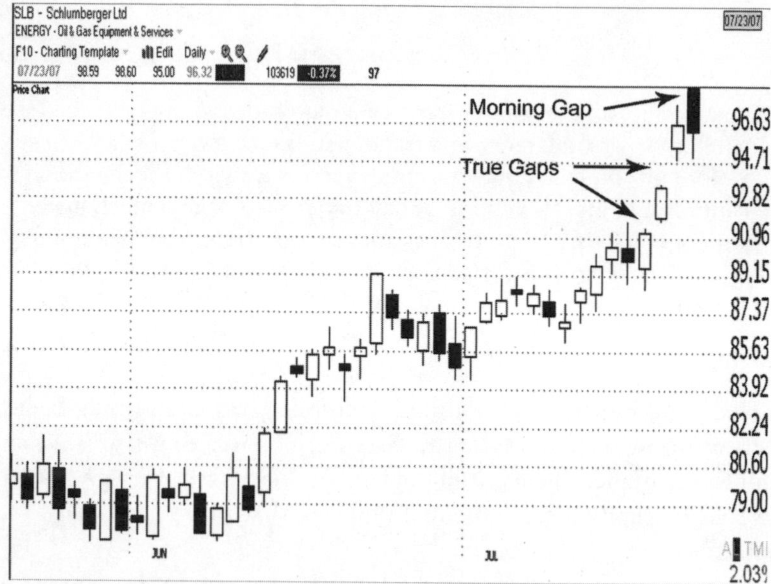

FIGURE 8.10 Price (true) gaps compared to a morning gap
Source: TeleChart 2007®

day's close (Figure 8.11). Price may even open above the prior day's high (Figure 8.12), but at a minimum, there must be a gap up between the two real bodies at the open. Some traders even refer to this gap as a *body gap*. For a downside morning gap, price must open below the prior day's close (Figure 8.13) or its low (Figure 8.14).

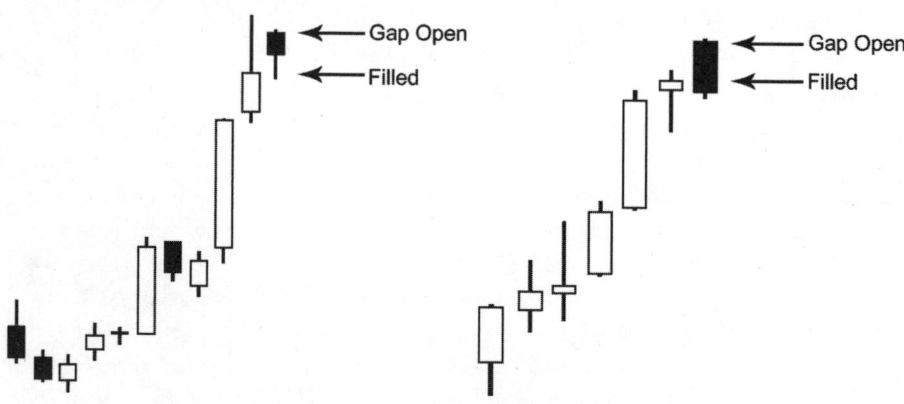

FIGURE 8.11 Morning gap up above the prior close

FIGURE 8.12 Morning gap up above the prior high

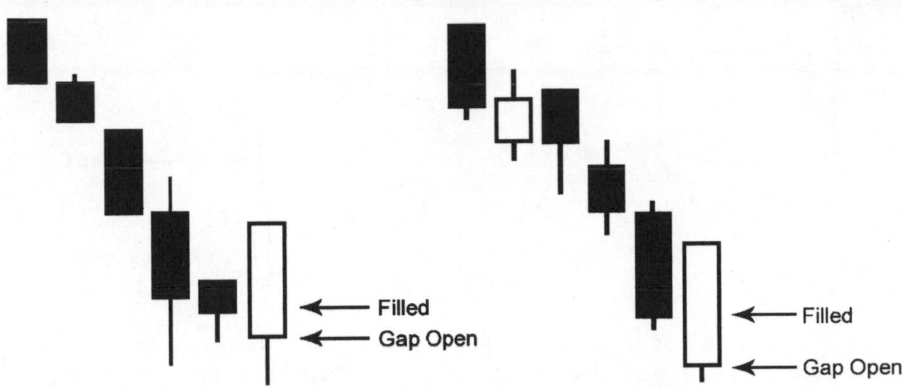

FIGURE 8.13 Morning gap down below the prior close

FIGURE 8.14 Morning gap down below the prior low

When Has a Morning Gap Been Filled?

A morning gap is filled when price reverses the opening direction intraday and trades back at least to the prior day's close. An upside morning gap is filled if any of the following is present on the chart by the close of market (the inverse is true for a morning gap down):

- The current day's low is the same, or very near the same, as the prior day's close (see Figure 8.11). The prior day's close is a natural support level so it is not unusual to see price stop falling there.
- The current day's lower shadow pierces the prior day's real body (not shown, but if the lower shadow in Figure 8.11 was longer it would be an example).
- The current day's real body touches, protrudes into, or engulfs, the prior day's real body (Figure 8.12).

The fact that there is an overlap between the real bodies, or their shadows, by the end of the session means it cannot be a true gap.

Variations of the Morning Gap

A variation of the morning gap occurs when price gaps up open above the prior bar's high, trades back to the prior bar's *high* or lower, but does not decline all the way back to the prior bar's *close* (Figure 8.15). This intraday price action closes the void on the daily chart that is created at the market open, but it does not close the entire intraday gap between the bodies.

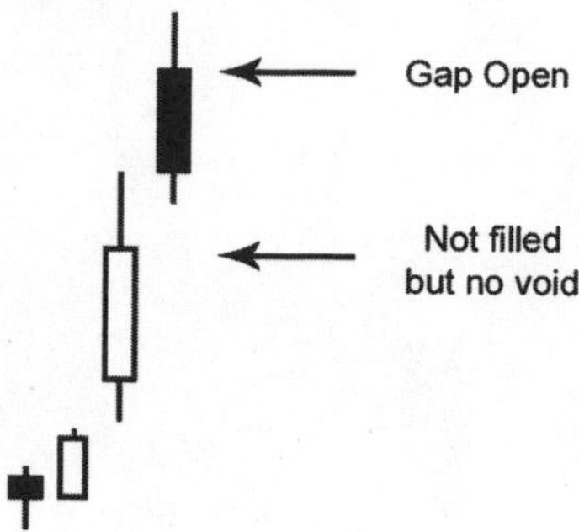

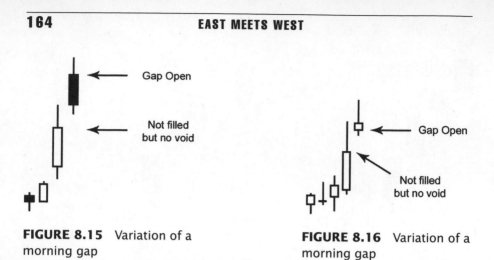

FIGURE 8.15 Variation of a morning gap

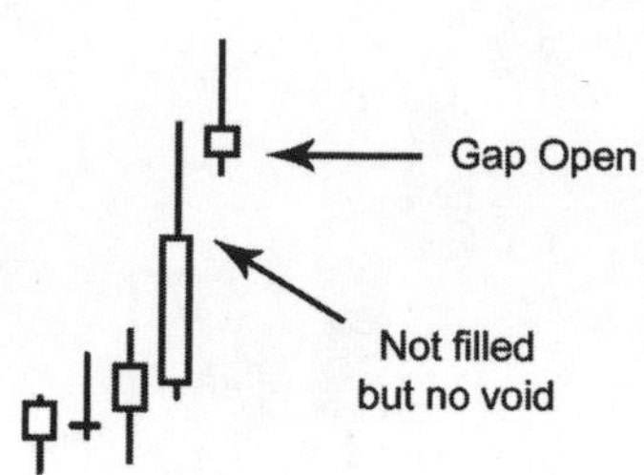

FIGURE 8.16 Variation of a morning gap

Another variation occurs when price gaps up open above the prior day's *close* and trades within that prior session's upper shadow. Price does not trade all the way back to the prior day's close, so again the intraday gap between the real bodies is not completely filled (Figure 8.16). In this case there is never an actual void on the daily chart because price does not open above the prior session's high; however, there is still a gap between the two bars' real bodies.

The inverse of the above variations may also occur with a downside morning gap.

Intraday View of a Morning Gap

Most opening gaps fill, or at least partially fill, within the trading session leaving no void on the daily chart. They often fill early in the day—frequently within the first hour of trading.

Example

Using the Schlumberger Ltd (SLB) chart from Figure 8.10 as an example, let's take a look at an intraday view of a morning gap. Figure 8.17 shows the daily price action on the left, which led up to the opening gap on July 23, 2007. On the right is a 5-minute chart showing the first 50 minutes after the open on July 23. The 5-minute chart demonstrates how price gapped up open but traded no higher. That is evident by the hanging man with a shaven top that formed in the first five minutes of trading. If price had traded higher after the open, that 5-minute hanging man (and the daily candlestick) would have an upper shadow. The stock declined from the open and filled the morning gap within the first 20 minutes of the trading session.

(*continues*)

Example *(continued)*

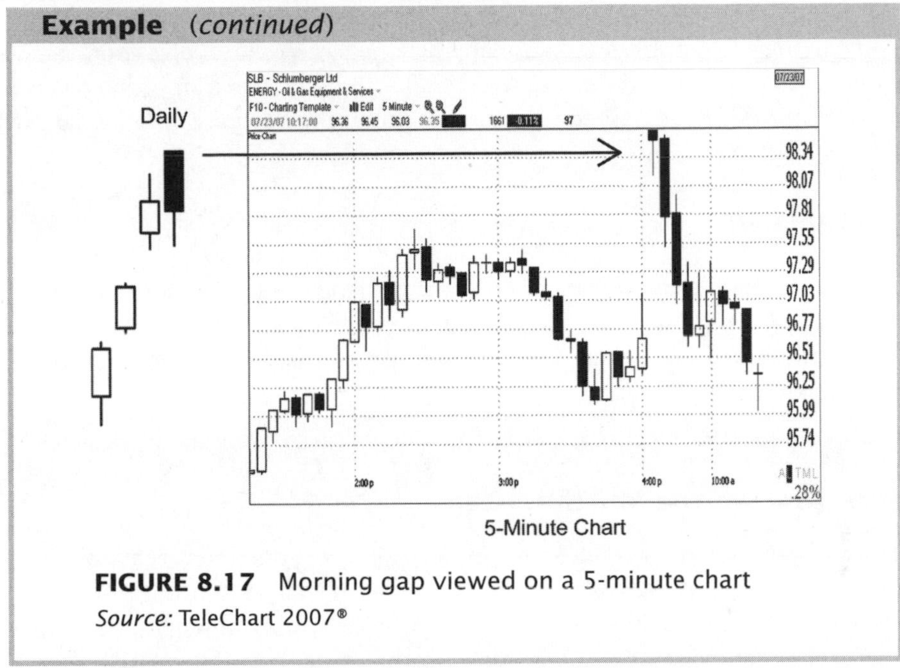

FIGURE 8.17 Morning gap viewed on a 5-minute chart
Source: TeleChart 2007®

Although you will no longer see a void on the *daily* chart once the gap has filled, you can see how and when price rolled over and filled the gap on the 5-minute time frame. Essentially, it is an intraday exhaustion gap if it occurs after a directional move. Depending on how fast the opening gap is filled, you may not see the actual void on all intraday time frames. For instance, the SLB gap in Figure 8.17 filled quickly, so no void would appear on the 30- or 60-minute charts; however, it is still visible on very low time frames. There will be some cases in which the gap is filled so quickly that it isn't even visible on the 5-minute time frame after the first 5-minute bar has closed.

Morning Gaps and Candlesticks

You may be thinking that the morning gap is an interesting and useful phenomenon, but what does it have to do with candlestick charting? Take a closer look at Figures 8.11 through 8.15. The morning gap up in Figure 8.11 occurred after a warning from a bearish upper shadow the prior session (long shadows were discussed in Chapter 5). In Figure 8.12 observe that the morning gap became a bearish engulfing pattern that surrounded the small real body of a hanging man that formed the prior day. The downside morning gap in Figure 8.13 turned into a bullish engulfing pattern by the end of the session. Figure 8.14 became a bullish piercing pattern. All of these events occurred after a price advance or a decline, so there was a move to reverse.

Not all morning gaps will turn into candlestick reversal patterns. However, you may be surprised at how many reversal patterns do evolve from, or include, a morning gap. Make sure to carefully study the criterion of the reversal patterns provided in Chapter 3 because several of them require an opening gap for a valid pattern.

Example

Both the dark cloud cover and the piercing pattern start with a morning gap; and the star patterns have a gap between the first and second real bodies in their formations. Most engulfing patterns also develop from a morning gap.

Interpreting the Morning Gap

Since all gaps start as opening gaps, you won't know at the time price gaps open how the day will unfold. Will a void remain on the chart (a true gap), or will the gap be closed, resulting in a morning gap? Remember, though, that morning gaps occur frequently; much more so than true gaps. Therefore, when a stock does gap open, it has a high likelihood of filling within the trading session and often early in the trading day. Keep that in mind when determining how you'll react to opening gaps.

The manner in which a trader chooses to react to an opening gap may vary from one situation to the next. Again, the following should be considered:

- The size of the gap
- The price action that preceded the gap
- The surrounding chart landscape
- The style of trading utilized
- The trader's risk tolerance and risk and money management rules
- The current volatility of the stock
- The current environment of the broader market

Since morning gaps are very common, traders who hold long-term positions may choose to ignore many opening gaps. Otherwise, they may exit a position prematurely. Even when holding longer term, though, situations may arise in which an opening gap should not be ignored. Always consider the context in which the gap formed.

Swing traders are much less inclined to ignore an opening gap. Because of the short hold time, the way they manage gaps may make a significant difference in their profitability. The remainder of this chapter is devoted to discussion of how morning gaps can affect short-term positions and how swing traders may choose to respond to such events. The discussion and examples refer to trading long positions; however, the same concepts apply inversely for shorting. Even if most of your trades are longer term, you should review the remaining pages, as you may pick up some valuable information.

The Opening Gap's Role in Swing Trading

The opening gap is an important concept to understand and is a component of many day-trading and swing-trading techniques and strategies. Trading decisions should not be based on emotions; they should be based on logical conclusions. Knowing that most opening gaps will reverse direction intraday should be a consideration when swing traders define their short-term strategies.

Location Matters

Just as it matters where a candlestick reversal pattern forms on a chart (it must have a move to reverse), it matters where an opening gap occurs. It is important to consider the price action that preceded the gap. If a trader holds a long position in a stock that has just started to move up, an opening gap, especially a small one, may not be a significant event. However, if price has already moved a good distance away from the average, an upside opening gap may be much more meaningful. It may represent a signal to exit all, or at least part, of a swing position, particularly if price gaps open substantially beyond the prior trading session's close.

Recall from Chapter 7 that price tends to revert to the mean. Thus, when price has moved away from the average on the daily chart, it becomes vulnerable to a pullback or at least a period of consolidation. Swing traders typically try to avoid getting caught in a pullback that may take back part of the gains achieved during a price advance (or sometimes all of the gains if proper risk management is not employed). They should be on the alert for warning signs that indicate a potential end of the short-term trend. In some cases, a warning comes in the form of an opening gap.

Since most opening gaps reverse direction intraday, that means it is common for price to decline back to the prior trading session's close, and potentially farther. When deciding whether to exit an opening gap, a trader should check the prior session's close and determine if he would be willing to hold back to that point. If not, the opening gap can be used to lock in additional profits. A stock's volatility should also be considered. If a stock is volatile, an opening gap may be bigger than it appears on a percentage basis. Looks can be deceiving where volatility is concerned.

Example

Figure 8.18 shows a daily chart of Biolase Technology Inc (BLTI). Price rallied for several days from July 23 to 30, 2007. On July 31, price gapped up open approximately 6 percent above the prior session's close. Price had already moved far away from the moving average prior to the appearance of the opening gap. The opening gap offered a swing trader an opportunity to sell near what may turn out to be the swing high. By the close of market, the opening gap had evolved into a bearish dark cloud cover pattern.

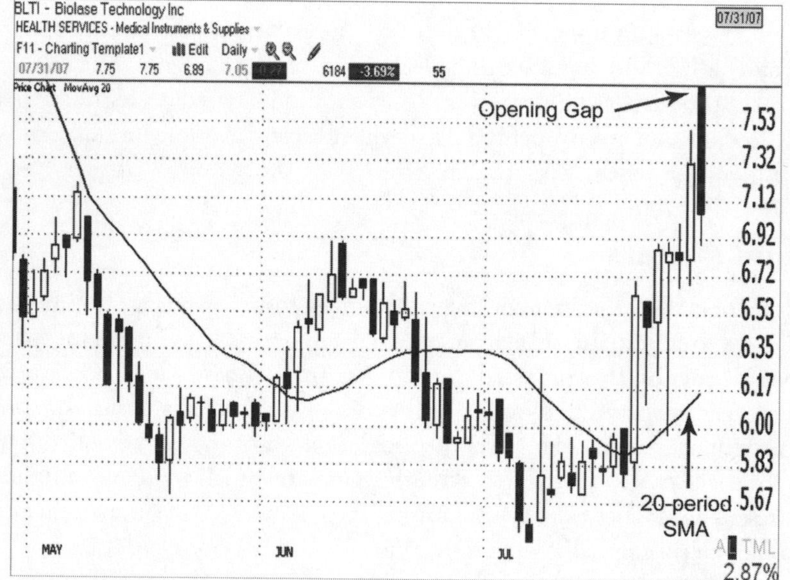

FIGURE 8.18 Upside opening gap turned into a bearish dark cloud cover pattern
Source: TeleChart 2007®

The surrounding chart landscape should also be evaluated. Look for technical signs that indicate where the trade may run into trouble. Swing traders typically determine targets in advance of initiating their trades. A ceiling above would provide a target. A gap up to that ceiling would indicate the target has been achieved. Conversely, if a short position is held and price gaps to a floor, in most cases the position should be covered.

Swing traders should monitor their trades closely and be vigilant at the open. Attention should be given to the circumstances in which the opening gap occurs. If a stock gaps up open to a level where price is vulnerable to a change in direction, it is not necessary to wait to see if the morning gap fills or if a candlestick pattern evolves by the end of the daily session. In many cases, the morning gap *is* an early reversal signal.

Example

Figure 8.19 shows a daily chart of Denbury Resources Ltd. (DNR). A swing trader who entered a long position when price pulled back to the 50-period simple moving average would have participated in the swing up from July 27 to August 1, 2007. The July high would be a logical target (dotted line). On August 2, price gapped up open approximately 7 percent to just above that ceiling. As you can see from the 15-minute price action shown in Figure 8.20, the stock fell rapidly after the opening gap, which pushed it back below the ceiling on the daily chart and filled the gap within the first 45 minutes of trading. It would not have been necessary to hold through that intraday decline had a swing trader determined the target in advance and used the opening gap to exit when that objective had been reached.

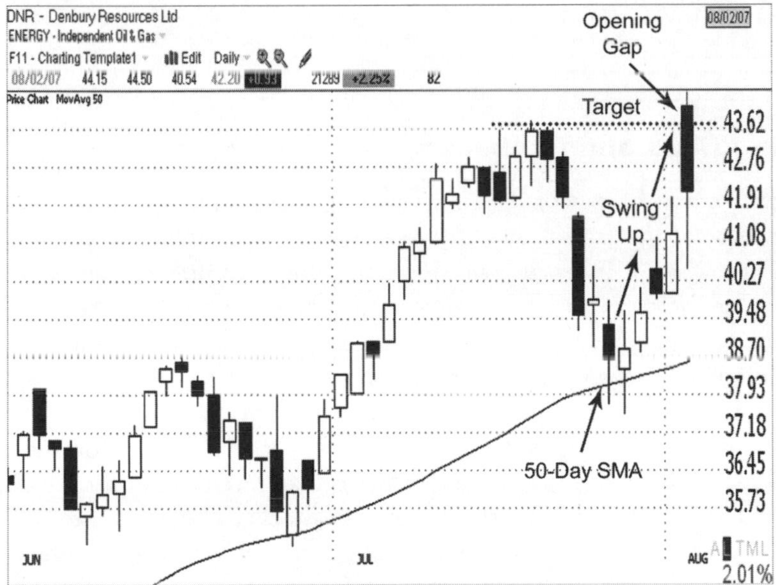

FIGURE 8.19 Price gapped up open to the swing target
Source: TeleChart 2007®

(*continues*)

Example *(continued)*

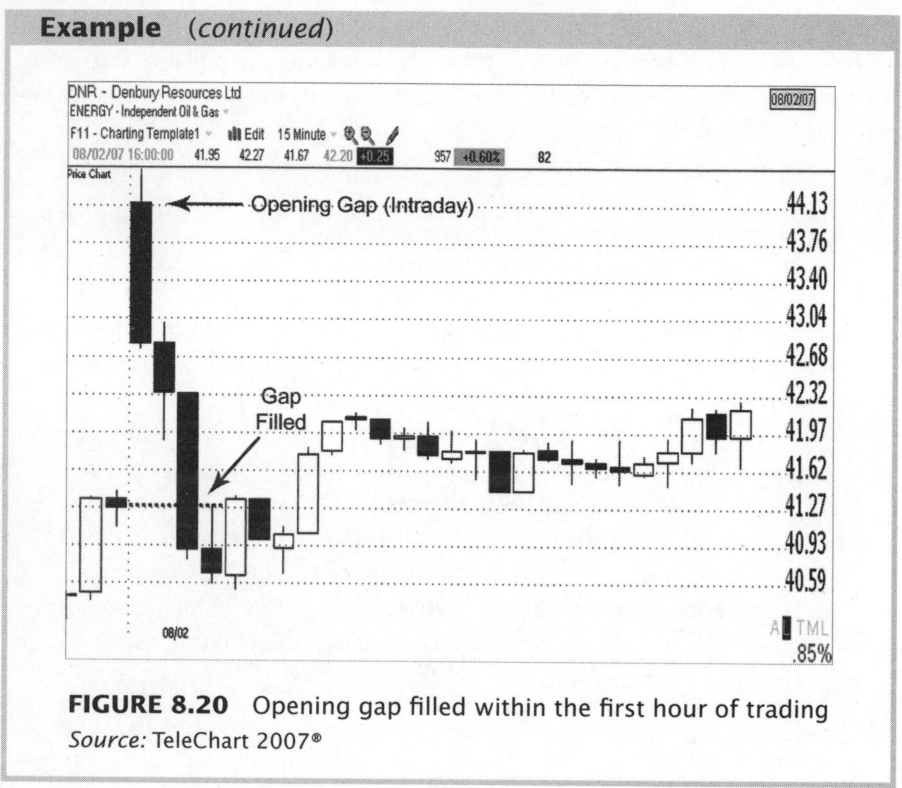

FIGURE 8.20 Opening gap filled within the first hour of trading
Source: TeleChart 2007®

Morning Gaps and Pullbacks

Swing traders may be concerned about opening gaps filling during the day and robbing them of the extra profits they could have had if they exited the trade earlier in the session. But that is not the only concern. Often, an opening gap marks the beginning of a pullback on the daily chart. So not only are the additional profits in the opening gap at risk, but the stock may decline further during the following days. As a general rule, a short-term trader seeks to exit after a price swing rather than holding through a pullback or consolidation.

Not all opening gaps will mark the beginning of a pullback. Morning gaps are very common. Even though most of them may reverse the opening direction intraday, it does not necessarily mean the stock will continue to decline during the following days. Sometimes opening gaps will occur day after day, filling (or partially filling) each day, but price continues in the direction of the trend. And even if a stock has moved well away from the average prior to the gap-up open, there will still be instances in which the stock will continue to rise instead of moving sideways or pulling back. Remember, though, that type of scenario is more the exception than the rule.

Example

Figure 8.21 shows a daily chart of Clarcor Inc. (CLC). After a long white shaven candle formed on August 8, 2007, price gapped up open in the following session far above the prior bar's high. Price turned down immediately and quickly filled the opening gap. By the end of the trading session, a dark cloud cover pattern had formed on the daily chart. Although price did not pierce halfway or more into the prior candle's white real body, the penetration was substantial enough to provide the same message as an ideal dark cloud cover pattern. The stock continued to decline over the next several days, retracing most of the prior swing up.

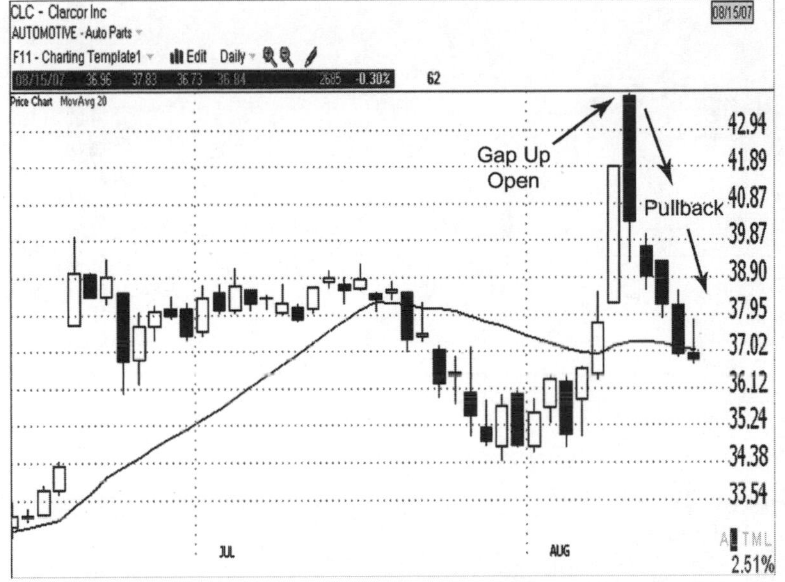

FIGURE 8.21 Price gapped up open, filled the gap, and continued to pull back
Source: TeleChart 2007®

There will always be situations where you exit a long position and then watch the stock move higher. That is simply part of doing business in the uncertain world of trading, in which we must make our decisions at the right edge of the chart instead of in the rearview mirror. Don't get caught up in wishful thinking by looking back at a stock like UIC in Figure 8.22 that you may have exited. If your strategy called for exiting, you should commend yourself for following your rules rather than chastising yourself for doing so. Disciplined traders survive in this business; undisciplined ones rarely do.

Example

Figure 8.22 shows a daily chart of United Industrial Corp. (UIC). UIC gapped up open every day for several days during May 2007 (arrows). Some of the morning gaps were very small, while others were more significant. Even though this stock got far away from the average, it continued to move higher.

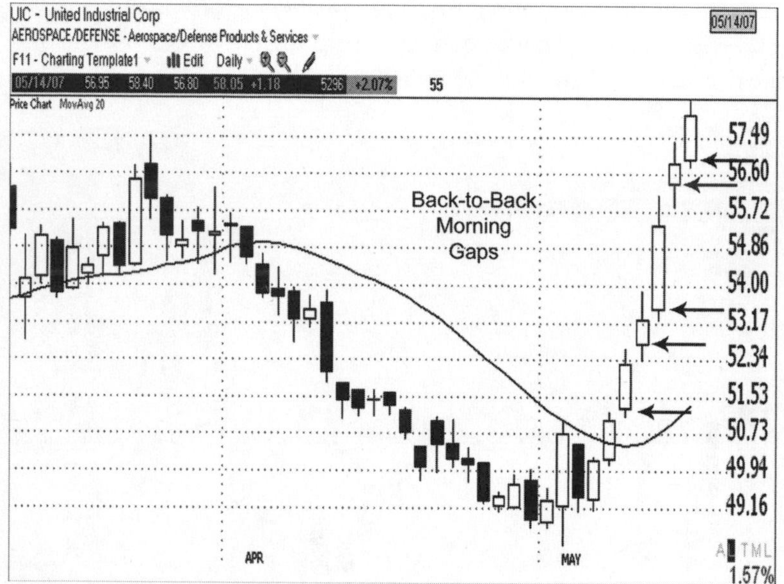

FIGURE 8.22 Multiple opening gaps occurred within the uptrend
Source: TeleChart 2007®

Some traders may elect to take partial profits in specific cases in the face of an opening gap. For instance, they may sell a quarter, half, or more of their shares and maintain a protective stop on the balance of the position. That action maintains a partial position in the event that the stock continues higher, while reducing the exposure in case price pulls back. Selling in increments is a practice referred to as *scaling out.* Other traders may prefer to utilize a strategy that includes raising the protective stop or implementing an automatic trailing stop, in lieu of exiting when an opening gap occurs. With practice, you'll determine the method that is best suited to your risk tolerance and trading style.

Exiting a Trade in Premarket

Since it is common for an opening gap to reverse within the first hour of trading, traders do not have a lot of time to ponder how to react to the gap. Traders should decide before the opening bell whether they'll wait until the open and observe the price action, or if they'll attempt to exit the position in premarket trading.

The regular trading session for the major U.S. stock exchanges runs from 9:30 AM to 4:00 PM Eastern Time. Premarket trading occurs for a couple of hours prior to the open of the regular trading session. Participation by market makers and electronic communications networks (ECNs) in premarket trading is voluntary. Thus, liquidity may be significantly less than during normal trading hours, and some stocks may not trade at all prior to the opening bell.

premarket trading
Trading that occurs prior to the open of the normal daily trading session.

Many novice traders are not familiar with, or have some fear of, trading in the premarket session. Traders should do so cautiously, as the bid-ask spreads can be significantly wider than during regular trading hours. However, if a trader owns a stock that is trading actively in premarket—heavily enough that the spread is not prohibitive—exiting in premarket is a viable option in many instances. Only limit orders will be filled during premarket hours. Market orders will be held in queue until the opening bell.

It is not usually necessary to wait until the opening bell in order to determine if a stock will gap open to the up or down side. If a stock is trading actively in premarket at a price higher than the prior trading session's close, then it has already gapped up. If it is trading at prices lower than the prior session's close, it has already gapped down. Unless something changes before the opening bell that pushes price back to the prior session's close, it is destined to gap open when the normal trading session begins.

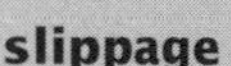

slippage
The difference between the price at the time a trader places an order and the price at which the order is actually filled.

Price may move quickly at the opening bell, and slippage can sometimes be severe in a fast-moving stock. Keep that in mind when determining your trading strategies.

Support and Resistance

If you wish to become skilled at technical analysis, it is imperative that you understand its primary focus. The crux of technical analysis is the study of trends. Chapter 7 was devoted entirely to discussion of trend analysis. In Chapter 8 you learned about price gaps, which can also play a part in a trend's development. This chapter adds one more layer to the study of trends by examining the role of support and resistance. Support and resistance play a crucial part in chart analysis, trade selection, and trade management.

support
An area beneath the current price in which demand should be sufficient to halt a price decline.

Support is an area below the current price that traders recognize as a level in which buying may be sufficient to overcome selling pressure (Figure 9.1). When price declines to a floor, it is referred to as a *test of support.* When support is tested and holds, the price decline is halted, at least temporarily. Bulls step into long positions and bears cover short positions, keeping price from descending further. Price may reverse direction after testing support, or it may move sideways. If price closes below a floor, it is referred to as a *breakdown* or a *break of support.* When support is broken, it is a sign of weakness and the downtrend may continue.

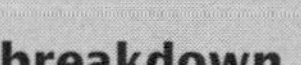

breakdown
Price closes below an identifiable support area.

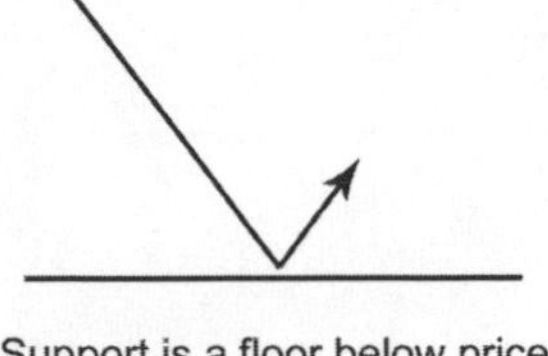
Support is a floor below price.

FIGURE 9.1 Support

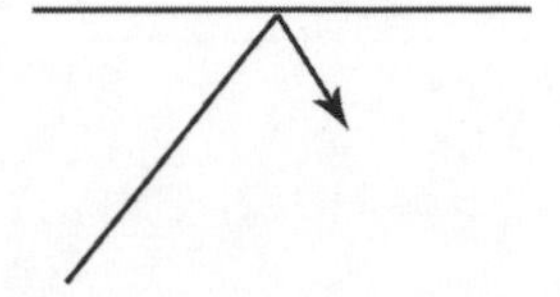
Resistance is a ceiling above price.

FIGURE 9.2 Resistance

resistance
An area above the current price in which supply should be sufficient to halt a price advance.

breakout
Price closes above an identifiable resistance area.

Resistance is an area above the current price which traders perceive to be a level where enough selling may occur to overcome buying pressure (Figure 9.2). When price rises up to a ceiling it is referred to as a *test of resistance.* When resistance is tested and holds, the price advance is halted, at least temporarily. Bears sell short and bulls exit long positions, keeping price from ascending further. Price may reverse direction or move sideways after testing resistance. If price closes above a ceiling, it is referred to as a *breakout* or a *break of resistance.* When price breaks through a ceiling, it is a sign of strength and the uptrend may continue.

Support and resistance levels are not arbitrary. They are areas on a chart that are known to have the potential of halting the trend. The most commonly referenced support and resistance areas are those created from price peaks and bottoms. Peaks and bottoms are formed during a trend's development, and they are also the building blocks of Western reversal and continuation patterns.

Resistance and Support at Peaks and Bottoms

As discussed in Chapter 7, peaks and bottoms are formed as a trend develops and during trendless phases (consolidation). Now it is time to expand upon the roles of peaks and bottoms as areas of resistance and support. Whether they have formed recently, or farther in the past, peaks and bottoms have the potential to provide resistance or support, respectively, when price approaches those areas again.

As an uptrend develops, price typically rises and then pulls back or consolidates. The price action from those short-term trends leaves a series of minor peaks and bottoms. Some of the peaks and bottoms will be more significant

Example

Figure 9.3 shows a daily chart of Berry Petroleum Co (BRY). From late March through mid-June 2007 price was in an uptrend. After each pullback or period of minor consolidation, price was easily able to surpass the prior peak (numbered 1 through 5) and move on to new highs. Notice how price frequently found support at the prior peak during subsequent pullbacks. For instance, after peak 4 formed price pulled back and used peak 3 as support. The same occurred again when peak 5 formed and pulled back to peak 4. Prior resistance often becomes new support. The pullback after peak 6 was deeper than the prior dips but held support at the prior swing low (at 4). Price moved up again from early to mid-July, but that time the momentum was not sufficient to break through the prior peak (at 6). Price declined back to support at the June 8 and June 27 bottoms (at 4 again).

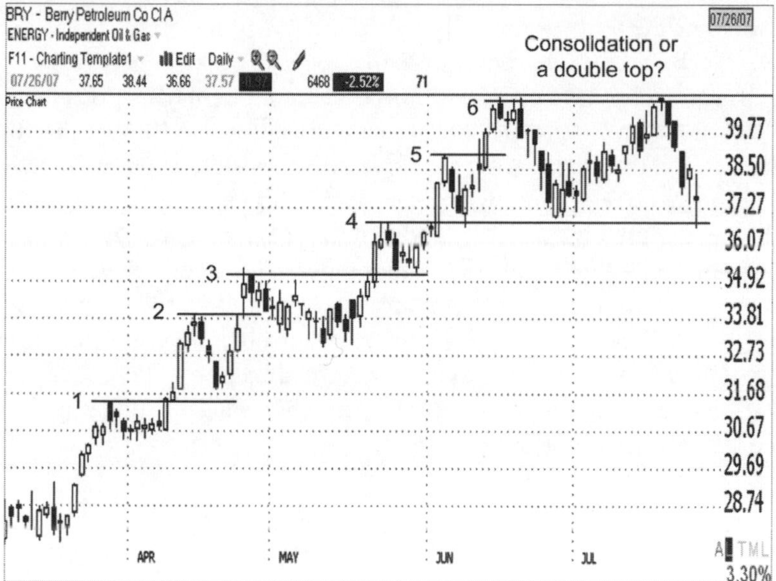

FIGURE 9.3 It is difficult to determine, at the right edge of the chart, whether the stock is consolidating or putting in a top
Source: TeleChart 2007®

than others, but each creates a potential resistance or support area. In order for the uptrend to continue, price must be able to break up through those newly formed peaks to new highs. In addition, when price pulls back it must hold prior support levels in order for the uptrend to remain intact. Once price is no longer able to take out the prior peak, the stock may either be transitioning into a trading range or putting in a top. Conversely, in order for a downtrend to continue, price must take out each newly formed bottom on subsequent declines. When it is no longer able to do so, the trend may be shifting into a trendless phase or bottoming out.

In a scenario like that, which occurred on the chart of BRY in Figure 9.3, when price is no longer able to surpass the prior peak, bearish traders may interpret it as a potential bearish Western double top setting up. They anticipate that a trend reversal is likely. Bullish traders may view the same chart and, rather than seeing a double top, they determine that price has entered a trading range. They anticipate that price will break to the upside at some point, continuing the prior uptrend. The double top that is present on the chart of BRY is just consolidation until it is confirmed with a close below the middle of the "M." Thus, it is difficult to determine, at the right edge of the chart, whether the stock is readying for a reversal or just resting before another move up. Only after price has broken down through support or up through resistance will you know whether the bears or the bulls were right.

As the BRY example shows, recently formed peaks and bottoms can be strong. Traders who have open positions will watch closely as price tests those areas. But don't underestimate the strength of ceilings and floors that formed farther back on the chart. Price may reverse at a visible support or resistance area that formed weeks, months, or even years in the past.

If you compress a daily chart and look back across its horizon, you'll often see very noticeable high and low points where the trend reversed direction. (Those major support and resistance areas may even be 52-week highs or lows for the stock.) When price approaches such an obvious ceiling or floor, the trend is vulnerable once again to a change in direction. Those areas may be tested again and again. It is a significant event when such a strong support or resistance area is finally broken.

Example

Figure 9.4 shows a daily chart of General Motors Corp (GM), which is compressed so that over a year of data is displayed. The horizontal trend lines show major support and resistance areas on the chart where the stock trended back and forth between \$28 and \$38. Those are not just minor peaks and bottoms within an up or down trend that can be surpassed easily. Those peaks and bottoms create a significant floor and ceiling for the stock (price was approaching the floor again at the time of this writing).

(continues)

Example *(continued)*

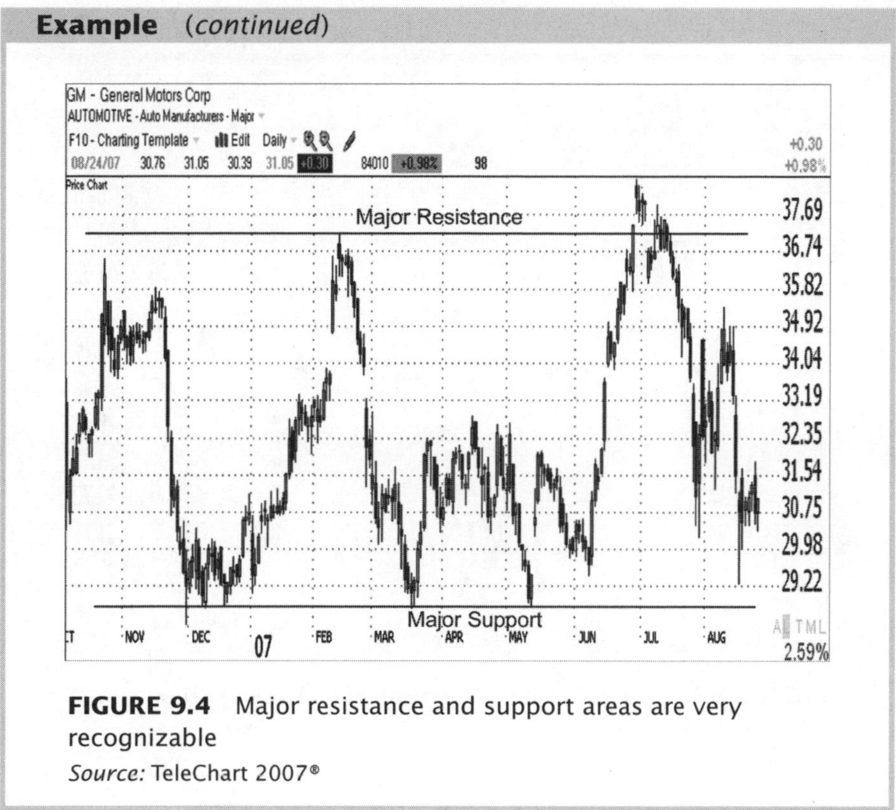

FIGURE 9.4 Major resistance and support areas are very recognizable
Source: TeleChart 2007®

If viewing only a few months of data on a daily chart, you may not recognize when a stock is traversing between a major floor and ceiling. The moves between those points are literally intermediate-term, or in some cases long-term, up and down trends on the daily chart. If you compress the daily chart to show a couple of years of data, or shift up to the weekly time frame, you'll have a clearer view of the big picture.

Example

Figure 9.5 shows a chart of General Motors Corp. again, but this time from a weekly vantage point. The intermediate-term up and down trends between $28 and $38 on the daily chart form a trading range, or rectangle, on the weekly chart. You can also see that the ceiling of that weekly trading range formed at prior resistance at a prominent ceiling from 2005.

(continues)

Example *(continued)*

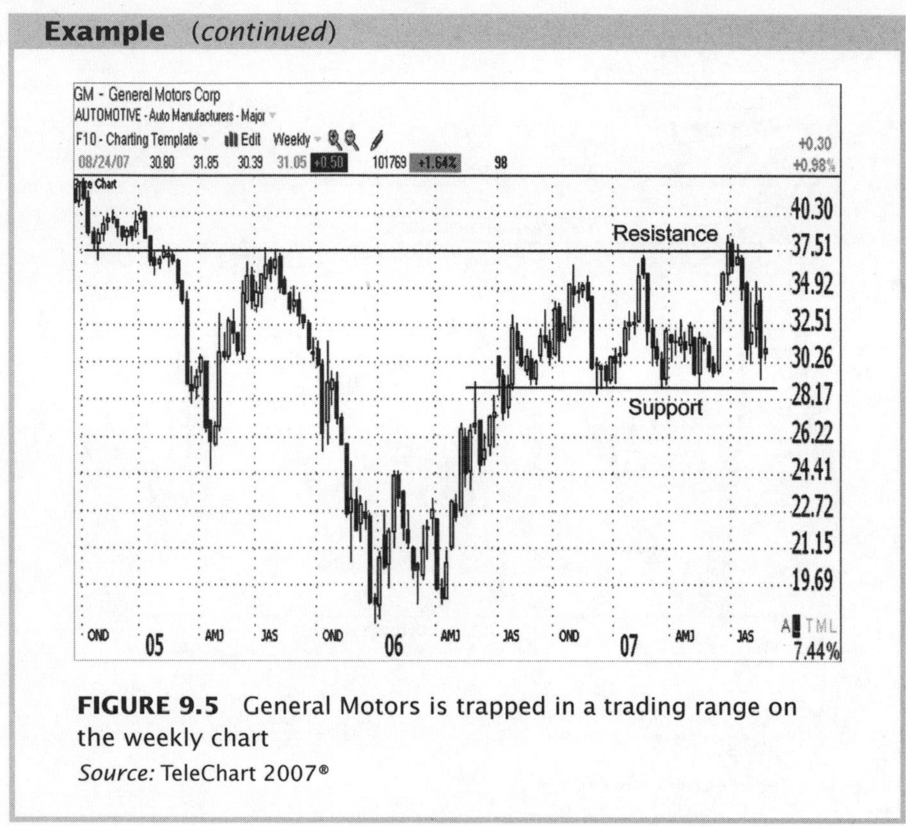

FIGURE 9.5 General Motors is trapped in a trading range on the weekly chart
Source: TeleChart 2007®

The GM chart in Figure 9.5 is a testament to the value of analyzing more than one time frame. When analyzing a chart of a stock, always glance at the time frame one level higher than the one you are trading on to check for prominent support and resistance areas that may not be visible on the lower time frame. For example, if the daily chart is the main time frame you trade, the weekly chart is the next higher time frame.

Round Numbers

Periodically, a stock will have trouble moving past a round number. This occurs most often at intervals of five or ten (prices ending in a five or a zero), for example

Example

Figure 9.6 shows a weekly chart of Rogers Corp. (ROG). A significant floor was formed back in 2005 that would not be visible on the daily chart. Price bounced at that floor in September 2007.

(*continues*)

Example (continued)

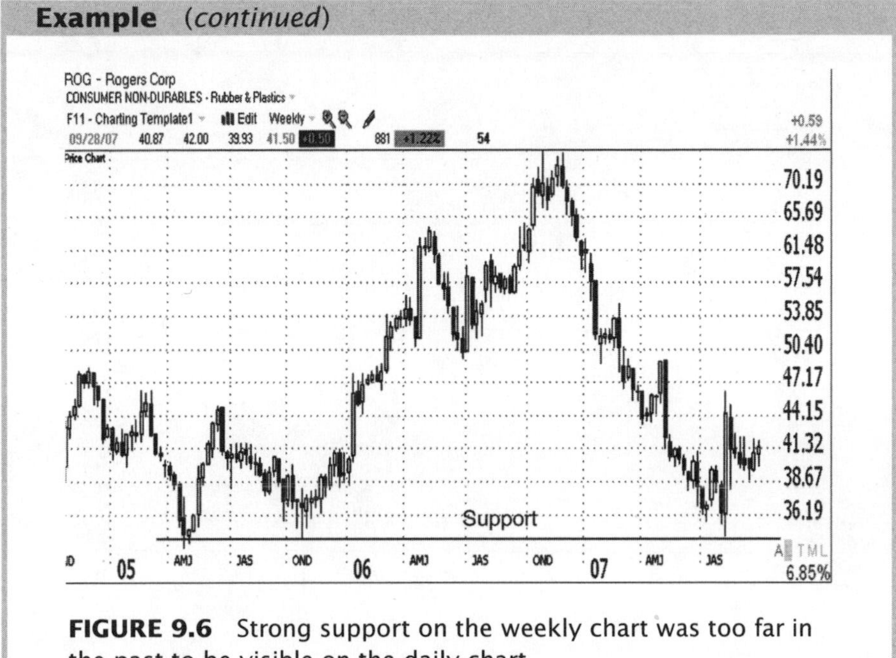

FIGURE 9.6 Strong support on the weekly chart was too far in the past to be visible on the daily chart

Source: TeleChart 2007®

25, 50, or 75. The 100 level (the "century mark") is significant, and it is not unusual to see a stock pull back after reaching that level. Round numbers are invisible barriers, and thus do not provide support or resistance nearly as often as visible barriers such as prominent peaks and bottoms. If a stock retreats from a round number one or more times though, that price action itself will set up a visible ceiling or floor at that level.

It is fairly common for major market averages to stall at levels that end in hundreds or thousands. They are psychologically charged numbers that are

Example

On the daily chart of Varian Inc. (VARI), shown in Figure 9.7, the uptrend halted at $60 in March 2007. The March high was tested again several times during April–May. The stock was unable to close above that resistance area. Finally, on July 27, price broke through $60 and closed above the strong ceiling.

(continues)

Example *(continued)*

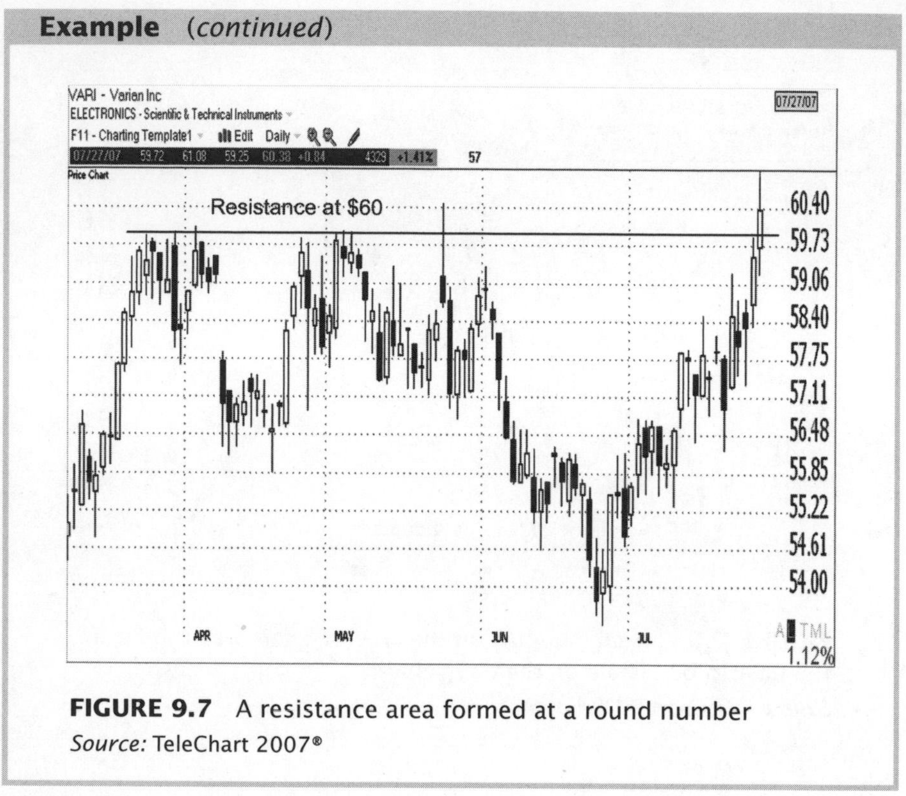

FIGURE 9.7 A resistance area formed at a round number
Source: TeleChart 2007®

watched closely by traders. For instance, it was a very significant event when the Dow Jones Industrial Average finally broke up through the 10,000 level.

Trend Lines

A trend line can be drawn below and connecting bottoms in order to highlight a support area, or above and connecting peaks in order to highlight a resistance area. The more times the support or resistance area is tested, the stronger it becomes. When a very long or strong trend line is broken, many traders will observe the event.

Trend lines may be drawn horizontally, connecting price peaks or bottoms to help identify the approximate boundaries of a trading range (see Figure 9.5), or a major ceiling or floor (see Figures 9.4 and 9.6) . They may also be drawn at an angle connecting rising or declining peaks and bottoms in order to identify the slope and length of the trend (refer to Chapter 7 and Figure 9.16 in this chapter). Trend lines make it easy to see when price has closed above resistance or below support.

Smart Investor Tip

Trend lines may be extended so that traders can anticipate where price might find potential support or resistance in the future. Your charting program may have an extension feature that automatically projects the line into the future, or you may elect to manually adjust the lines.

Other Areas of Support and Resistance

In addition to peaks and bottoms, price may also find support or resistance at the beginning of a gap and at strong moving averages.

Gaps May Provide Support or Resistance

As discussed in Chapter 8, a true gap is formed between two consecutive bars when the current bar gaps above (gap up) or below (gap down) the prior bar's range. This price action leaves a void on the chart in which no trading took place. It is common for price to trade back through that void and close it.

When a stock gaps up, the bottom of the void may provide support when price declines back down to that level. The beginning of the gap up is the high of the bar prior to the gap-up bar. Price may trade below the gap intraday (leaving a lower shadow) but it should close the session above it. If price closes below the gap, the support area has been violated and the implication is bearish.

Example

Figure 9.8 shows a daily chart of Crane Co. (CR). Horizontal lines have been drawn to indicate where price gapped up and later filled the gap, which provided support from which price moved higher. That scenario occurred twice on this chart—first in March 2007 and again in May.

(*continues*)

Example *(continued)*

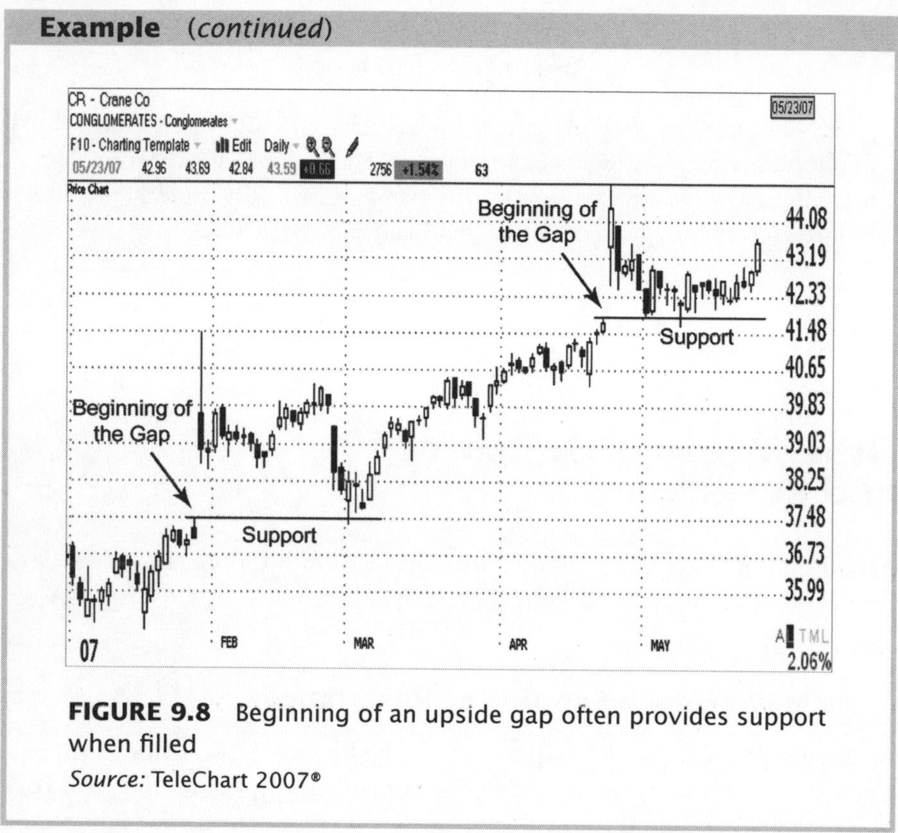

FIGURE 9.8 Beginning of an upside gap often provides support when filled
Source: TeleChart 2007®

When a stock gaps down, the top of the void may provide resistance when price rises back up to that level. In this case, the beginning of the gap is the low of the bar prior to the gap-down bar. Price may trade above the gap intraday (leaving an upper shadow), but it should close the session below it. If price closes above the gap, the resistance area has been overcome and the message is bullish.

Example

Figure 9.9 shows a daily chart of Estee Lauder Companies Inc. (EL). The horizontal line indicates the resistance area at the beginning of the gap, which was tested (1) on August 27, 2007. Price retreated and then tested the resistance area again (2) in late September.

(continues)

Example *(continued)*

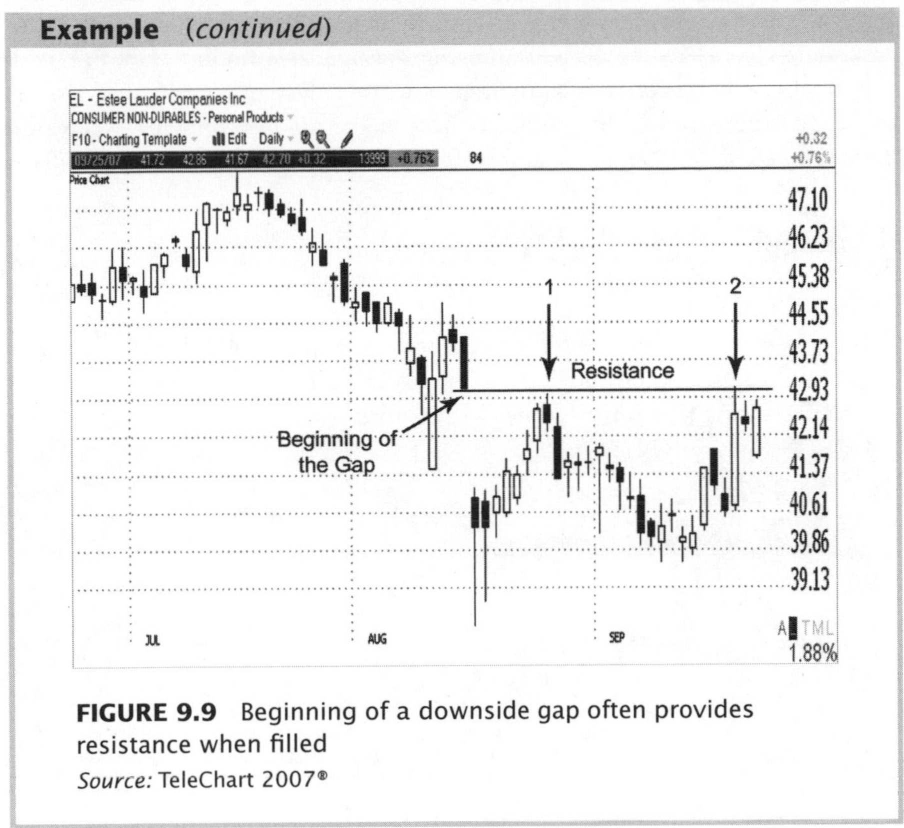

FIGURE 9.9 Beginning of a downside gap often provides resistance when filled
Source: TeleChart 2007®

Regardless of whether a gap is filled shortly after it has formed or weeks or months later, the beginning of the gap has the potential to provide support (gap up) or resistance (gap down). Price will not always fill the whole gap. The entire vacuum between the two consecutive price bars may act as a zone of support or resistance.

Moving Averages May Provide Support or Resistance

Unlike most other indicators that are plotted in panels below the chart (or above it in some charting programs), moving averages are plotted directly in the chart window. As the use of technical analysis has become more popular and widespread, certain moving average lengths have gained recognition. For instance, the 50- and 200-period moving averages are closely monitored by traders. These moving averages have the potential to provide support or resistance because traders tend to react (buy or sell shares) as price approaches them.

The 50-day moving average is a strong intermediate-term average. It is approximately equal to the 10-week moving average (five trading days per week × 10 = 50), which is often used by traders who view charts on the weekly time frame. In other words, when price bounces at the 10-week moving average on the weekly chart, it is bouncing at the 50-day moving average on the daily chart.

Example

Figure 9.10 shows a daily chart of AMB Property Corp (AMB). The stock was in a downtrend from May through August 2007. Every attempt to break up through the 50-period simple moving average (SMA) during that time was met with failure.

FIGURE 9.10 Price found resistance several times at the 50-day SMA
Source: TeleChart 2007®

The 200-day is a long-term moving average. It is approximately equal to the 40-week moving average (5 × 40 = 200), so it is also monitored by many traders who utilize daily and/or weekly charts. Price tends to gravitate toward it during a correction of a trend.

Moving averages are derived from price. They do not generally provide support and resistance as readily as price peaks and bottoms that are created from the actual price action. However, do not underestimate the ability of the 50- and 200-period moving averages to stop a stock's move, at least temporarily. Those two moving average lengths tend to be strong on all time frames, even though the correlation to the weekly chart mentioned previously is applicable only on the daily time frame. Many novice traders are not aware of the correlation and simply adopt the use of the 50- and 200-period moving averages, assuming they will work on various time frames, and often they do.

Debate over Simple versus Exponential The simple method of calculating a moving average was presented in Chapter 7 and is the most commonly used. The simple method assigns equal weight to each day's price that is included in the average. There are other ways to calculate a moving average, including assigning a different weight to one or more of the prices in the set. One such method that is popular among traders is an exponentially smoothed moving average that weights the most recent prices heavier than the older prices. Whether you use simple or exponential moving averages is a matter of personal preference. Fortunately, mainstream charting programs do the calculations for us, and users are given the option of selecting either simple or exponential.

SMAs are used exclusively in the chart examples provided in this book for consistency, and to avoid displaying a "busy" chart that may distract from the technical event(s) being emphasized. However, I do monitor both simple and exponential moving averages (EMAs). Many mainstream charting programs offer users the ability to configure multiple chart templates. Different indicators can be assigned to the various templates if desired to avoid indicator overload on one template. One of my templates includes both the exponential and simple version of the 50- and 200-period moving averages. I can quickly jump to that template whenever I need to determine which version of the average appears to be more powerful for the particular stock or index that I am evaluating. Some stocks may find support or resistance at the SMA, and some at the EMA, or both. Therefore, it certainly doesn't hurt to plot both versions in the chart window.

Smart Investor Tip

If plotting both an SMA and an EMA of the same length, I recommend assigning the same color for each but identifying one with a solid line and one with a dashed or dotted line. For instance, I use dark green for a 50-period moving average (against a white chart background) and purple for a 200-period. The SMA is assigned a solid line because it is easy to remember that they both start with the letter "s" (simple equals solid). The EMA is plotted as a dotted line.

Some traders may argue that the SMA is the only one that matters and there is no sense in looking at the EMA. I do not agree and could provide numerous examples in which the EMA was quite strong.

Example

A case in point is a stock that I trade periodically: Shaw Group Inc. (SGR). Figure 9.11 shows a daily chart of SGR. In the past, this stock has had a tendency to obey both the 200-day SMA and the 200-day EMA (see circled turning points). Without viewing both versions, one would not be aware of this fact.

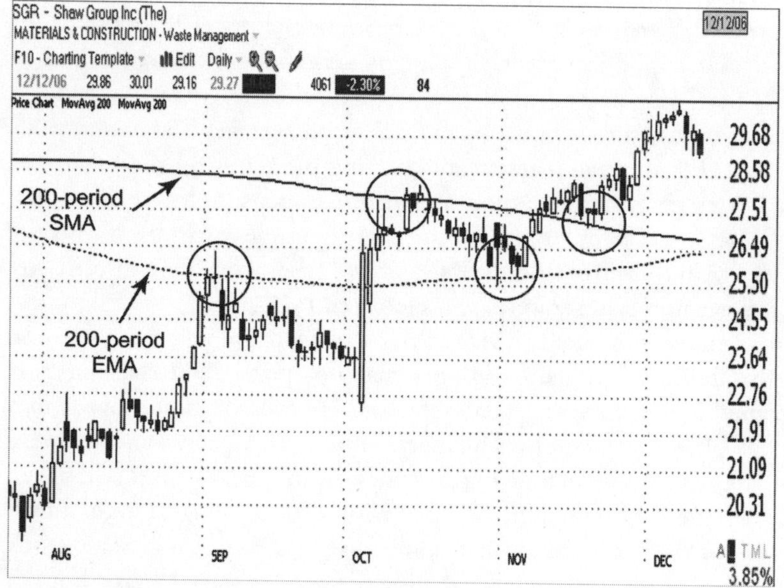

FIGURE 9.11 For several weeks, the stock found support or resistance at both the 200-day EMA and the 200-day SMA
Source: TeleChart 2007®

Example

If you still are not certain that the EMAs are worth monitoring, take a look at Figure 9.12, which shows a daily chart of the Nasdaq Composite Index. In February and March 2007, the broad market sold off sharply

(*continues*)

Example *(continued)*

and then bottomed out. The Nasdaq Composite Index formed a bullish double bottom (dotted line) at the 200-period EMA. Similar events occurred on the charts of the following indexes during that time period: the Dow Jones Industrial Average, the S&P 500 Index, and the Russell 2000 Small-Cap Index.

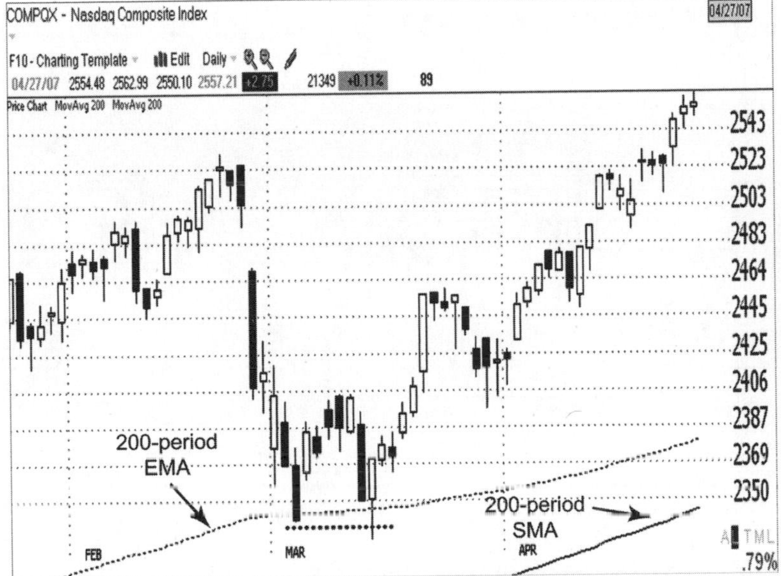

FIGURE 9.12 Index found support at the 200-day EMA
Source: TeleChart 2007®

Support and Resistance Areas Are Not Rigid Barriers

Support and resistance levels are not rigid, inflexible barriers. Don't expect price to always make an abrupt turn precisely at a floor or ceiling. Price may turn a bit before, or move slightly beyond, those boundaries. Therefore, they should be considered zones of support and resistance rather than exact turning points.

Example

Figure 9.13 shows a daily chart of Dril-Quip Inc. (DRQ), which was trapped in a trading range for a few months. The horizontal trend lines illustrate the approximate upper and lower boundaries revealing the rectangular shape.

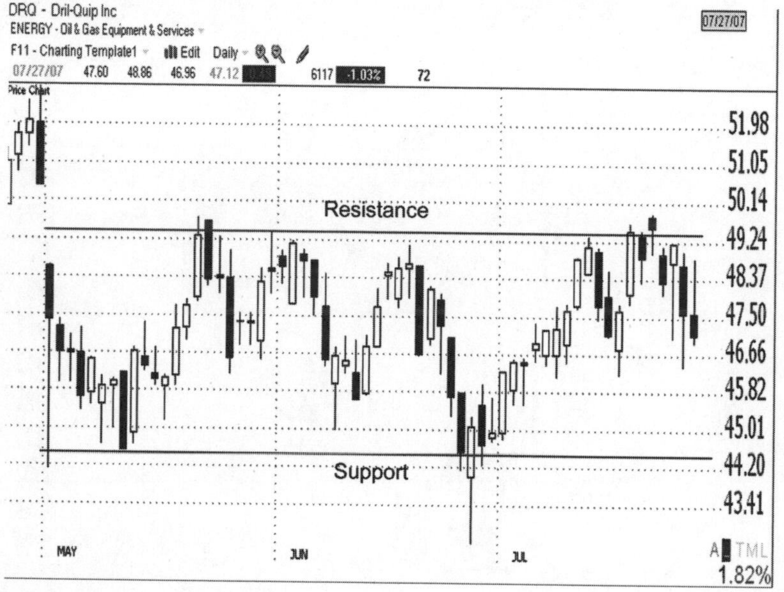

FIGURE 9.13 Visible support and resistance areas
Source: TeleChart 2007®

Failure of Support or Resistance Levels

As mentioned previously, minor support and resistance levels are formed as price surges and then consolidates or pulls back. Price typically forms a series of peaks and bottoms in the general direction of the trend. Those short-term moves create temporary interruptions of the trend. In order for the trend to continue its direction, those barriers must eventually be overcome.

Even very strong support or resistance areas are not infallible. Support and resistance levels are not permanent barriers. Investors' expectations change over time. Eventually, most support and resistance levels are broken and traders accommodate the new higher, or lower, prices. There are a variety of events that may cause the break of a strong floor or ceiling, including the following:

- News may be released that impacts a company's stock.
- Funds are regularly rotated from one asset class, sector, or industry group to another based on economic principles such as the business cycle or monetary policy.
- An actual or anticipated change in a company's fundamentals. For example, a stock may break out above resistance, or break down below support, when earnings are announced or if the company releases guidance for upcoming quarters.
- A broad market rally or sell-off may raise or lower most stocks, regardless of their financial worthiness. When the Dow Jones Industrial Average fell over 400 points on February 27, 2007, support levels were irrelevant. All of the major averages sold off and many stocks plunged through previously strong support levels that day, or in the following days.

Support and Resistance Reverse Roles

Once support or resistance has been broken, it is very common for it to reverse roles on the other side. When a stock breaks down through a floor, it often becomes a ceiling above price, and vice versa. This phenomenon is commonly seen when price peaks or bottoms are broken.

The support-resistance role reversal may occur soon after the breakout or breakdown. Often, price turns right back for a test of the prior ceiling or floor (see Figure 9.14). That price action offers traders a low-risk opportunity to get aboard the trend when price pulls back rather than chasing a runaway stock. The stock often continues in the direction of the breakout or breakdown after pulling back. Volume may offer an important clue as to the strength of the new move.

Example

The upside breakout on the daily chart of Myriad Genetics Inc. (MYGN) in Figure 9.14 was accompanied by heavy volume. Volume declined during the pullback, dropping below average as the prior ceiling was tested as support. That was a good indication that the new higher price level had been accepted.

(*continues*)

Example *(continued)*

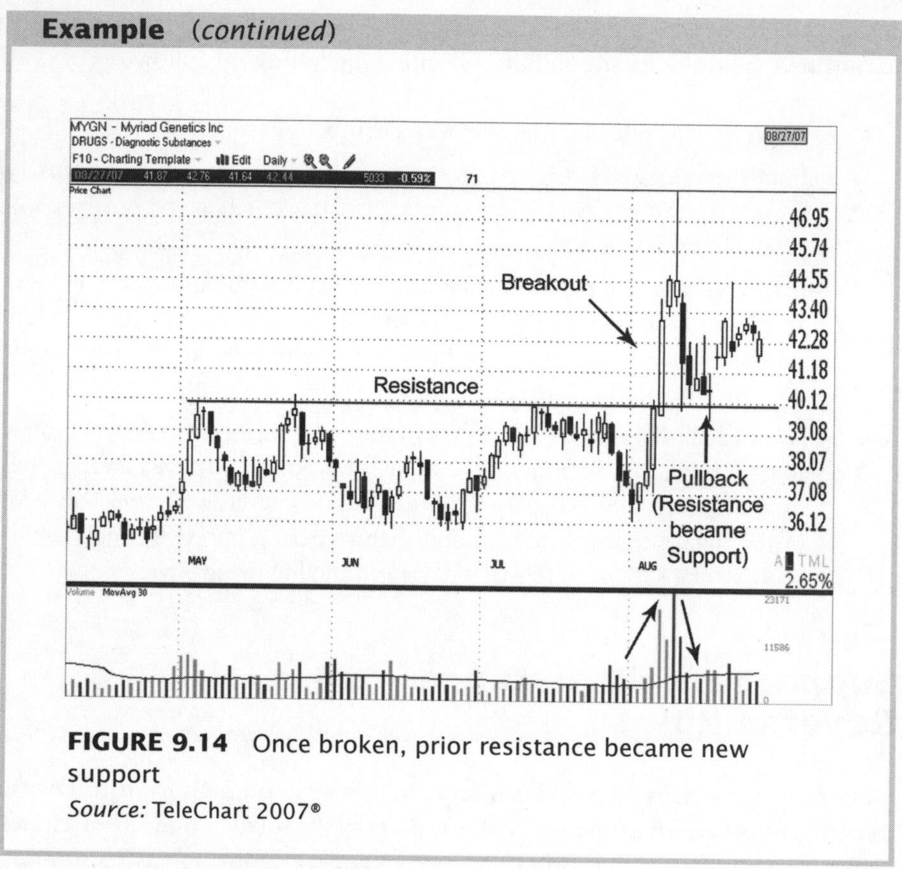

FIGURE 9.14 Once broken, prior resistance became new support

Source: TeleChart 2007®

Even if price does not pull back immediately, it is common to see a prior ceiling or floor tested weeks or even months later during a correction of the trend. Sometimes support and resistance reverse roles multiple times. The more tests of support and resistance, the stronger that area becomes; price is likely to reverse or consolidate there again in the future.

Example

On the daily chart of Ryerson Inc. (RYI), shown in Figure 9.15, resistance that formed in March 2007 was broken in April and became new support. Once that support level was broken in May, it became resistance once again.

(continues)

Example *(continued)*

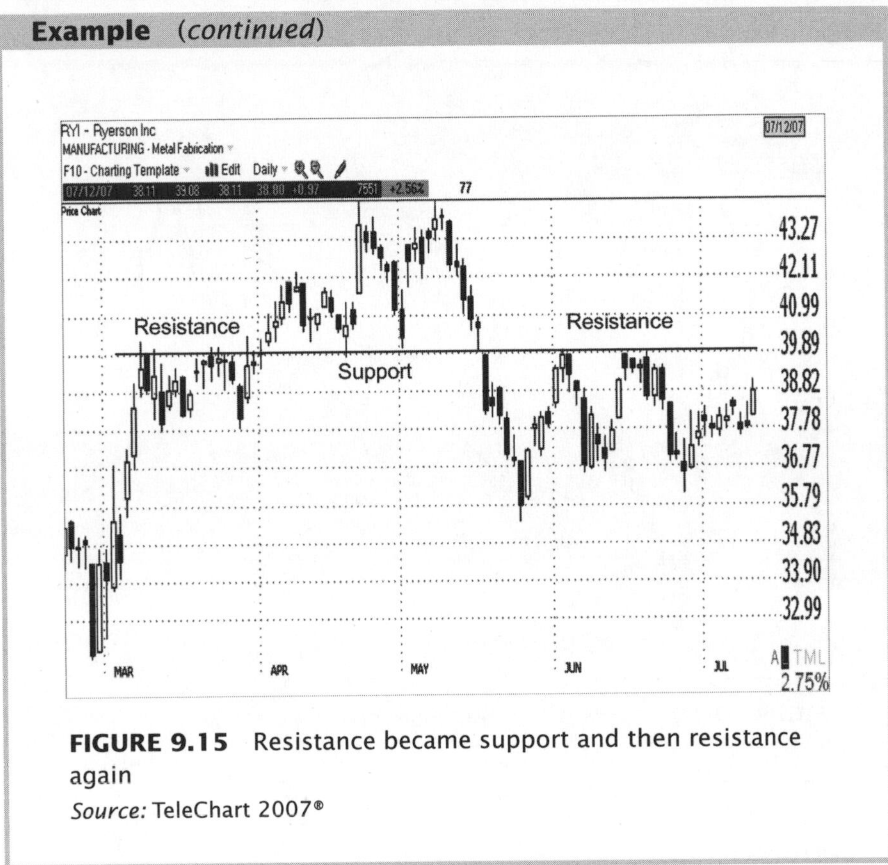

FIGURE 9.15 Resistance became support and then resistance again
Source: TeleChart 2007®

The reversal of roles may occur when horizontal support or resistance is broken, but it may also occur when an angled trend line is broken.

It is also not unusual for a strong moving average, such as the 50- or 200-period, to reverse roles when broken.

Example

On the daily chart of Omni Energy (OMNI) shown in Figure 9.16, price trended up for several weeks off the January 2007 low. That strong support trend line was broken in April. Once the uptrend resumed in May, that prior support trend line was tested as resistance several times.

(continues)

Example *(continued)*

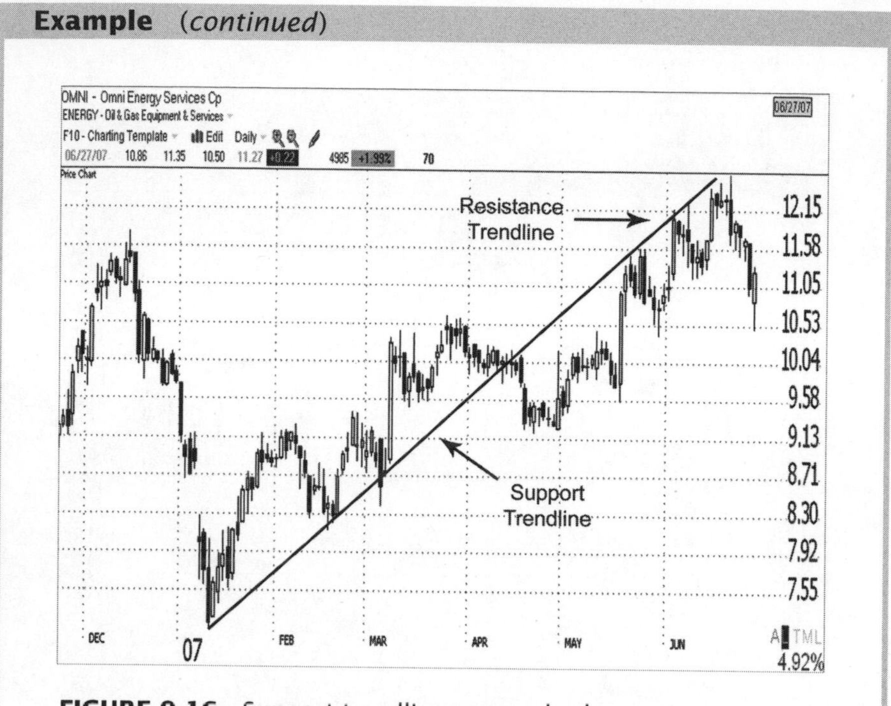

FIGURE 9.16 Support trendline reversed roles
Source: TeleChart 2007®

Example

Figure 9.17 shows a daily chart of Golinhas Aereas (GOL). In February 2007, price rallied up to the 200-period SMA (1). Price retreated from that strong average for a few weeks and then rose up to test it again. On March 31, price gapped up open above the average but the bulls could not sustain the new high and price closed below it (2). Not only was the 200-period SMA tested (at 2), but the February high (1) was at about that same level, offering even more resistance. Finally, in May, price punched up through the average and moved to a new high before pulling back toward the average. On June 8, price gapped down open (3) after the short-term decline and pierced the prior session's long black real body, leaving a bullish piercing pattern with the 200-period SMA below for support.

(*continues*)

Example *(continued)*

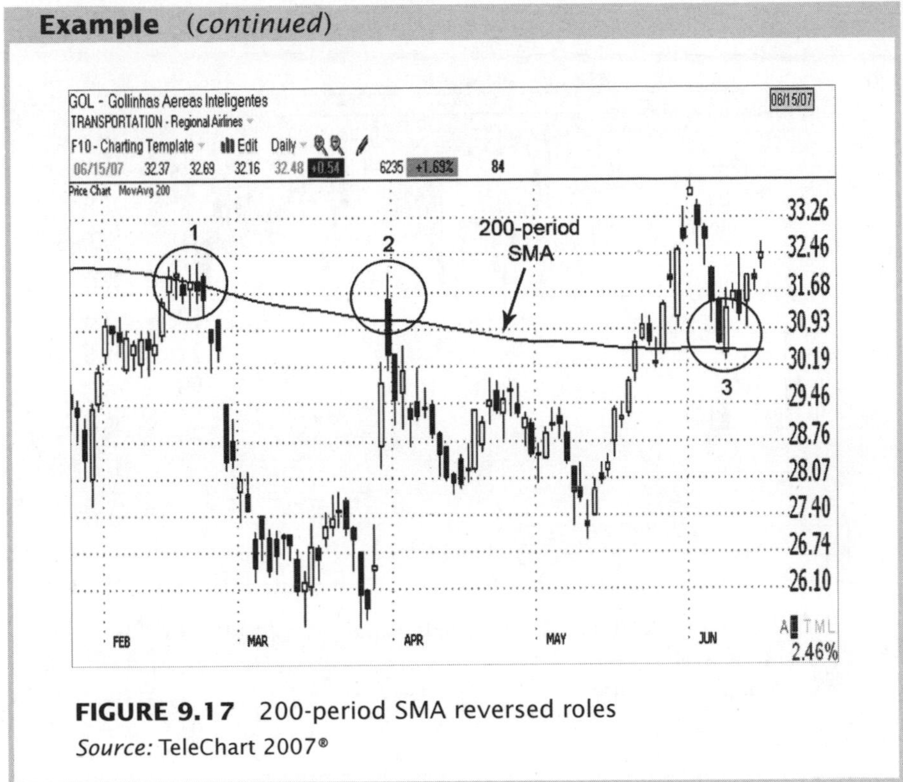

FIGURE 9.17 200-period SMA reversed roles
Source: TeleChart 2007®

Candlesticks at Support and Resistance

You may be surprised to discover how often candlestick reversal patterns form at or near support and resistance areas. And recall from Chapter 5 that long shadows are common at those areas, whether or not the candlestick line(s) meets the criteria of a specific reversal pattern. One or more long shadows are evidence of traders reacting when price tests a support or resistance area.

A daily chart of McDonald's (MCD) is displayed in Figure 9.18. The stock has been consolidating for a few months. The horizontal trend lines identify the ceiling and floor of the trading range. The following analysis explains the events that occurred at the turning points as the trading range developed between May and July 2007. The numbers that follow correspond to the numbers on the chart:

1. A bearish hanging man (1) formed after two long white candles. Because the candle prior to the hanging man was a long white candle it

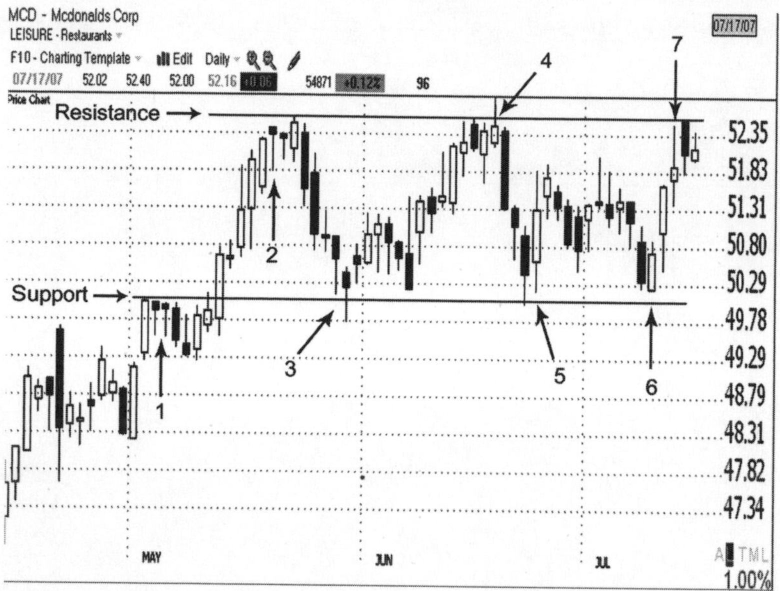

FIGURE 9.18 Candlestick reversal signals at support and resistance areas
Source: TeleChart 2007®

could also be interpreted as a bearish harami pattern. Price pulled back for a couple of days before moving higher.

2. After a strong swing up, a bearish hanging man (2) formed on May 18. Price declined from there back to the May 2 peak (at 1) where it found support.
3. Two long lower shadows (3) formed on May 29 and 30 as the May 2 peak was tested as new support. The May 30 lower shadow was long enough for many traders to interpret it as a hammer.
4. Price rallied back up and found resistance at the May high. A long upper shadow (4) formed there on June 19. It was nearly long enough to be a shooting star. That shadow showed that there was an intraday breakout above the May high but the bulls were not able to sustain the breakout.
5. Price declined back to the floor that had been established by the May 2 peak (at 1) and the May 30 bottom (at 3). Notice the long lower shadows (5) that formed as price tested support. That showed the willingness of bulls to step into long positions at the support area.
6. Price did not make it all the way back to the top of the trading range before turning back down to test the floor again. A bullish piercing pattern (6) formed on July 11 at support.

7. Price made another swing up across the channel. The long upper shadow (7) on July 13 was an indication of selling near the strong resistance level. The stock gapped up open the next morning, reversed immediately at the ceiling (shaven top), and filled by the end of the session leaving a morning gap.

Not all reversals at support and resistance levels will include a candlestick signal, but many do.

Chapter 10

Putting Candlestick Reversal Patterns to Work

Now that you have learned about the primary candlestick reversal patterns and some basics of Western charting, it's time to determine how you'll put the reversal signals to work. The candlestick reversal patterns may be used by traders in several ways, including the following:

- *Trading opportunities.* Traders may initiate trades based solely on the presence of a candlestick pattern.
- *Reinforce another setup.* Traders may look for candlestick signals that form in conjunction with larger price setups, or where price is testing support or resistance.
- *Warning to take profits.* Traders may interpret a reversal pattern as a warning to exit an open position, or at least take a defensive stance.

This chapter will address these uses for the reversal signals, as well as provide some suggestions for finding patterns and controlling risk to your capital. In-depth instruction on risk management and trade management is beyond the scope of this book. Novice traders are strongly advised to pursue additional study of those topics.

Practice Spotting Candlestick Patterns

It takes practice to convert knowledge to skill. Before you can utilize the candlestick patterns, you must be able to recognize them. Schedule some time to immediately start evaluating charts in order to develop your pattern recognition skills. You may need to review Chapter 3 a few times first so you feel certain that you understand the psychology behind each of the primary reversal patterns. A quick reference guide is also provided in Appendix A.

Smart Investor Tip

If you don't already use a charting service, you'll need to subscribe to one that either provides end-of-day or real-time data. TeleChart, MetaStock, TradeStation, QCharts, and eSignal are a few of the many fine charting services available. Many vendors offer a 30-day free trial to allow potential subscribers to explore their platforms. Stockcharts.com provides limited charting with end-of-day data at no charge; so there is no reason you can't start evaluating charts right away.

The goal is to train your eye to quickly spot candlestick reversal patterns. Evaluate many charts, one after another; the repetition will be helpful. If you are not sure what stocks to evaluate, select some symbols from the S&P 500 Index component list included in Appendix B. Focus primarily on the turning points (peaks and bottoms) on a chart and you'll locate reversal patterns. If a chart is messy and hard to decipher, just skip past it. When you locate a reversal pattern, make note of the surrounding chart landscape. Did the pattern form at a support or resistance area? Did the stochastic oscillator confirm the signal? Was it an ideal reversal pattern, or was it a nonideal pattern or variation? Was a strong reversal pattern, such as an engulfing pattern or a hammer, accompanied by heavy volume? Eventually, it will not only be very easy for you to recognize the reversal patterns, but you'll learn to look for supporting Western technical occurrences that assist you in determining which signals are most likely to follow through. Once you are able to recognize the patterns, you can determine how you'll implement them in your trading.

As part of your analysis, don't forget about the bigger picture. Consult the charts of the broad market averages: the Dow Jones Industrial Average, the S&P 500 Index, and the Nasdaq Composite Index. While browsing through charts, you may notice that between certain dates a lot of bullish patterns seemed to fail. That may result in your questioning the validity of the signals. But perhaps that occurred during a time when the broad market was selling off. Remember that stocks, regardless of how bullish a setup or how good the company fundamentals, may be pulled down during a broad market decline. Conversely, if the market is rallying, even stocks with weak charts and/or poor fundamentals may get a temporary boost.

Reversal Patterns Provide Trading Opportunities

The candlestick reversal patterns can be utilized for trade setups. Recall that a setup is an identifiable price formation that presents a potentially profitable trading opportunity. Among the numerous setups for traders to choose from are candlestick patterns. A strategy is the method a trader uses to trade a setup. Some traders may wish to devise a strategy for trading one or more of the candlestick reversal patterns. Bullish reversal patterns can be used to initiate long positions, and bearish patterns for short positions.

Traders cannot be certain that a candlestick pattern is present until the close of the trading session. Therefore, if trading a candlestick signal, a position may be entered very near the end of the session on the signal day, or after the open of the following session. As indicated in Chapter 3, for some reversal patterns it is best to wait for confirmation before entering a position. Make sure to carefully review the criteria and psychology of each candlestick pattern you wish to trade.

Searching for Reversal Patterns

For centuries, the Japanese did not have the aid of computers for chart analysis. They fared quite well using a trained eye to find the formations on charts that were drawn by hand. Of course, that was before the days when there were thousands of stocks available to trade.

If you trade a single instrument, such as the S&P e-mini, or a limited number of stocks, you won't need to run computerized scans to find reversal patterns. Patterns can be located simply by evaluating the charts. In fact, it would be beneficial to recognize and understand all of the reversal patterns presented in Chapter 3 in order to expand the trading opportunities rather than waiting for just one specific pattern to form.

Some traders may prefer to trade one or more specific candlestick patterns. In that case, they'll need to flush out the stocks that meet the pattern's criteria so they can choose good-looking setups from among them. There are currently about 7,000 stocks traded on the three major U.S. exchanges: the New York Stock Exchange (NYSE), the American Stock Exchange (AMEX), and the Nasdaq. Traders who wish to find a particular reversal pattern among hundreds or thousands of stocks can save a tremendous amount of time by allowing the computer to do most of the work.

Computerized Screening The ever-increasing power and speed of personal computers has made searching for candlestick patterns easy. Many of the mainstream charting programs offer users the capability to code the criteria that identifies the patterns. Users can quickly scan for candlestick patterns among the thousands of stocks traded on the exchanges.

Coding the Candlestick Patterns Those who wish to trade one or more of the candlestick reversal signals and scan for them among a large number of stocks will need to define the criteria for each formation. For instance, TeleChart users can create Personal Criteria Formulas (PCFs) for the patterns. The PCFs can then be used to sort or scan for stocks that meet the pattern's criteria.

Fortunately, the criteria of all the patterns have already been defined by traders who were generous enough to share that information with others. TeleChart users can access www.tradeon.com, a free web site, to obtain the formulas for candlesticks. The web site includes the code for all of the candlestick lines and the reversal patterns discussed in this book (as well as several reversal and continuation patterns that were not covered). On the home page, click the down arrow to the right of "Beginners & Misc. Information" and select Candlestick PCF Tutorial (Figure 10.1). On the candlesticks page, use the scroll bar to the right to search for the candlestick pattern(s) you wish to trade (Figure 10.2). A PCF must be created in TeleChart for each candlestick pattern. The code can be highlighted and copied from the tradeon.com web page and pasted directly into a PCF in TeleChart. For more information on TeleChart, visit the web site at www.telechart.com.

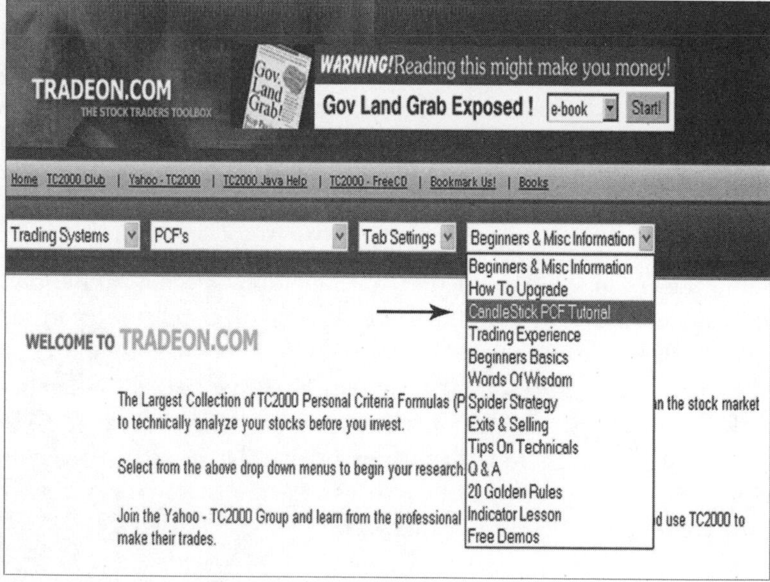

FIGURE 10.1 Tradeon.com web site
Source: www.tradeon.com

FIGURE 10.2 Code for candlesticks is available free at www.tradeon.com
Source: www.tradeon.com

Traders who do not use TeleChart should contact the vendor of their charting service to inquire if there are similar online resources where users share code in that program's language. Even if you cannot find such a resource, you can use the code from tradeon.com to extrapolate the criteria for the various patterns and write it in the language of your charting software. The language for each charting platform may differ some; however, the coding concepts are usually similar. For example, TradeStation is a powerful charting platform. Their proprietary EasyLanguage® allows users to designate criteria for screening. For more information on TradeStation, visit the web site at www.tradestation.com. Those who wish to utilize the TradeStation platform can get a substantial discount off the monthly fee by opening a brokerage account with them; the software is linked to their brokerage services. If you are a MetaStock user, the code has been written and is available for purchase as a plug-in. For more information about MetaStock, visit the web site at www.metastock.com.

Filter for Price and Volume Traders can also reduce the number of stocks to be analyzed by utilizing a price and volume filter. This is a great technique to use in conjunction with a scan that isolates a specific pattern from among a large number of stocks. Such a filter can be used to narrow down the stocks in *any* scan or list of stocks, not just candlestick scans.

First, determine the price range of stocks you wish to trade. The desired price range may vary widely from one trader to the next. If you are not sure what price range to select, consider using a simple model based on account size. Say Trader A has a trading account of $50,000. For that account size, I don't recommend investing more than 20 percent of the account in the stock of one company. Therefore, no more than $10,000 could be used to purchase one stock and the trader could purchase up to five stocks in this account (or more if less than $10,000 is committed per stock). Personally, I don't typically buy a stock that I cannot afford at least 200 shares of, but at a minimum, I'd recommend figuring for no less than 100 shares (less than 100 shares is referred to as an *odd lot*). Divide $10,000 by 100 shares for a maximum price per share of $100, or divide $10,000 by 200 shares for a maximum of $50 per share. Next, determine the minimum share price. For instance, many traders elect to trade stocks that are $5 per share or higher because stocks below $5 may not be marginable. Using these parameters, the price range would be $5 to $50 if you wish to trade a minimum of 200 shares, or $5 to $100 for a minimum of 100 shares.

Think of the model outlined above as trading within the means of your account. Most aspiring traders who do not succeed in this business fail due to poor risk and money management methods. Diversification and position sizing are two very important factors to consider.

Example

Google (GOOG) is currently trading above $500 per share. Buying shares of Google could tie up a substantial amount of capital, which may not be a challenge for a large account, but could be problematic for a smaller account. Trader A would have to invest his entire account of $50,000 in Google just to buy 100 shares. That would be an error in judgment, as the account would be over-allocated to one stock. If Google got unexpected news one evening and dropped 10 percent the next day, Trader A's entire account would be drawn down by 10 percent. However, if Trader A limited the purchase of one stock to 20 percent of the account, and the stock fell 10 percent, the trader's account would be drawn down by only 2 percent. In addition, implementing a rule for diversification will keep him focused on stocks that are priced appropriately for the account size.

Trader B has a larger account of $250,000. Putting 20 percent, or $50,000, into one stock would mean lot more exposure in one company. Trader B should break her account down further, for example, into 10 blocks of $25,000 or 15 blocks of approximately $16,500. That means managing more trades in order to get the account fully invested—that is a "quality problem"!

There are different schools of thought on the best way to determine position sizing and for diversifying one's account. The above-referenced model was presented because it is simple for novice traders to understand and implement.

As traders gain experience, they should study various risk management models to determine which is best suited for their trading style and risk tolerance. Regardless of how you ultimately decide to invest your account, it is paramount that protection of capital be the top priority. Using stop loss orders to limit loss is another way to protect your capital.

Once you have determined the price range for the stocks you'll trade, it is time to think of the stock's liquidity. Decide on the minimum average volume per day you'll require for a stock to be deemed liquid enough to comfortably trade. Again, that level may vary from one trader to the next.

Example

With few exceptions, I trade stocks ranked in the 50 to 99 percentile for average daily volume over the past 90 days. That equates to a minimum of approximately 125,000 shares per day. I periodically trade stocks below the 50 percentile, but the majority of my trades are above that level. Novice traders may elect to start with more heavily traded stocks to avoid problems with order fills and excessive slippage. For instance, stocks in the 70 to 99 percentile trade a minimum of about half a million shares per day.

Combine the two concepts outlined above into one filter and you have the following price-volume criterion for an account of $50,000: average daily volume of 125,000 shares or higher (if designating the 50 to 99 percentile) and stocks that are priced between $5 and $50. By using such a filter, you'll eliminate all the stocks that don't fall into your price-volume parameters. Then you can scan the remaining stocks for the candlestick pattern(s), or other set-ups, that you wish to trade.

Your charting program may have a feature that allows you to create a price-volume filter and apply it to any list of stocks. In TeleChart, both the price and volume filters can be designated by creating a single Easy Scan. The price-volume Easy Scan can then be laid over any watch list, or over any other Easy Scan, using TeleChart's sublist feature.

If you use TeleChart and are not familiar with the scanning and sublisting processes mentioned in this chapter, contact the vendor for training materials or feel free to e-mail me for assistance. You can reach me at tina@tinalogan.com or through my web site at www.tinalogan.com.

If you use a program other than TeleChart, I encourage you to contact the vendor and inquire if similar filtering techniques are available in their platform. It is not my intention to steer you toward using TeleChart. Many mainstream

Example

Figure 10.3 shows the TeleChart watch list window. A scan for bullish engulfing patterns was run with a price-volume sublist applied. On the day this scan was run (October 5, 2007), only 168 of over 7,000 stocks met the criteria of a bullish engulfing pattern. But once the price-volume sublist was applied, only 33 stocks remained. You can see how this dramatically reduces the number of stocks to be evaluated.

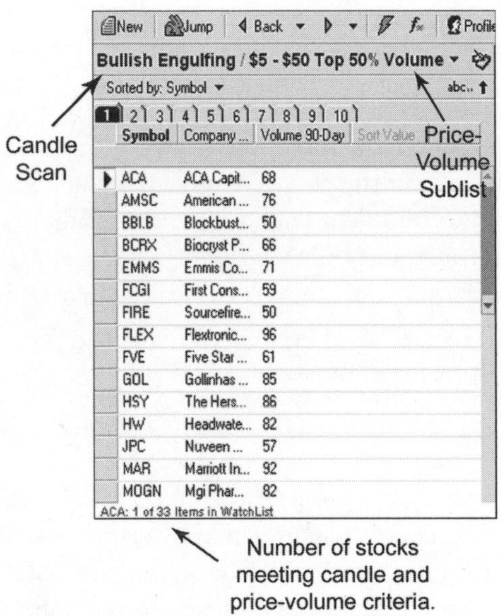

FIGURE 10.3 TeleChart watch list window
Source: TeleChart 2007®

charting platforms include some type of screening mechanism. You must decide which charting service is best suited to your trading needs. It is important, though, if you intend to search for setups among a large number of stocks, that you understand such tools and features are available with a good charting program. It may help you distinguish one platform from another when determining where you'll spend your money.

Limitations of Computerized Scanning Computers can reduce the amount of work required to isolate stocks that exhibit a certain candlestick pattern. That does not release the trader from the responsibility of knowing the psychology of the pattern, as well as an understanding of Western technical analysis.

A computer cannot discern whether one pattern appears to be a more *viable* candidate than another. A computer cannot look across the chart landscape and see where areas of support and resistance lie that may help or hinder a stock's movement. It cannot spot a divergence, nor can it tell you whether there is an adequate reward-to-risk ratio to justify a trade. A computer can only narrow down a large list of stocks to a much smaller list of potential trade opportunities. After that, it is up to you to review that list, making a visual inspection of each chart, and further reducing the number of stocks to only those that merit the commitment of your funds.

Another challenge with computerized screening is that a nonideal pattern, or a slight variation of a pattern, may be excluded because it falls short of meeting the requirements designated in the formula. Remember that nonideal patterns and variations can be just as strong as some ideal patterns when considered in the context of the surrounding price action.

Reward versus Risk

In Chapter 3, reference was made in regard to several of the reversal patterns that, by the time the signal is apparent, there may not be an adequate reward-to-risk ratio to justify a trade. The reward versus the risk should be considered *before* entering a trade, regardless of whether it is a candlestick pattern or some other price setup. If the potential reward does not outweigh the risk involved by a sufficient amount, a trader should pass on the trade or wait for a better entry opportunity to set up.

The *reward* is the potential profit on the trade. It is the gain that a trader will recognize if a trade moves from the entry price to an exit point he has determined based on analysis of the chart. That exit point is referred to as the *target* or *price objective.*

The *risk* for a trade is the amount of money that will be lost if the trade does not follow through as anticipated. It is the distance from the entry price to the point where the trader has determined that the position will be exited because it has failed. The failure point is where the initial protective stop-loss order would be placed.

The reward compared to the risk is often referenced as a ratio. To calculate the *reward-to-risk ratio,* simply divide the amount of potential reward by the amount of potential risk. For example, if the distance to the target is four points, and the distance to the protective stop is two points, the reward-to-risk ratio is 2. There is twice as much potential reward as risk. A ratio of 1 means that the potential risk is as great as the potential gain—that is a poor ratio. The higher the reward-to-risk ratio, the better the trading opportunity. I suggest always trying to select trade setups that will net at least twice as much potential gain as loss. And ideally, that ratio will be 3:1 or better on many trades.

Example

Figure 10.4 shows how to compare the reward to the risk. A trader is considering entering near the close of the bullish engulfing pattern at the right edge of the chart. There is an area of resistance overhead that offers a reasonable target for a swing trade. The low of the bullish engulfing pattern is the failure point for this setup. The distance to the target (reward) is about 2.5 times the distance to the failure point (risk).

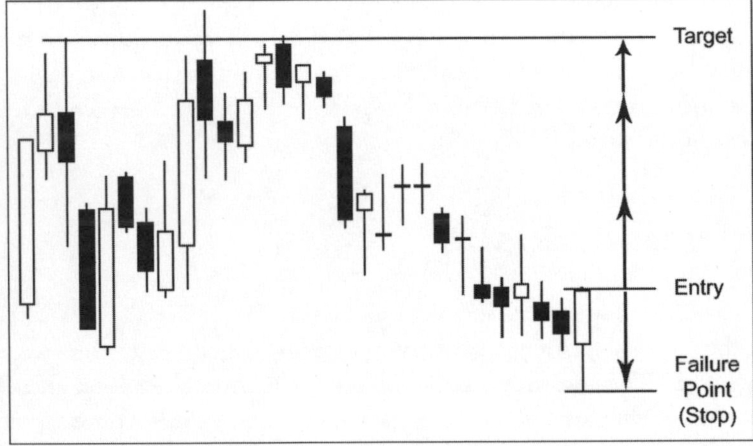

FIGURE 10.4 Reward versus risk
Source: TeleChart 2007®

Example

Figure 10.5 shows a daily chart of Pier 1 Imports Inc. (PIR). The stock was in a downtrend during July 2007. Price accelerated to the downside in late July and early August, moving far away from the 20-period SMA. That short-term oversold condition was alleviated by a rally from August 6 to 9. On August 9, a spinning top formed after the prior day's long bullish candle creating a bearish star pattern and alerting that the rally may be running out of steam. It was followed in the next session by a strong bearish engulfing pattern. A swing trader might use the engulfing setup to initiate a short position. The swing target (reward) would be to resistance at the August low. The failure point (risk) would be to the high of the engulfing candle. The reward-to-risk ratio would be only about 1.5, not enough to justify the trade.

(*continues*)

Example *(continued)*

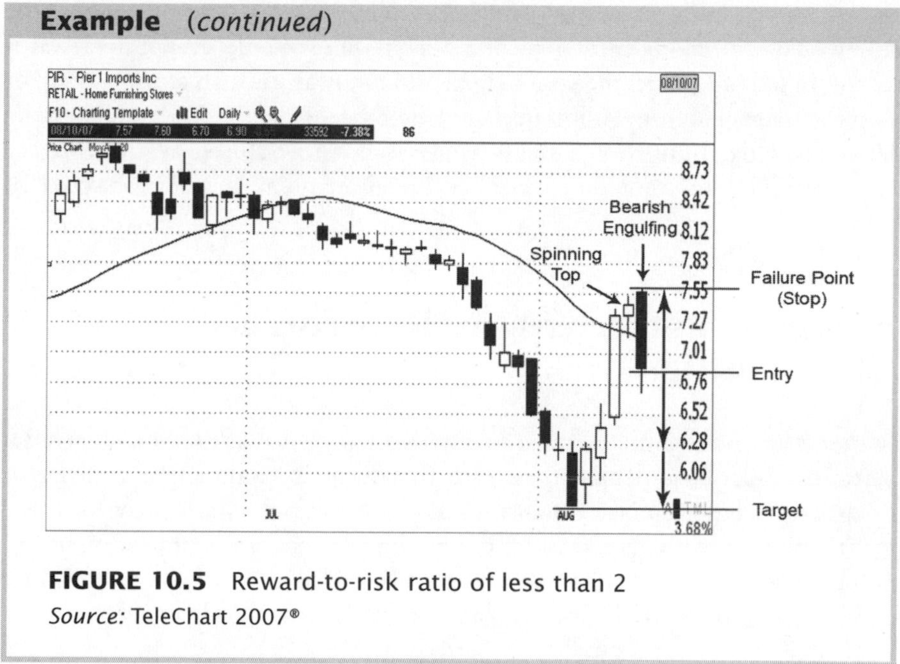

FIGURE 10.5 Reward-to-risk ratio of less than 2
Source: TeleChart 2007®

Swing trading strategies typically call for determining the failure point and price target. Thus, determining the reward to risk ratio in advance of initiating a trade is part of a swing trader's work when evaluating the viability of a setup.

Trend-following strategies may not call for determining price objectives since the goal is to enter a trending stock and ride the trend until it reverses. Even if a trader does not have a specific price objective for a trade, it is still prudent to enter where the initial stop would not be prohibitively far away.

Don't Forget about Volatility

Even if a setup provides an adequate reward-to-risk ratio, it does not necessarily mean it merits an entry. Using the example of PIR in Figure 10.5, if a short position were entered near the close of market, with the protective buy-to-cover stop a little bit above the high of the bearish engulfing pattern, the stop would be about 10 percent away. For swing trades, I have a general risk control rule that my stop should never be more than 10 percent away from the current price of the stock. Thus, the PIR entry would be right at my maximum allowed for a stop. I prefer to trade setups that offer an entry that is closer to the failure point to minimize the potential loss and improve the reward-to-risk ratio.

I look at both the reward-to-risk ratio and how far, percentage-wise, the stop would be from my entry price. If a stock is quite volatile, even if the reward-to-risk ratio is adequate, the stop may be too far away. In such a case, I'll either skip the trade or shift to an intraday strategy to trade the stock. Remember, the 10 percent maximum for a swing trade is not to be used as an arbitrary stop level. The stop should be placed at the failure point, but not to exceed 10 percent.

Reversal Patterns May Reinforce Other Setups

Rather than entering trades based solely on the presence of candlestick reversal patterns, traders may look for patterns that form in conjunction with larger price setups. For example, a bullish candlestick reversal pattern may form the second bottom of a larger Western double bottom pattern as shown in several examples throughout this book. I refer to these setups as a "pattern within a pattern." This is one of the uses for candlestick patterns that I favor.

The presence of a candlestick pattern within a larger pattern, such as the hammer that formed the potential double bottom in the STJ example (Figure 10.6), provides an opportunity for an assertive entry into a long position for traders who prefer not to wait for the larger double bottom pattern to confirm. (For a double bottom to confirm, price must close above the peak between the two bottoms.) Bottoming patterns often form as a long downtrend is coming to an end, or at that completion of a correction of a long-term uptrend, and vice versa for topping patterns. Traders wishing to get aboard a new trend, or a resumption of the trend, as early as possible, may favor setups such as the STJ example. Protective stops should be used to limit loss in the event the bottoming pattern is not successful at reversing the trend.

Support and Resistance

Another application for the candlestick reversal patterns is to choose setups that form at support (bullish patterns) or resistance (bearish patterns). As discussed in Chapter 9, price often finds support (or resistance) at prior price peaks and bottoms, strong moving averages, and at the beginning of a gap window.

Some traders (myself included) may feel more comfortable entering bullish patterns, such as those shown in the FLR example (Figure 10.7), where there is support below rather than if they form during a decline in which there is no visible support that will attract the attention of market participants. This approach works well for swing trading strategies, but also can be employed for entry into longer-term positions.

Example

Figure 10.6 shows a daily chart of Saint Jude Medical Inc. (STJ). In February–March 2007, price declined and found support at the 200-period simple moving average (SMA) on March 14. Another test of the 200-period SMA occurred on March 30, setting up the potential for a Western double bottom reversal pattern (dotted line). The March 30 candle was a hammer.

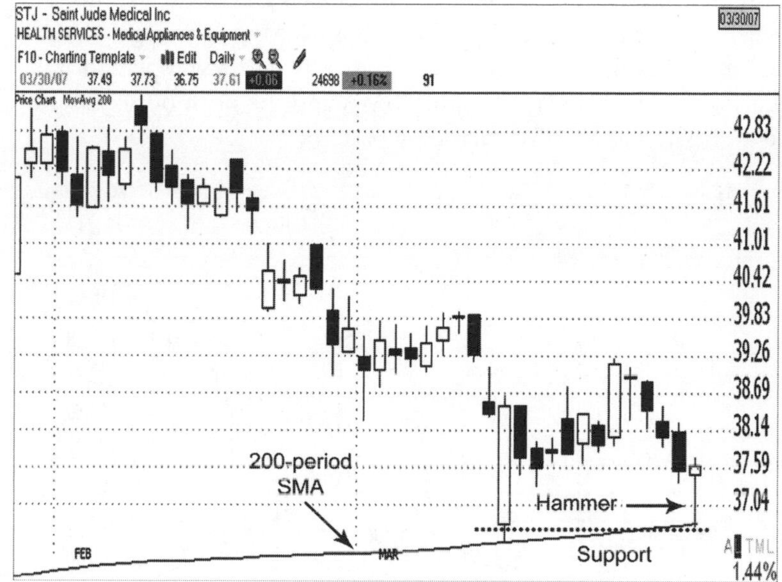

FIGURE 10.6 Hammer formed at support at the prior bottom and the 200-period simple moving average
Source: TeleChart 2007®

Convergence of Signals

The setup shown in Figure 10.6 was very desirable because there was a *convergence of signals.* Signals converge when there are two or more bullish (or bearish) events that intersect. In this case, not only was there a candlestick reversal signal (hammer) within a Western reversal pattern (double bottom), but there was support below provided by the 200-period SMA. Figure 10.7 also provided a convergence of signals.

Even with a convergence of signals there is no guarantee that the setup will follow through as anticipated; however, with several signals present many traders will notice the setup increasing the likelihood of a successful outcome.

Example

Figure 10.7 shows a daily chart of Fluor Corp. (FLR). After a price decline, price gapped down open on June 8 to near the 50-day SMA, reversed direction, and closed well into the prior black candle's real body leaving a bullish piercing pattern. In addition to the strong moving average just below, the horizontal line drawn on the chart shows that there was additional support provided by prior minor peaks and bottoms that formed in April–May. Another swing up followed the piercing pattern ending with a northern doji near the June high. Price pulled back again from June 18 to 26. Price gapped down open on June 27, tested support again at the 50-day SMA and the prior bottoms, and closed the session as a bullish engulfing pattern.

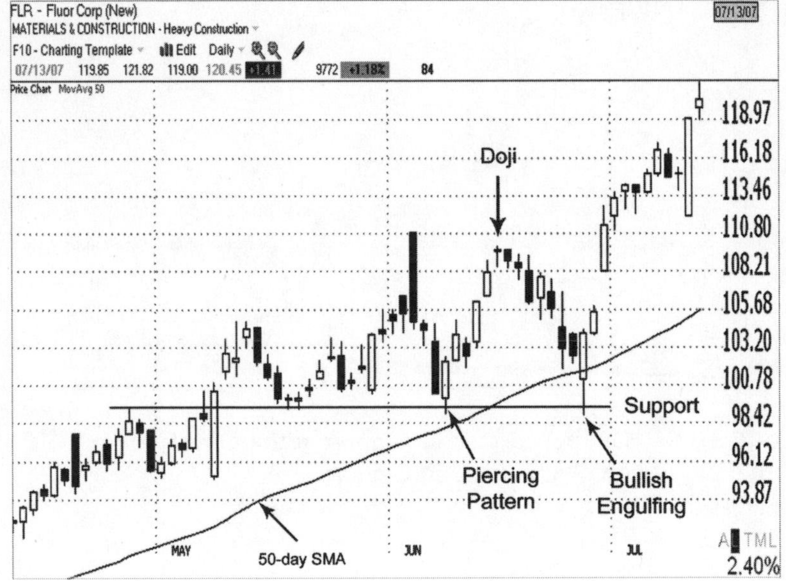

FIGURE 10.7 Bullish reversal patterns formed at support
Source: TeleChart 2007®

In summary, although I will periodically trade a candlestick pattern in isolation, it is my preference to trade those that form where there is additional ammunition for a move in the anticipated direction. As long as there are many trade opportunities to choose from, I'll always gravitate toward the setups that offer a higher likelihood of following through. When I do trade based strictly on the appearance of a candlestick signal, I look for confirmation from other technical tools, such as volume and/or the stochastic oscillator. Even traders who wish to run computerized scans looking for specific candlestick patterns can apply these Western techniques in order to isolate the most promising setups.

Reversal Patterns can Provide Warnings

Another effective way to utilize the candlestick reversal signals is for warnings to lighten up, or exit, an open position. This is especially helpful for swing traders who hold positions for a few days to a few weeks. Rather than holding on as the market zigs and zigs like a longer-term investor may do, the swing trader exploits the short-term moves within a trend.

Candlestick reversal signals can be used to exit a trade, or at least take a defensive stance, for those who do not wish to hold through a potential pullback or period of consolidation. Swing traders holding long positions should watch for bearish reversal signals. Those holding short positions should watch for bullish reversal signals.

A challenge with utilizing the reversal signals in this manner is that you won't know until the close of the trading session that the pattern is present. As discussed in Chapters 2 and 4, the candlestick can change shape throughout the session so a close is necessary in order to identify the pattern. For some reversal patterns, that means price may have moved significantly against your position by the session's end (for example, a dark cloud cover or an engulfing pattern) as you wait to see how the candle looks by the end of the session. Recall from discussion in Chapter 8, though, that many times a reversal pattern will begin as an opening gap. Swing traders may elect to exit a position that gaps after a directional move. By the end of the session, it won't matter if a strong reversal candlestick pattern has formed because you'll have used the gap to exit early in the day. Another option is to lighten up by selling part of the position on the opening gap (or in pre-market trading) and maintain a protective stop on the balance of the position.

Short Selling

Several times in this book you've seen reference to "shorting" a stock. For instance, some traders may utilize bearish candlestick signals to initiate short positions. Shorting is a confusing concept for many novice traders, but it really need not be. Selling short is the opposite of going long. Instead of buying and then selling, the trader is selling and then buying. When a trader enters a long position, shares of the stock are purchased in anticipation that the price will rise and the stock will be sold at a higher price. When a trader enters a short position, the shares are sold in anticipation of a price decline. If the stock declines, the shares can be bought at a lower price, which is referred to as *covering.*

Example

If a long position is taken on a stock at $50 and the stock rises to $60 and is sold, the trader recognizes a gain of $10 per share. If a stock is sold short at $60 and covered at $50, the trader recognizes a profit of $10 per share.

Short selling has some restrictions:

- The shares must be borrowed from the brokerage firm in order to sell short. The broker may not have shares in their inventory to lend, so traders should not assume they'll always be able to execute a short position. If demand is high to short the stock, the broker may not have shares available at the time you wish to borrow them. You may be notified later by the broker when shares do become available; however, in some cases, by the time that occurs, the trade is no longer desirable.
- A margin account is required in order to sell short because the shares must be borrowed. Therefore, short selling is not allowed in tax-deferred retirement accounts because they are nonmargin accounts.

margin account A brokerage account that permits an investor to buy or sell securities on credit and to borrow against securities held in the account.

Until recently, there was an uptick rule for shorting stocks. That meant price must trade higher than the last price before an order to sell short could be filled. The rule, which was implemented by the Securities and Exchange Commission (SEC) back in the 1930s in order to curtail a bear raid on a stock, was eliminated in July 2007.

Novice traders often shy away from shorting due to lack of understanding and a sense that it is a risky practice. Some traders cite the concern that there is no limit to how high the stock's price could rise, thus setting up the potential for unlimited loss. However, traders should not find themselves in this position if they implement proper risk and money management rules. It is not the practice of shorting that is risky, but rather the actions of the trader who fails to protect his capital. Just like with a long position, a protective stop order can be used to limit loss on a short position. A protective stop-loss order for a long position is called a *sell stop*. It is placed *below* the current price at a level where the trader would no longer wish to hold a position in that stock. For a short position, a buy stop (or buy-to-cover stop) is placed *above* the current price at a level where the trader would no longer wish to be short the stock.

Short selling offers traders the opportunity to take advantage of a declining market. I once heard it said that "the bull walks up the stairway but the bear jumps out the window." This is a clever way of saying that prices tend to fall faster than they rise. Experienced traders can profit handsomely in a down market. For new traders, though, it is usually best if they become skilled at trading the long side first and then begin to develop their shorting skills.

ProShares ETFs

Exchange-traded funds (ETFs) have become increasingly popular with investors over the past decade or so. Originally designed to track a stock index, such as the S&P 500 Index, ETFs have expanded and now track commodities, sectors, and so on.

exchange-traded fund (ETF)
A security that tracks an index, a commodity, or a specific group of stocks, for example, semiconductors. An ETF represents a basket of stocks, like an index fund does, but it is traded like a stock.

There are now ETFs available that offer an alternative to shorting. ProShares offers a unique breed of ETFs that are designed to *go up when their underlying indexes go down* (and vice versa). In other words, a long position is taken in the ETF while the market is declining because the ETF moves the opposite direction of the market. These inverse ETFs offer a solution to market participants who want to take advantage of a declining market but do not wish to short stocks, or cannot do so in their tax-deferred retirement accounts.

ProShares has introduced several such ETFs in recent years. The first inverse ETFs introduced correspond to the major averages. Traders have a choice of short or ultra-short ETFs. The ultra-short ETFs are designed to double the performance of the index. The short and ultra-short symbols for the market averages are listed below:

Dow Jones Industrial Average: DOG and DXD
S&P 500 Large-Cap Index: SH and SDS
S&P 400 Midcap Index: MYY and MZZ

Nasdaq 100 Index: PSQ and QID

Russell 2000 Small-Cap Index: RWM and TWM

ProShares has since designed several more such ETFs that correspond to sectors and industry groups, such as DUG that is the symbol for the ProShares UltraShort Oil & Gas ETF. For more information on these ETFs, visit the ProShares web site at www.proshares.com.

Trading Requires Commitment

The markets do not hand out riches easily. The odds of winning are stacked against the novice trader. Becoming a successful trader requires persistence and discipline, and the willingness to commit to learning how the markets work. This book, because of its "getting started in" focus, provides novice traders a foundation from which to get started with candlestick charting as well as Western technical analysis. If you wish to survive in this competitive business, be tenacious; continue your study beyond these pages, and develop experience through lots of practice with real-world chart analysis and trading. If you would like to pursue further training with me, please visit my web site at www.tinalogan.com. I have dedicated many years to developing training materials and methods to help traders succeed.

Chapter 11

Practice Sets

Now that you have been introduced to both Eastern candlesticks and Western technical analysis, and realize how powerful they are when blended, it is time to recap and reinforce what you have learned.

Pattern Recognition Quiz

Let's start with a quick test of your recall of the primary reversal patterns introduced in Chapter 3. The arrows in the chart examples (Figures 11.1 through 11.8) point to reversal patterns. See how many of the patterns you can identify. Record your answers below each chart or on a separate sheet of paper. Don't worry if you don't remember some of them at first glance. With practice, you will soon know them all. The answers are included following the set of charts, but try to figure out the patterns on your own before checking the answers. Refer to the quick reference guide in Appendix A if needed.

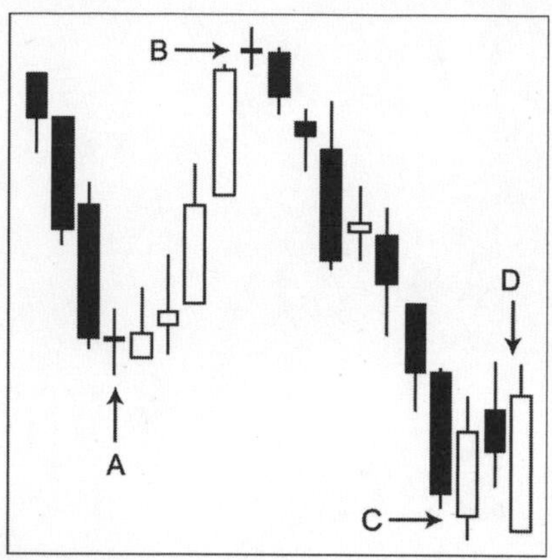

FIGURE 11.1 Chart Example 1

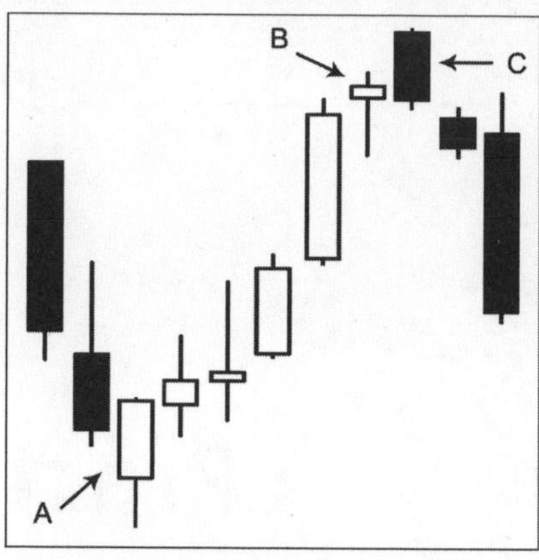

FIGURE 11.2 Chart Example 2

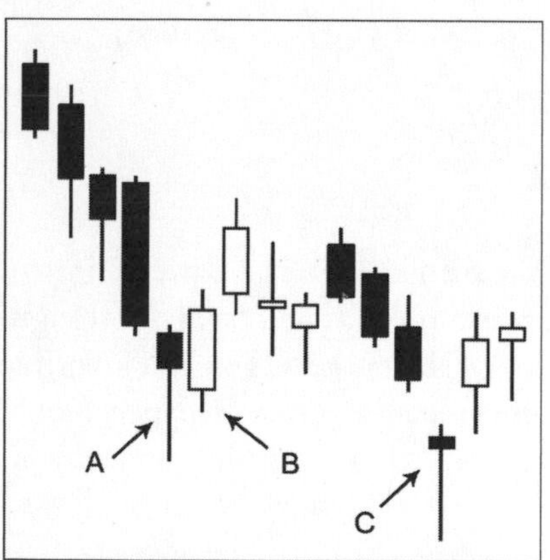

FIGURE 11.3 Chart Example 3

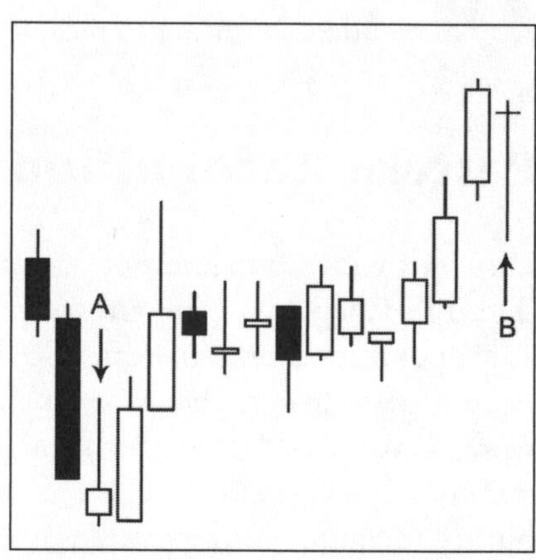

FIGURE 11.4 Chart Example 4

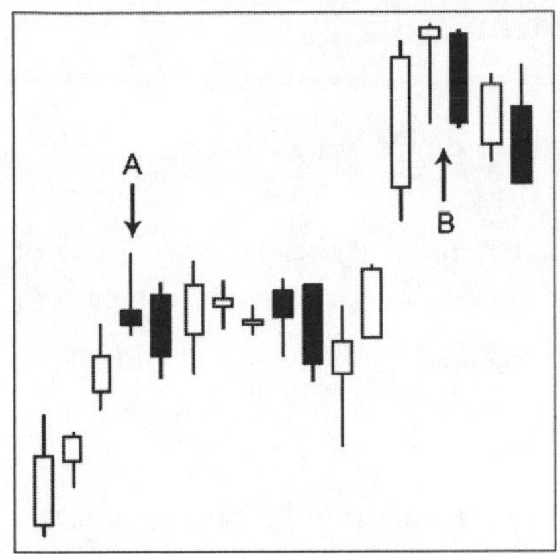

FIGURE 11.5 Chart Example 5

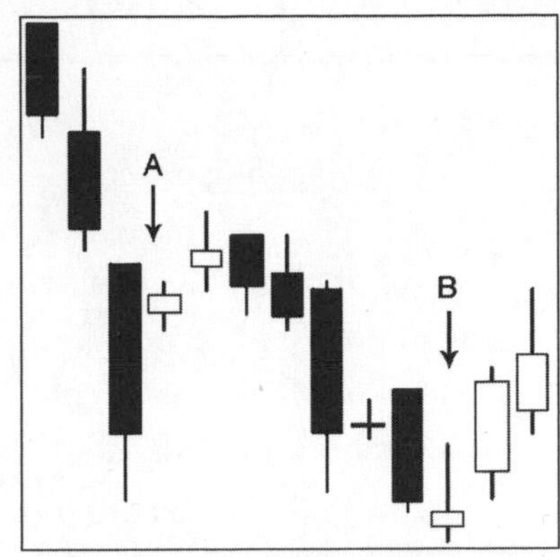

FIGURE 11.6 Chart Example 6

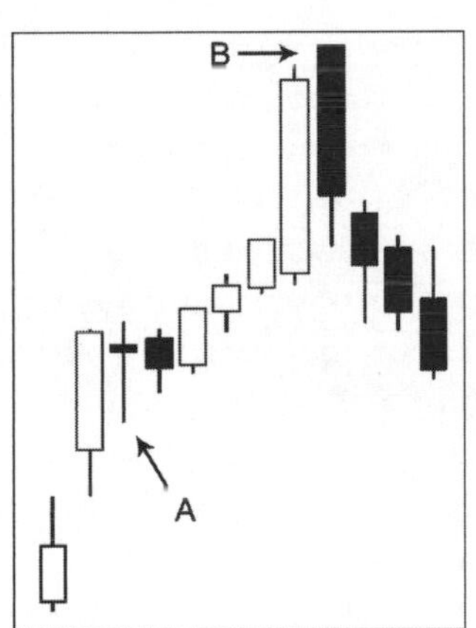

FIGURE 11.7 Chart Example 7

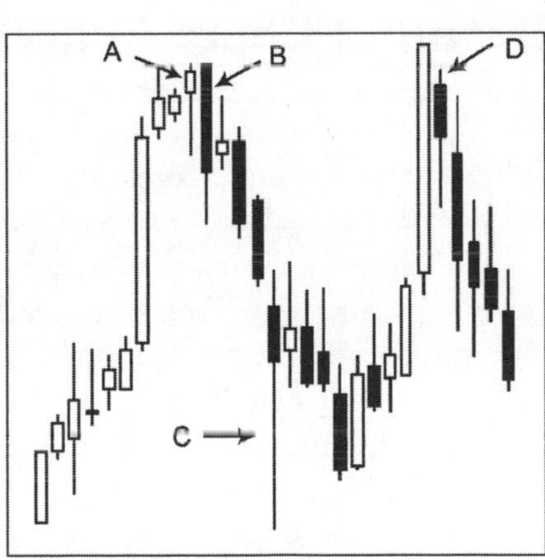

FIGURE 11.8 Chart Example 8

Answer Key for Pattern Recognition Quiz

Figure 11.1: A = southern doji; B = northern doji; C = piercing pattern; D = bullish engulfing pattern

Figure 11.2: A = piercing pattern (but not quite to the half-way point of the prior black real body); B = hanging man; C = bearish engulfing pattern

Figure 11.3: A = hammer; B = bullish engulfing pattern; C = hammer

Figure 11.4: A = inverted hammer; B = bearish harami cross (second candle is also a dragonfly doji)

Figure 11.5: A = shooting star; B = evening star (middle candle is also a hanging man)

Figure 11.6: A = bullish harami; B = morning star (middle candle is also an inverted hammer)

Figure 11.7: A = bearish harami cross (second candle is also a near dragonfly doji); B = dark cloud cover

Figure 11.8: A = hanging man; B = bearish engulfing pattern; C = hammer; D = bearish harami

Detailed Chart Analysis

Now it is time for you to analyze some charts in more detail. Three case studies follow that incorporate candlestick lines and reversal patterns covered in Part I of this book, as well as Western technical occurrences presented in Part II.

Analyze each numbered event and record your observations below the chart or on a separate sheet of paper. Each number on the chart may refer to a distinctive candle line or a reversal pattern, and/or a Western technical event such as a test of support-resistance or an overextended condition. Volume bars with a 30-day simple moving average of volume, and the stochastic oscillator (12-3-3 setting), are plotted in the panels below each chart example to assist with your analysis. Once you have finished evaluating each chart, compare your analysis to the commentary at the end of the chapter to see the author's perspective of the same set of charts.

The goal of this exercise is to guide you toward the significant technical occurrences on the charts so that you can condition what you have learned. Numerous technical incidents may occur on a daily chart over a period of a few months or more. Not every single event on every chart (Figures 11.9 through 11.11) was singled out, so you may observe some technical events that are not numbered. And don't worry if you aren't able to identify every event at first;

with continued practice you'll be amazed at how quickly and thoroughly you'll be able to evaluate a chart.

One of the challenges inherent with visual analysis is that there will be a certain amount of subjectivity. Traders may have different interpretations of the same chart. For instance, one trader may feel that a bullish hammer with a lower shadow of less than two times the length of the body still generates a valid signal, while another trader may argue that the shadow should be longer. When determining the validity of a reversal pattern, don't forget to consider the context in which it formed. Keep in mind these two questions:

1. What price action *preceded* the event?
2. Are there Western technical occurrences present on the chart that may have an impact on the direction of price?

Example

A nonideal candlestick reversal pattern may form within a larger Western pattern; when a strong ceiling or floor is tested; or after price has become overextended. There's a good chance in these instances that the pattern will follow through in spite of falling short of meeting the criteria of an ideal pattern.

CASE STUDY 1: SUNOCO INC. (SUN)

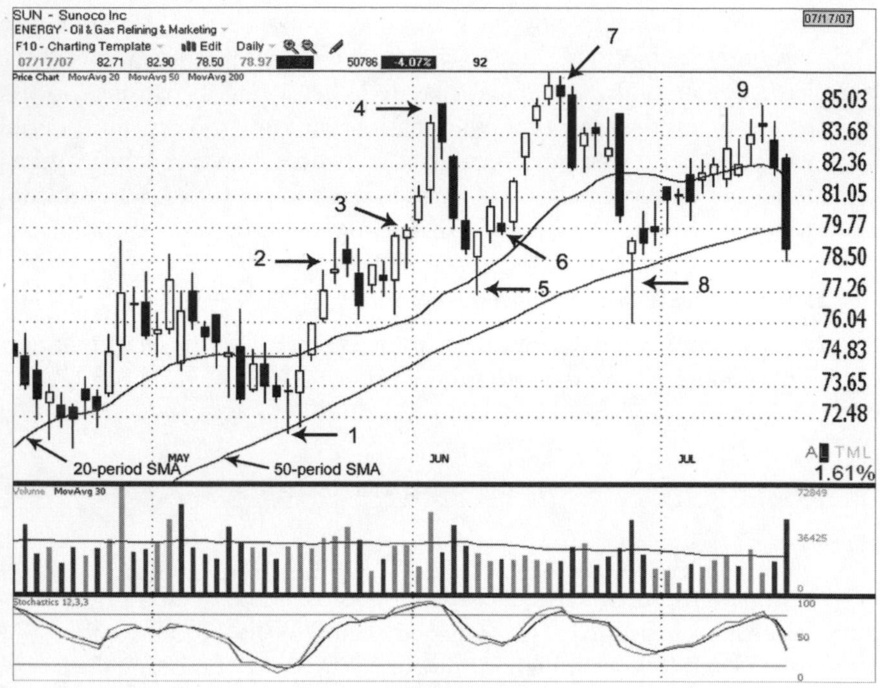

FIGURE 11.9

Source: TeleChart 2007®

1. ______________________________

2. ______________________________

3. ______________________________

4. ______________________________

5. ______________________________

6. ______________________________

7. ______________________________

8. ______________________________

9. Bonus: The peaks at 4, 7, and 9 form what Western pattern?

CASE STUDY 2: METHANEX CORP. (MEOH)

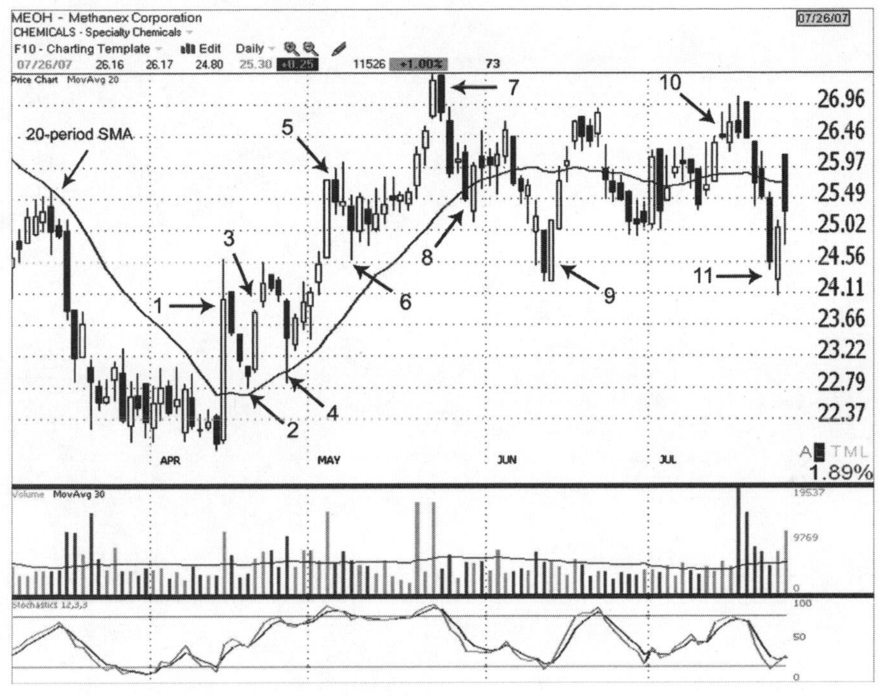

FIGURE 11.10
Source: TeleChart 2007®

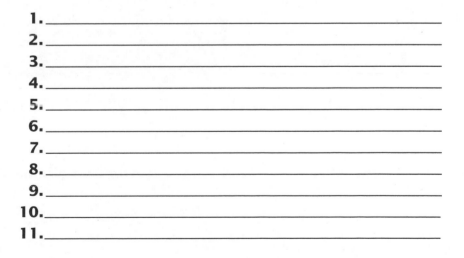

1. ______________________

2. ______________________

3. ______________________

4. ______________________

5. ______________________

6. ______________________

7. ______________________

8. ______________________

9. ______________________

10. ______________________

11. ______________________

CASE STUDY 3: GREAT WOLF RESORTS (WOLF)

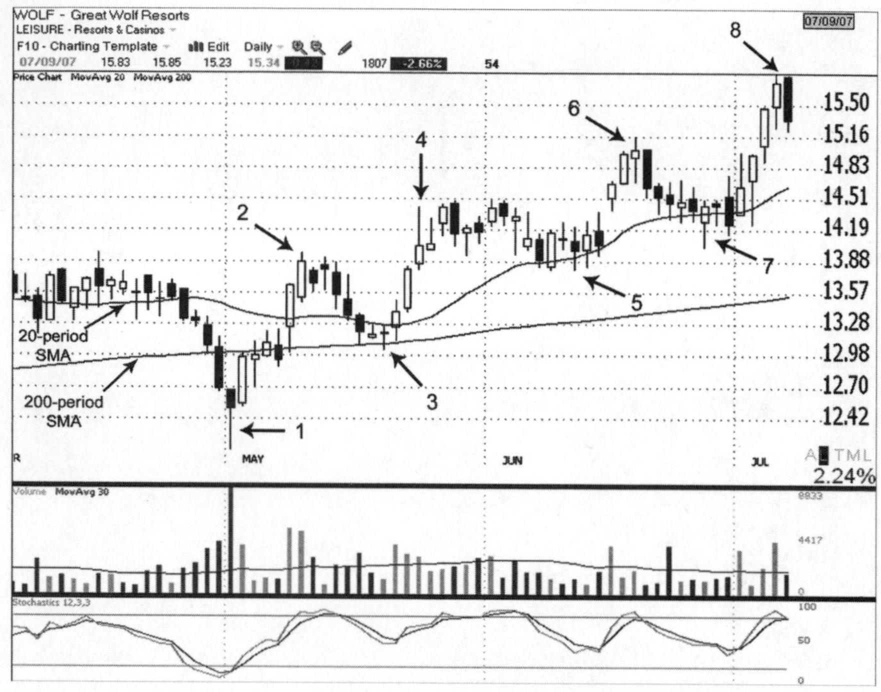

FIGURE 11.11

Source: TeleChart 2007®

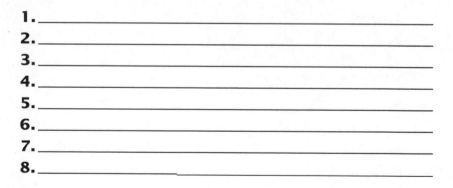

1. ______________________________
2. ______________________________
3. ______________________________
4. ______________________________
5. ______________________________
6. ______________________________
7. ______________________________
8. ______________________________

Author's Analysis—Case Study 1: Sunoco Inc. (SUN)

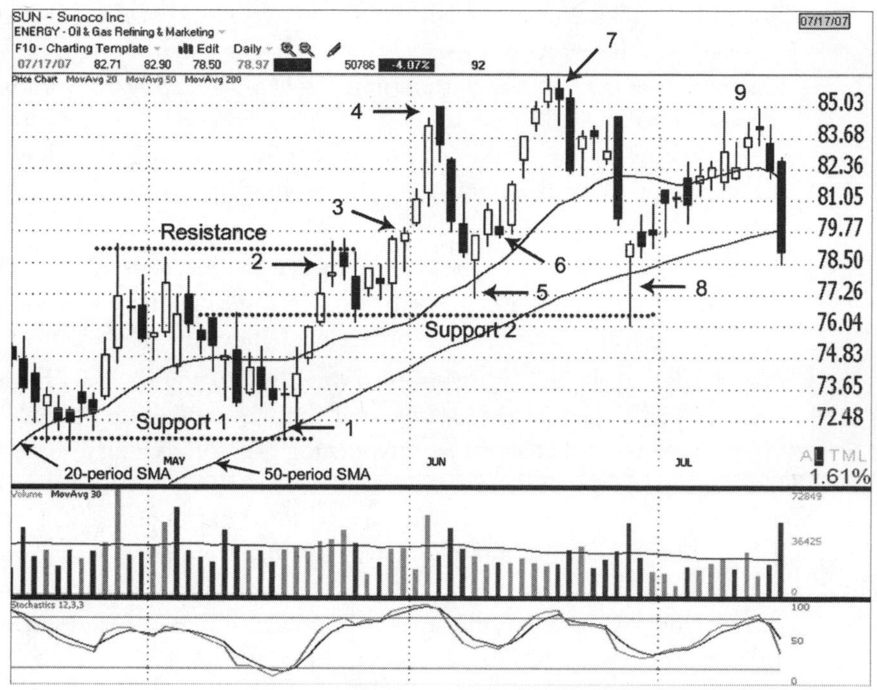

FIGURE 11.12
Source: TeleChart 2007®

The following commentary refers to the daily chart of Sunoco Inc. (SUN) from May through July 2007 (Figure 11.12). The numbered items below correspond to the numbered areas on the chart:

1. *May 16–17:* After a price decline a dragonfly doji formed at support at the 50-period simple moving average (SMA) on May 16 (1). There was additional support at that area provided by the swing low formed in April (dotted line labeled Support1). The stochastic oscillator had reached the oversold line as well offering further confirmation of a viable setup for a long position. The 50-period SMA was tested again during the session following the dragonfly doji. The long lower shadows on those two days alerted that the bulls were stepping into long positions at support. An entry at the close of the doji session, or the following day, would have provided an adequate reward-to-risk ratio for a short-term trade up to resistance at the April–May highs (dotted line labeled Resistance), or an entry for a longer-term position.

2. *May 17–29:* Price rallied for a few days then formed a shooting star (2) on May 22 near resistance at the April–May highs (dotted line labeled Resistance). The shooting star's real body was very small so some traders would have called it a gravestone doji. The shooting star's high was tested the next session with a morning gap up leaving a spinning top and signaling indecision among bulls and bears and further reinforcing the resistance area. Price pulled back some during the following session and then stabilized over the next two sessions before starting another leg up.
3. *May 31:* A hanging man formed, (3) but price had just started to move up again, so its presence was not very significant. Its signal was negated in the next session when price closed above the hanging man.
4. *May 30–June 5:* Price made a strong swing up, moving far away from the average (20-period SMA). On June 5, price gapped up open (4) but reversed immediately filling the opening gap and leaving a shaven head on the daily candle. By the end of the session, price had closed well into the prior day's bullish real body. Price did not close at least half way into the white body, so it was not an ideal dark cloud cover pattern. However, since price had moved a good distance away from the moving average, and the stochastic oscillator was in overbought territory, the signal was just as strong as an ideal pattern.
5. *June 5–8:* Price pulled back to the 20-period SMA. The lower shadow that formed on June 8 (5) was nearly long enough to qualify as a hammer. The signal was confirmed the following day when price closed higher.
6. *June 12:* A shooting star formed (6); however, price had just begun to move up again, so this pattern was not very significant. It turned out to be just a consolidation day and price closed higher in the following day's session.
7. *June 8–19:* Price made another swing up from June 8–18 once again moving far away from the 20-period SMA. Notice that the real bodies got smaller toward the end of that upswing (forming short candles, or spinning tops) followed by a bearish hanging man (7) on June 19. The stochastic confirmed with an overbought reading.
8. *June 20–27:* Price declined again ending with a gap down on June 27 (8). Price broke down through the June low (at 5) and the 50-period SMA intraday on June 27; however, there was a dramatic turnaround, and by the end of the session the stock recovered and closed near the high. The result was a bullish hammer with a very long lower shadow (that formed at support line 2). It was accompanied by heavy volume.

9. ***Bonus:*** The peaks numbered 4, 7, and 9 form a larger bearish Western chart pattern called a triple top. The middle peak (7) was slightly higher than the peaks on either side, so some traders would interpret it as a head-and-shoulders top. Either way, it warned of a *potential* trend reversal. Remember that many double and triple top patterns turn out to be periods of consolidation. In this case, though, the trend did end up reversing direction (not shown).

Author's Analysis—Case Study 2: Methanex Corp. (MEOH)

The following commentary refers to the daily chart of Methanex Corp. (MEOH) from April through July 2007 (Figure 11.13). The numbered items below correspond to the numbered areas on the chart:

1. *April 16:* After consolidating for a few weeks from late March through mid-April, price broke out on heavy volume on April 16 leaving a very long bullish candle with a long upper shadow (1).

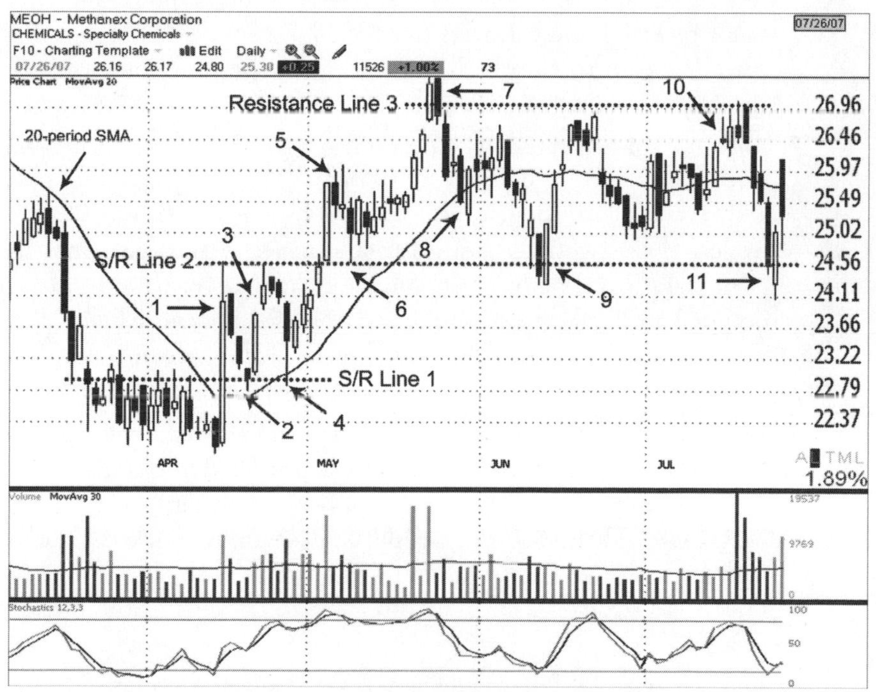

FIGURE 11.13
Source: TeleChart 2007®

2. *April 17–19:* Price pulled back for the next three sessions and tested support at the top of the March–April consolidation area and the 20-period SMA (labeled S/R Line 1). Volume declined to below average as price pulled back.
3. *April 20–23:* Price rallied (3) for two days and found resistance at the top of the long upper shadow that formed on April 16 (labeled S/R Line 2).
4. *April 24–26:* Price turned back down and declined sharply intraday on April 26 (4) back to support (S/R Line 1) but closed well off its low. Shorts were covered and buyers stepped into long positions, as evidenced by the long lower shadow.
5. *April 27–May 7:* Price rallied strongly and was able to break above the prior peaks (at S/R Line 2). A long bullish candle with a shaven head and bottom formed on May 3. In the following session, a small black real body formed within the prior session's long white real body, creating a bearish harami (5). The next session was a shooting star, another bearish sign
6. *May 8:* The following day, price declined back to the peaks that formed in April (S/R Line 2). As they often do, support and resistance reversed roles. Buyers stepped in at support (6) and pushed price back up to close well off the low as the long lower shadow indicates.
7. *May 9–23:* Price consolidated for a few days and then rallied again, surpassing the prior peak (at 5). On May 23, price gapped up open and reversed immediately, as evidenced by the shaven top (7). The session closed with the bearish candle penetrating deeply into the prior bullish real body, creating a dark cloud cover pattern. Had it declined a little farther it would have engulfed the entire body of the prior candle. Note that the stochastic oscillator was in overbought territory.
8. *May 23–30:* Price declined for a few days and gapped down open on May 30 (8). By the close of that session, price had penetrated deeply into the prior black candle's long real body, creating a bullish piercing pattern. There was not a significant downtrend to reverse; the decline from the May high was only a short-term decline. Nonetheless, price stabilized for a few days after the appearance of the piercing candle.
9. *May 31–June 13:* Price made very little headway for a few days and then declined again from June 6 through 12. On June 12, price tested support at the April high (S/R Line 2). The next day price

gapped down open (9), reversed immediately, and closed the day as a bullish engulfing pattern. The shaven head and bottom on the engulfing day show the clear leadership of the bulls during the session. The low of June 12 and the low of the engulfing bar (9) on June 13 were exactly the same. When the lows of two or more consecutive candles match, the Japanese call it a *tweezer bottom.* Two or more consecutive matching highs create a *tweezer top.* The tweezer formation alone is not a significant reversal pattern; however, when it occurs in combination with another reversal pattern, in this case the bullish engulfing pattern, it strengthens the signal.

10. *June 13–July 18:* Price swung back and forth in a trading range during June and July. A shooting star (10) formed on July 16 as the June high was tested (resistance Line 3). Long upper shadows during the following two sessions, on July 17–18, showed the inability of the bulls to push price above the June high.
11. *July 19–25:* Price declined again. A long bearish candle formed on July 24, closing near support at the bottom of the trading range (S/R Line 2). Price gapped down open the following day (11) and closed deeply into the prior candle's long black real body, creating a bullish piercing pattern.

Author's Analysis—Case Study 3: Great Wolf (WOLF)

The following commentary refers to the daily chart of Great Wolf Resorts (WOLF) from May through July 2007 (Figure 11.14). The numbered items below correspond to the numbered areas on the chart:

1. *April 25–May 1:* After consolidating for several days in April, price rolled over declining below the 200-period SMA. The decline ended on May 1 with a bullish hammer (1). The stochastic oscillator was in oversold territory and the very high volume that accompanied the hammer increased the likelihood of a reversal.
2. *May 2–11:* Price rallied back above the 200-period SMA. A bearish harami (2) formed on May 9–10 at the ceiling of the consolidation area from April (S/R Line 1). The following day a hanging man formed, further defining the resistance area.
3. *May 14–18:* Price declined for a few days, ending with a spinning top on May 17 followed by a doji (3) on May 18. The fact that those indecision candles formed at the 200-period SMA support provided a good entry opportunity for a long position.

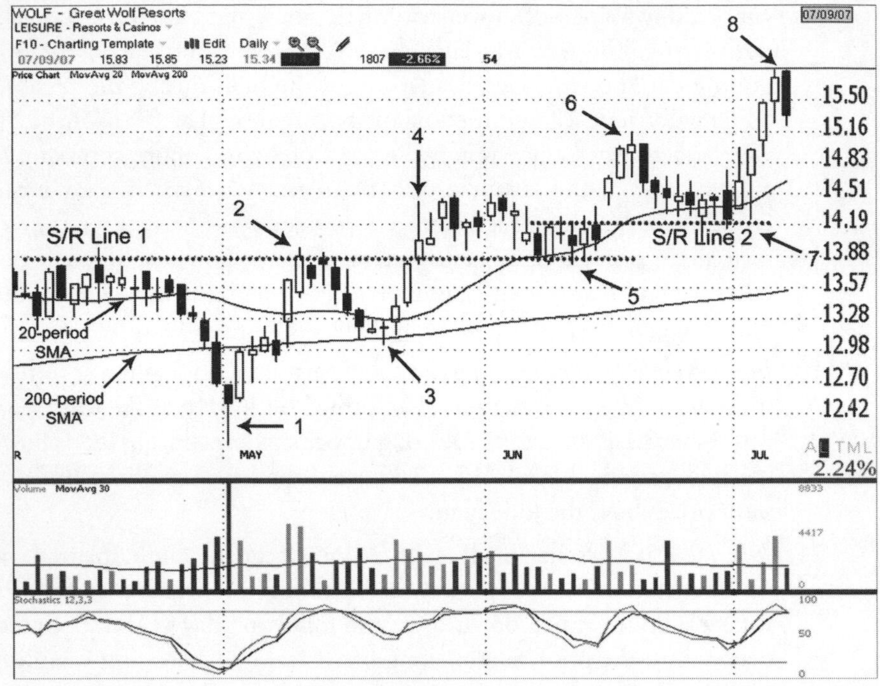

FIGURE 11.14

Source: TeleChart 2007®

4. *May 21–June 4:* Price rallied above resistance at the prior peak (S/R Line 1). A long upper shadow on May 23 (4) formed a bearish shooting star indicating that the short-term swing up was running out of steam. That was supported further during the following session with the presence of another bearish shooting star and a bearish engulfing pattern two days later on May 29. The peak of the engulfing pattern was tested on June 1 and 4.
5. *June 5–14:* Price declined a bit back to support (at S/R Line 1) and consolidated there (5) for a few days. Prior resistance had become new support.
6. *June 15–19:* On June 15, price gapped up above the minor consolidation (at 5) and closed above the prior peaks (at 4), continuing the uptrend. On June 19, a nonideal hanging man formed (6). It was not ideal because the upper shadow was not extremely short; nonetheless, price had moved up from the average and was vulnerable to a pullback. The pullback began during the following session with the formation of a bearish engulfing pattern.

7. *June 20–29:* Price declined back to the top of the small base that formed from June 6 to 14 (S/R Line 2).
8. *July 2–9:* Price rallied again, surpassing the prior peak (at 6), and moved a good distance away from the average. On July 9, a bearish engulfing pattern formed (8), indicating that price may pull back again.

On each of the upswings during this trend, the stochastic oscillator moved to the oversold line when price got somewhat overextended.

Moving Forward

Analyzing charts in the "rearview mirror" is helpful for learning. When it comes to taking live trades, though, you must make your trading decisions at the right edge of the chart without the benefit of hindsight. It is imperative that you start right away practicing what you have learned in this book with the aid of real-time charts. The repetitive process of observing price action as it unfolds, and analyzing how price moves after the formation of a pattern or other technical event, is a critical part of the learning process.

The value of the candlestick lines and signals is the message they provide about the psychology of market participants. Ironically, you'll learn a lot about *your own psychology* when you start taking actual trades with your hard-earned money on the line.

Conclusion

By carefully reviewing the content in this book, and studying the accompanying illustrations, you'll develop a valuable foundation from which to get started using candlestick charting. Read the book as many times as needed in order to feel confident that you understand the concepts. A mistake made by many aspiring traders is that they read a book, usually only once, and then move on to another book or seminar without taking the time to reinforce the new information. I am not trying to discourage you from learning as much as you can about this industry—quite the contrary. Even after years of study and practice, I am amazed at how there is always something new to be learned. What I am discouraging is the practice of moving continuously from one topic to another without first making sure that you have absorbed and can apply what you have learned. It is a mistake that I made myself at times early in my trading career, which I later corrected. Whenever I study a new topic now, I review the information multiple times and begin immediately to put it to work.

While studying new information, it may seem as if it is embedded solidly in your mind. The real test comes, however, when you attempt to put that knowledge to work with real-time charts and live trades. You may discover that you don't know the information as well as you thought; or you may find that you miss certain technical events at first when analyzing charts. That will improve with continued review and practice.

Knowledge by itself is not powerful; it is the application of knowledge that is powerful. Completion of this book is only the first step, albeit a crucial one. You will learn equally as much by applying the information. Only through repeated practice will this knowledge become permanent and serve to increase your charting proficiency and profitability.

When you are ready to add to your knowledge base, please visit my web site at www.tinalogan.com. In addition to instruction on technical analysis (charting), I offer training on a variety of topics including trade management, trading strategies, and organizing and structuring your work. Your feedback regarding this book is also welcome and appreciated. If you have any comments or questions, you may e-mail me directly at tina@tinalogan.com.

Trading is not a fast path to riches. It takes time and patience to develop a strong skill set that will result in consistent profits. But for those who commit to learning and stay the course, it can be very rewarding both financially and intellectually. I'll leave you with a quote from a gentleman named Herbert Otto, a wise trader whom I've learned a lot from: "It ain't easy. If it were easy everyone would be doing it and it could not pay well."

Appendix A

Brief summaries of the criteria of the primary bearish and bullish candlestick reversal patterns introduced in Chapter 3, along with illustrations, are included in this section. The real bodies that are shown in gray indicate that that the body may be either black or white. Review Chapter 3 for more discussion and variations of these patterns.

Bearish Reversal Patterns

Hanging man: This bearish counterpart to the hammer forms after a price advance. It has a small real body that forms at, or very near, the upper end of the candlestick's range. The small real body may be either black or white. There should be no upper shadow or a very small one. The long lower shadow is typically two or more times the length of the real body. A hanging man may appear after a short-term upward move, but it is more significant if it appears after a long or sharp rally or at an all-time high.

Shooting star: This bearish counterpart to the inverted hammer forms after a price advance. It has a small real body that forms at, or very near, the lower end of the candlestick's range. The small real body may be either black or white. There should be no lower shadow or a very small one. The long upper shadow is typically two or more times the length of the real body. An ideal pattern will have a real body that gaps up open away from the prior real body. It is acceptable, though, for the real body of the shooting star to overlap the prior candle's real body.

Doji (northern): This bearish counterpart to the southern doji forms after a price advance. The opening and closing prices are the same, or very near the same, meaning it has no real body. The length of its upper and lower shadows may vary. This doji's signal is even stronger if it follows one or more long bullish candles. The northern doji is often a component of other bearish patterns, such as the evening doji star and the bearish harami cross.

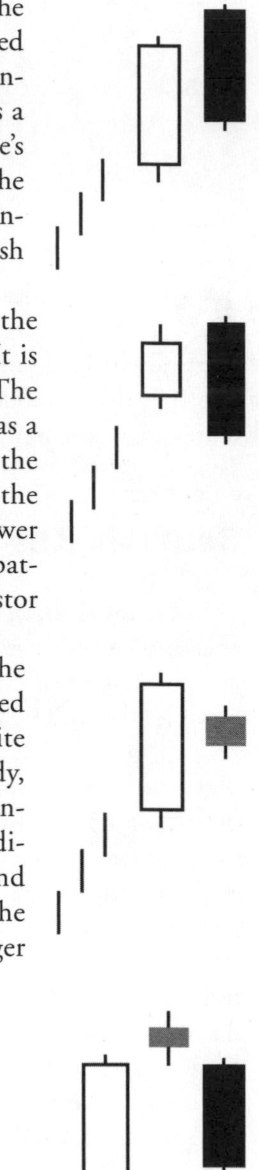

Dark cloud cover: This bearish counterpart to the piercing pattern forms after a price advance. It is formed from two candlestick lines of opposite color. The first candle has a strong bullish real body. The second candle has a black real body. Price gaps up open above the prior candle's high and closes deeply (ideally at least half-way) into the prior candle's white real body. The deeper the second candle's bearish real body penetrates the prior candle's bullish real body, the stronger the signal.

Bearish engulfing: This bearish counterpart to the bullish engulfing pattern forms after a price advance. It is formed from two candlestick lines of opposite color. The first candle has a white real body. The second candle has a longer black real body that completely surrounds the prior candle's white real body. It is not necessary that the second candle envelop the prior candle's upper and lower shadows, just the real body. This is a strong reversal pattern that exemplifies an abrupt turnaround in investor psychology.

Bearish harami: This bearish counterpart to the bullish harami forms after a price advance. It is formed from two candlestick lines. The first candle's long white real body is followed by a noticeably smaller real body, either black or white, that resides within the prior candle's longer body. The appearance of a harami is an indication that the market may be losing momentum and should signal caution. If the second candle is a doji, the pattern is called a *bearish harami cross* and sends a stronger signal.

Evening star: This bearish counterpart to the morning star forms after a price advance. It is comprised of three candlestick lines. The first candle has a long white real body. The second candle gaps up open and forms a small real body, either black or white, or a doji, creating the star portion of the pattern. The third candle has a black real body that intrudes deeply into the first candle's long bullish real body. The deeper the intrusion, the more likely a reversal will follow, especially if the third candle is accompanied by heavy volume.

Bullish Reversal Patterns

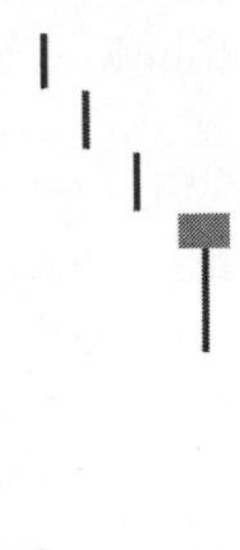

Hammer: This bullish counterpart to the hanging man forms after a price decline. It has a small real body that forms at, or very near, the upper end of the candlestick's range. The small real body may be either black or white. There should be no upper shadow or a very small one. The long lower shadow is typically two or more times the length of the real body. The hammer is a strong reversal signal. It is meaningful whether it forms after a short-term downside move or after a more significant decline.

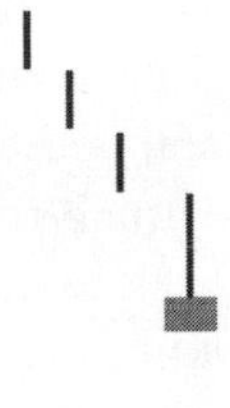

Inverted hammer: This bullish counterpart to the shooting star forms after a price decline. It has a small real body that forms at, or very near, the lower end of the candlestick's range. The small real body may be either black or white. There should be no lower shadow or a very small one. The long upper shadow is typically two or more times the length of the real body.

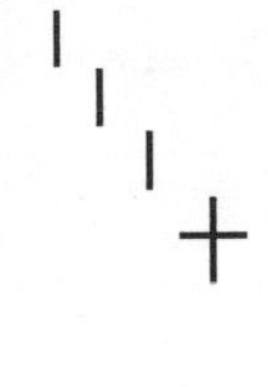

Doji (southern): This bullish counterpart to the northern doji forms after a price decline. The opening and closing prices are the same, or very near the same, meaning it has no real body. The length of its upper and lower shadows may vary. A doji that appears after a downward move may result in a change in price direction; however, doji tend to lose some of their potency in a declining market. The southern doji is often a component of other bullish patterns, such as the morning doji star and the bullish harami cross.

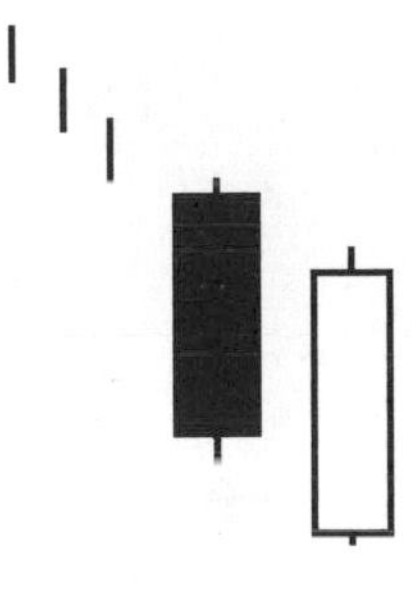

Piercing pattern: This bullish counterpart to the dark cloud cover pattern forms after a price decline. It is formed from two candlestick lines of opposite color. The first candle has a strong black real body. The second candle has a white real body. Price gaps down open below the prior candle's low and closes deeply (at least halfway) into the prior candle's black real body. The deeper the second candle's bullish real body penetrates the prior candle's bearish real body, the stronger the signal.

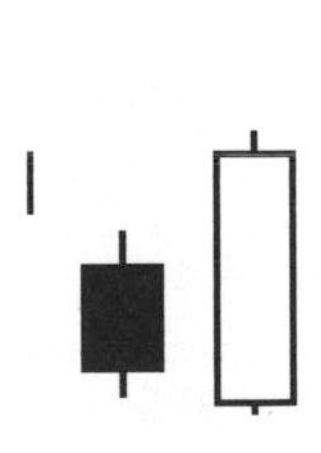

Bullish engulfing: This bullish counterpart to the bearish engulfing pattern forms after a price decline. It is formed from two candlestick lines of opposite color. The first candle has a black real body. The second candle has a longer white real body that completely surrounds the prior candle's black real body. It is not necessary that the second candle envelop the prior candle's upper and lower shadows, just the real body. This is a strong reversal pattern that exemplifies an abrupt turnaround in investor psychology.

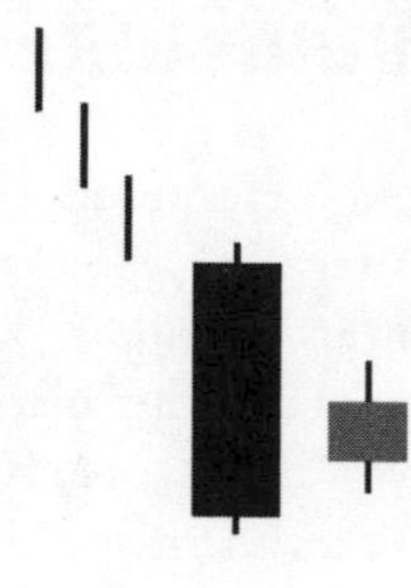

Bullish harami: This bullish counterpart to the bearish harami forms after a price decline. It is formed from two candlestick lines. The first candle's long black real body is followed by a noticeably smaller real body, either black or white, that resides within the prior candle's longer body. The appearance of a harami is an indication that the market may be losing momentum and should signal caution. If the second candle is a doji, the pattern is called a *bullish harami cross* and sends a stronger signal.

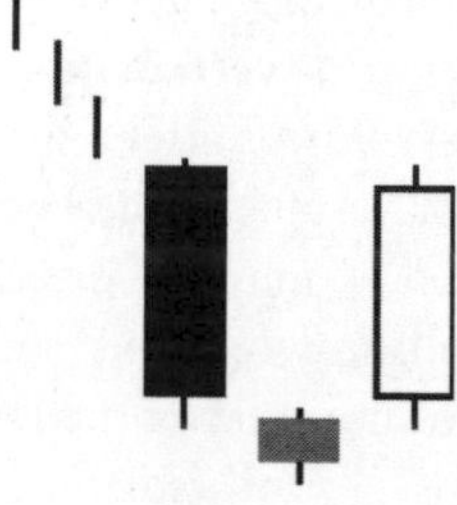

Morning star: This bullish counterpart to the evening star forms after a price decline. It is comprised of three candlestick lines. The first candle has a long black real body. The second candle gaps down open and forms a small real body, either black or white, or a doji, creating the star portion of the pattern. The third candle has a white real body that intrudes deeply into the first candle's long bearish real body. The deeper the intrusion, the more likely a reversal will follow, especially if the third candle is accompanied by heavy volume.

Appendix B

S&P 500 LARGE-CAP INDEX COMPONENTS (AS OF OCTOBER 2007)

A
AA
AAPL
ABC
ABI
ABK
ABT
ACAS
ACE
ACS
ADBE
ADI
ADM
ADP
ADSK
AEE
AEP
AES
AET
AFL
AGN
AIG
AIV
AIZ
AKAM
ALL
ALTR
AMAT
AMD
AMGN
AMP
AMZN
AN
ANF
AOC
APA
APC
APD
APOL
ASD
ASH
ASN
AT
ATI
AV
AVB
AVP
AVY
AW
AXP
AYE
AZO
BA
BAC
BAX
BBBY
BBT
BBY
BC
BCR
BDK
BDX
BEN
BF.B
BHI
BIG
BIIB
BJS
BK
BLL
BMC
BMS
BMY
BNI
BOL
BRCM

BRL
BSC
BSX
BTU
BUD
BXP
C
CA
CAG
CAH
CAT
CB
CBE
CBG
CBH
CBS
CC
CCE
CCL
CCU
CEG
CELG
CFC
CHK
CHRW
CI
CIEN
CINF
CIT
CL
CLX
CMA
CMCSA
CME
CMI
CMS
CNP
CNX
COF
COH
COL
COP
COST
COV
CPB
CPWR
CSC
CSCO
CSX
CTAS
CTL
CTSH
CTX
CTXS
CVG
CVH
CVS
CVX
CZN
D
DD
DDR
DDS
DE
DELL
DF
DFS
DGX
DHI
DHR
DIS
DJ
DOV
DOW
DRI
DTE
DTV
DUK
DVN
DYN
EBAY
ECL
ED
EDS
EFX
EIX
EK
EL
EMC
EMN
EMR
EOG
EP
EQ
EQR
ERTS
ESRX
ESV
ETFC
ETN
ETR
EXC
F
FCX
FDC
FDO
FDX
FE
FHN
FII
FIS
FISV
FITB
FLR
FNM
FO
FPL
FRE
FRX
GAS
GCI
GD
GE
GENZ
GGP
GILD
GIS
GLW
GM
GNW
GOOG
GPC
GPS
GR
GS
GT
GWW
HAL
HAR
HAS
HBAN
HCBK
HCR
HD
HES
HET
HIG
HLT
HNZ
HOG
HON
HOT
HPC
HPQ
HRB
HSP
HST
HSY
HUM
IACI
IBM
IFF
IGT
INTC
INTU
IP
IPG
IR

ITT
ITW
JAVA
JBL
JCI
JCP
JDSU
JNJ
JNPR
JNS
JNY
JPM
JWN
K
KBH
KEY
KFT
KG
KIM
KLAC
KMB
KO
KR
KSS
LEG
LEH
LEN
LH
LIZ
LLL
LLTC
LLY
LM
LMT
LNC
LOW
LSI
LTD
LTR
LUK
LUV
LXK
M
MAR
MAS
MAT
MBI
MCD
MCHP
MCK
MCO
MDP
MDT
MER
MET
MHP
MHS
MI
MIL
MKC
MMC
MMM
MNST
MO
MOLX
MON
MOT
MRK
MRO
MS
MSFT
MTB
MTG
MU
MUR
MWV
MXIM
MYL
NBR
NCC
NE
NEM
NI
NKE
NOC
NOV
NOVL
NSC
NSM
NTAP
NTRS
NUE
NVDA
NVLS
NWL
NWS.A
NYT
ODP
OMC
OMX
ORCL
OXY
PAYX
PBG
PBI
PCAR
PCG
PCL
PCP
PDCO
PEG
PEP
PFE
PFG
PG
PGN
PGR
PH
PHM
PKI
PLD
PLL
PNC
PNW
PPG
PPL
PRU
PSA
PTV
PX
Q
QCOM
QLGC
R
RAI
RDC
RF
RHI
RIG
RL
ROH
ROK
RRD
RSH
RTN
RX
S
SAF
SBUX
SCHW
SE
SEE
SGP
SHLD
SHW
SIAL
SII
SLB
SLE
SLM
SLR
SNA
SNDK
SNV
SO
SOV
SPG
SPLS

SRE
SSP
STI
STJ
STR
STT
STZ
SUN
SVU
SWK
SWY
SYK
SYMC
SYY
T
TAP
TDC
TE
TEG
TEK
TEL
TER
TEX
TGT
THC
TIF
TIN
TJX
TLAB
TMK
TMO
TRB
TROW
TRV
TSN
TWX
TXN
TXT
TXU
TYC
UIS
UNH
UNM
UNP
UPS
USB
UST
UTX
VAR
VFC
VIA.B
VLO
VMC
VNO
VRSN
VZ
WAG
WAT
WB
WEN
WFC
WFMI
WFR
WFT
WHR
WIN
WLP
WM
WMB
WMI
WMT
WPI
WU
WWY
WY
WYE
WYN
X
XEL
XL
XLNX
XOM
XRX
XTO
YHOO
YUM
ZION
ZMH

Glossary

After hours trading Trading that occurs after the close of the normal daily trading session.

Area gap A gap that occurs within a period of consolidation. An area gap may also be called a *common gap* or *pattern gap.*

Average An average, or mean, is determined by summing a set of values and dividing the result by the total number of values in the set.

Blow-off top A sharp upward thrust in an uptrend is followed by aggressive selling. The move is accompanied by heavy volume and often results in a change in the direction of the trend.

Bollinger Bands Developed by John Bollinger, these bands are plotted at standard deviation levels above and below a moving average of price.

Breakaway gap A gap that forms when price breaks out above resistance or below support. Breakaway gaps are typically accompanied by heavy volume.

Breakdown Price closes below an identifiable support area.

Breakout Price closes above an identifiable resistance area.

Capitulation A phenomenon in which investors "give up" and are willing to sell a declining stock at almost any price in order to exit their long positions. True capitulation involves very high volume and a sharp decline as panic selling occurs. Capitulation is often followed by a change in the direction of the trend.

Close The final price at which a security trades during a trading session.

Consolidation A condition in which price moves sideways for a period of time. See also **Rectangle** and **Triangle.**

Continuation gap A gap that forms while price is trending up or down. A continuation gap may also be called a *runaway gap* or a *measuring gap.*

Cover (buy-to-cover) An order placed with a broker to exit a short position.

Divergence A scenario in which the price peaks of an asset moves in the opposite direction of an indicator's peaks.

Double bottom A common bullish reversal pattern that occurs when two prominent, parallel (or nearly parallel) bottoms form in a downtrend. The pattern resembles the letter "W." It is a valid reversal pattern when it is confirmed by a close above the middle of the "W."

Double top A common bearish reversal pattern that occurs when two prominent, parallel (or nearly parallel) peaks form in an uptrend. The pattern resembles the letter "M." It is a valid reversal pattern when it is confirmed by a close below the middle of the "M."

Exchange-traded fund (ETF) A security that tracks an index, a commodity, or a specific group of stocks, for example, semiconductors. An ETF represents a basket of stocks, like an index fund does, but it is traded like a stock.

Exhaustion gap A gap that forms at the end of a trend. Exhaustion gaps are typically accompanied by heavy volume.

Exponential moving average (EMA) The most recent prices in the average are weighted more heavily than the older prices.

False breakout Price closes above an identifiable resistance area, or below an identifiable support area, but does not have enough momentum to continue the move. Price reverses direction invalidating the breakout.

Fibonacci A sequence of numbers discovered by Leonardo Fibonacci, a thirteenth-century mathematician.

Gap Empty space on a chart where no trading has occurred.

Head-and-shoulders top A variation of a triple top pattern in which the center peak is noticeably higher than the two peaks on either side. It is a valid reversal pattern when price closes below the neckline. The neckline is a support line that connects the swing lows on both sides of the head.

High The highest price reached by a security during a trading session.

Inside bar A price bar that forms within the range of the bar that precedes it.

Island reversal An exhaustion gap is followed soon after by another gap in the opposite direction.

Long (long position) The purchase of a stock or other trading instrument with the expectation that price will rise.

Low The lowest price reached by a security during a trading session.

Margin account A brokerage account that permits an investor to buy or sell securities on credit and to borrow against securities held in the account.

Market order An order for immediate execution at the best price available when the order reaches the market.

Mean reversion A statistical concept that suggests that a value eventually moves back toward the mean, or average. For price, the mean can be a historical average of the price.

Morning gap A gap that occurs at the open of a daily trading session and is filled before the close of the session.

Moving average A trend-following indicator that smoothes out price action by averaging price over a designated period of time.

Negative divergence When price continues to form higher peaks in an uptrend, while the peaks in an indicator begin to decline, it indicates the uptrend may be weakening.

Open The price at the start of a trading session.

Opening gap See **Morning gap.**

Oscillator A technical indicator that signifies when a stock or market is in an overbought or oversold condition.

Overbought A condition in which a stock or market has risen too far too quickly and is likely to suffer at least a short-term decline or period of consolidation.

Outside bar The price bar's range completely encompasses the range of the bar that precedes it.

Oversold A condition in which a stock or market has fallen too far too quickly and is likely to experience at least a short-term rally or period of consolidation.

Positive divergence When price is making lower bottoms in a downtrend, while the indicator bottoms are rising, it indicates the downtrend may be weakening.

Premarket trading Trading that occurs prior to the open of the normal daily trading session.

Price The perceived value of a security at a given time.

Price gap See **Gap.**

Price objective See **Price target.**

Price target A projected price level where, if it is reached, a trader intends to exit an open position.

Probability The likelihood, but not a certainty, of something's happening or being true.

Rally A fairly sharp rise after a decline or a period of consolidation. Demand overwhelms supply resulting in a rise in value.

Range A price bar's range is the difference between the highest and lowest prices reached during a given trading period, for example, a daily session.

Rectangle A pattern that forms on a chart when price moves sideways swinging back and forth in a bounded range. The top of the range becomes resistance and the bottom of the range becomes support. A rectangle represents a pause within a trend and is usually resolved with a breakout in the direction of the trend; however, at times it will precede a trend reversal.

Resistance An area above the current price where supply should be sufficient to halt a price advance.

Reward-to-risk ratio A ratio used by traders to determine the potential reward (profit) compared to the potential risk (loss) if a position is taken in a stock or other trading instrument. The ratio is calculated by dividing the potential reward by the potential risk.

Selling climax A sharp sell-off in a downtrend is followed by aggressive buying. The move is accompanied by heavy volume and often results in a change in the direction of the trend.

Sell-off Rapid selling of a stock or other trading instrument. Supply overwhelms demand resulting in a decline in value.

Setup An identifiable price formation that presents a potentially profitable trading opportunity.

Short (short position) The sale of a stock or other trading instrument with the expectation that price will decline.

Simple moving average (SMA) Equal weight is assigned to each price that is included in the average.

Slippage The difference between the price at the time a trader places an order and the price at which the order is actually filled.

Stochastic oscillator A popular momentum indicator developed by George Lane. It is based on the premise that when price is trending up, the closing prices will tend to be near the high of the price range. In a downtrend, the closing prices will be nearer the low of the price range.

Stock index An indicator used to track the composite value for a particular group of stocks. For example, the S&P 500 is a very well-known large-cap index, that is commonly used as a benchmark for the stock market.

Stop-loss order An order placed with a broker to exit an open position if a stock reaches a certain price. The order is intended to limit the loss an investor takes if the stock moves against him. Stop loss orders become market orders when triggered.

Strategy A set of rules and conditions that determine such factors as what generates a signal and how to enter, manage and exit the trade.

Support An area beneath the current price where demand should be sufficient to halt a price decline.

Tail A candlestick line with a long upper or lower shadow.

Three Buddha top See **Head-and-shoulders top.**

Three mountain top See **Triple top.**

Three river bottom See **Triple bottom.**

Trend The direction of a price move. A trend may move up or down and is often classified by its duration as either short, intermediate, or long term.

Trend line A straight line drawn on a chart to determine the direction and slope of the current trend, or to identify the boundaries of a consolidation area.

Triangle A chart pattern that forms when price moves sideways. The swings across the consolidation area tighten as price moves toward the apex of the triangle. There are three types of triangles: ascending, descending, and symmetrical.

Triple top A bearish reversal pattern that occurs when three prominent, parallel (or nearly parallel) peaks form in an uptrend. It is a valid reversal pattern when price closes below the lowest point between the three peaks.

True gap See **Gap.**

Volatility The tendency for price to fluctuate.

Volume The number of shares or contracts that are traded during a specified period of time.

Bibliography

Bigalow, Stephen W. *Profitable Candlestick Trading.* New York: John Wiley & Sons, 2002; *High Profit Candlestick Patterns*, Houston, TX: Profit Publishing, LLC, 2005.

Bollinger, John. *Bollinger on Bollinger Bands.* New York: McGraw-Hill, 2002.

Bulkowski, Thomas N. *Getting Started in Chart Patterns.* Hoboken, NJ: John Wiley & Sons, 2006.

Lane, George C. *Using Stochastics, Cycles, and RSI.* Des Plaines, IL: Investment Educators, 1986.

Morris, Gregory L. *Candlestick Charting Explained,* 3rd ed. New York: McGraw-Hill, 2006.

Murphy, John J. *Technical Analysis of the Financial Markets.* New York: New York Institute of Finance, 1999.

Nison, Steve. *Japanese Candlestick Charting Techniques,* 2nd ed. New York: New York Institute of Finance, 2001; *Beyond Candlesticks.* New York: John Wiley & Sons, 1994.

Person, John L. *Candlestick and Pivot Point Trading Triggers.* Hoboken, NJ: John Wiley & Sons, 2007.

About the Author

Tina Logan is the president of Tina Logan, Inc. (www.tinalogan.com). She has over 15 years of combined experience as a trainer in corporate settings and as a tutor for traders. For the past several years she has provided stock market training through private tutoring, seminars, and web-based sessions. Tina has mentored traders from across the United States and abroad. Her course graduates range from beginners, who aspire to enter this tough business, to more advanced traders who wish to improve their returns and fine-tune their skills.

Tina began trading by timing mutual funds in her retirement account before moving on to trading stocks. She left the corporate workplace in early 2000 in order to pursue full-time trading and study of the financial markets.

Tina was a contributing author to Stephen Bigalow's second book, *High Profit Candlestick Patterns* (2005). She holds a bachelor of arts from the University of Nevada–Reno, where she majored in communications and minored in business administration.

Index